IMMIGRANTS IN PRAIRIE CITIES:
ETHNIC DIVERSITY IN TWENTIETH-CENTURY CANADA

Over the course of the twentieth century, sequential waves of immigrants from Europe, Asia, Latin America, and Africa settled in the cities of the Canadian prairies. In *Immigrants in Prairie Cities*, Royden Loewen and Gerald Friesen analyse the processes of cultural interaction and adaptation that unfolded in these urban centres and describe how this model of diversity has changed over time. The authors argue that intimate prairie cities fostered a form of social diversity characterized by vibrant ethnic networks, continuously evolving ethnic identities, and boundary zones that facilitated intercultural contact and hybridity.

Impressive in scope, *Immigrants in Prairie Cities* spans the entire twentieth century, and encompasses personal testimonies, government perspectives, and even fictional narratives. This engaging work will appeal to both historians of the Canadian prairies and those with a general interest in migration, cross-cultural exchange, and urban history.

ROYDEN LOEWEN is a professor in the Department of History at the University of Winnipeg.

GERALD FRIESEN is a distinguished professor in the Department of History at the University of Manitoba.

IMMIGRANTS
IN PRAIRIE CITIES

Ethnic Diversity
in Twentieth-Century Canada

Royden Loewen and Gerald Friesen

UNIVERSITY OF TORONTO PRESS
Toronto Buffalo London

© University of Toronto Press Incorporated 2009
Toronto Buffalo London
www.utppublishing.com
Printed in Canada

ISBN 978-0-8020-9908-2 (cloth)
ISBN 978-0-8020-9609-8 (paper)

Printed on acid-free, 100% post-consumer recycled paper with vegetable-based inks.

Library and Archives Canada Cataloguing in Publication

Loewen, Royden, 1954–
  Immigrants in prairie cities: ethnic diversity in twentieth-century Canada / by
  Roydon Loewen and Gerald Friesen.

  Includes bibliographical references and index.
  ISBN 978-0-8020-9908-2 (bound)   ISBN 978-0-8020-9609-8 (pbk.)

  1. Immigrants – Prairie Provinces – History – 20th century.   2. Multiculturalism
  – Prairie Provinces – History – 20th century.   3. Prairie Provinces – Emigration
  and immigration – History – 20th century.   4. Prairie Provinces – Ethnic
  relations – History – 20th century.   I. Friesen, Gerald, 1943–   II. Title.

  FC3250.A1L63 2009   971.20086'912   C2009-905443-4

University of Toronto Press acknowledges the financial assistance to its publishing program of the Canada Council for the Arts and the Ontario Arts Council.

   Canada Council   Conseil des Arts   ONTARIO ARTS COUNCIL
                for the Arts   du Canada   CONSEIL DES ARTS DE L'ONTARIO

University of Toronto Press acknowledges the financial support for its publishing activities of the Government of Canada through the Book Publishing
Industry Development Program (BPIDP).

This book has been published with the help of a grant from the Canadian
Federation for the Humanities and Social Sciences, through the Aid to
Scholarly Publications Program, using funds provided by the Social Sciences
and Research Council of Canada.

Contents

Acknowledgments

We would like to thank the many individuals who assisted us in the writing of this book. We are very grateful for the research and counsel of six post-doctoral and graduate students in the Winnipeg Immigration History Research Group, Esyllt Jones, Peter Nunoda, Jennifer Rogalsky, Ken Sylvester, Janis Thiessen, and Hans Werner. We were also aided by student research assistants Dora Dueck, Joe Friesen, Carl Martens, Mallory Richard, and Jen Simons. Many people who had direct experience with immigration and settlement agreed to be interviewed and we thank these individuals for their contributions. Gerald Friesen's debts to Masako Kawata and Saul Cherniack will be apparent in the chapters that discuss their life histories and he wishes to pay special tribute to them. We met members of the immigration settlement community in Edmonton and Winnipeg, and we would especially acknowledge the help of Tom Denton, Marty Dolin, Beatrice Watson, Lawrence Whitehead, Marlene Reguly, Monika Feist, D'Arcy Phillips, Ximena Munoz, Paul McGeachie, and the staff at the International Centre of Winnipeg.

Officers and colleagues at universities gave us support in many ways. We thank members of the University of Manitoba and University of Winnipeg administrations Alaa Abd-El Aziz, Barbara Crutchley, Raymond Currie, John Hofley, John Kendle, Mary Kinnear, Robert O'Kell, and George Tomlinson. We also were helped by academic colleagues in a number of universities, including David Burley, Tom Carter, Petra Dolata-Kreutzkamp, John Lehr, Leo Driedger, Alexander Freund, Shiva Halli, Ursula Lehmkuhl, Tamara Meyers, Tom Nesmith, Nolan Reilly, Eliakim Sibanda, and Brian Young. We gratefully acknowledge the support of Baha Abu Laban of the University of Alberta and the Prairie Centre for the Study of Immigration and Integration. We relied on the librarians at the University of Winnipeg and University of Manitoba, and the archivists in the Archives of Saskatchewan, Glenbow Museum (Calgary), Archives of Manitoba, and University of Manitoba Archives, and thank them for their generous aid.

Many people helped prepare this manuscript for publication. Anonymous reviewers provided invaluable help, as did Frances Swyripa, Lyle Dick, Neil Besner, and Paul Bramadat, who read all or parts of it. Len Husband at the University of Toronto Press has backed our work and we want to thank him for his consistent interest in the manuscript and his determination that we eventually relinquish it. Also at UTP, Frances Mundy, the managing editor, Jenna Germaine, and Patricia Simoes have guided it into book form. Pat Sanders, our expert editor, fitted us into her busy schedule and for this we are in her debt.

The book has been constructed on dozens of coffee-shop conversations and we would like to acknowledge our many hosts. Loewen thanks Mary Ann for all those chats linking history and CanLit. Friesen thanks Jean for recommending the Illingworth Kerr painting on the cover and for everything.

Royden Loewen
Gerald Friesen

IMMIGRANTS IN PRAIRIE CITIES

Introduction

Multiculturalism has become an internationally recognized symbol of contemporary Canada. It is often associated with a 1971 federal policy supporting ethnic groups and the expression of heritage cultures, an initiative introduced just as waves of newcomers from Asia, Africa, the Caribbean, and Latin America were remaking the country. Canada's diversity is also linked to the kaleidoscope of peoples in the country's largest cities – Vancouver, Montreal, and especially Toronto – and to the writing of novelists and scholars who have worked in these challenging communities.[1] This book discusses another group of cities and a longer span of time to illustrate a different version of the country's experiment in cultural mixing. It contends that the immigrant phenomenon can be seen with particular clarity in Canada's prairie cities, medium-sized inland centres that received sequential waves of newcomers throughout the twentieth century. These cities were nearly as multi-ethnic at the outbreak of the First World War as they were in the 1990s. They were relatively small, requiring sustained inter-group contact. Within their boundaries, the intensity of the immigrant experience and the power of the immigrant challenge to convention shaped a distinct variation on the Canadian model of cultural diversity.[2]

Our contention is that, despite long-lived rural stereotypes inherited from previous generations – grand open spaces and pioneer farms – prairie cities were noteworthy sites in the making of regional and national history. A particular pattern of social diversity developed here, a pattern distinguished by significant changes in both host and migrant societies. Prairie Canada was not a melting pot, as depicted in the American cliché, nor was it the site of Anglo-conformism, wherein newcomers abandoned their former cultures and adopted a singularly

British–Canadian one. And, despite current assumptions, neither was it 'multicultural,' at least according to definitions of the term that place a priority on immigrants' retaining all the attributes of an historic ethnocultural group.[3] Each of these images captures part of the story, but none expresses its full meaning.

This book follows two approaches to the prairie cities' model of cultural diversity by suggesting that the genesis of their hybrid cultures lay in the vibrant ethnic networks developed by the immigrant communities and in the dynamic boundary zones where established Canadians encountered immigrants and their children. Chapters 1, 3, 5, 6, and 8, written by Royden Loewen, examine the ethnic group's social and cultural 'webs.' This image reflects the inner workings of ethnic community adjustment, the networks composed of familial, religious, inter-ethnic, and transnational links that shape newcomer strategies of integration. Within these social networks, the newcomers also develop their cultural webs; that is, their shared symbols and systems of meaning. Chapters 2, 4, and 7, written by Gerald Friesen, discuss the urban community as a whole, focusing on the first major western city, Winnipeg. The emphasis in these chapters is on relations between ethnic groups and host society, particularly the atmosphere of a market, a schoolyard, or a political forum where moments of cross-cultural contact take place in an imagined 'boundary zone.' The two images – the boundary zone and the ethnic web – highlight different aspects of immigrant and ethnic experience in the small cities of Canada's prairie interior.

The idea of ethnic web resonates with Clifford Geertz's view of culture as consisting of 'webs of significance.' It seeks the point of view of the newcomer, the 'inter-worked systems of constructable signs,' the way immigrants knew and understood the meaning of their migration.[4] It probes their imagination, seeks to understand their vocabularies, retells their stories. And it subverts the notion of the hapless victim of assimilation or the 'sugar coated, multicultural,' reified, immigrant subject. Echoing the work of Edward Said on 'the dominated cultural others,' this particular approach seeks to 'centre' the immigrant in the story.[5] Acculturation in this account is not especially important, not because it didn't happen but because it never ceased happening. As Fredrik Barth notes in one of his later works, all communities embrace 'interdependencies that generate a degree of order'; this web develops over time as newcomers seek 'knowledge [which] is a modification of earlier knowledge.'[6] But the ethnic web is also spatial: 'people pursue purposes, schemes and conscious design stubbornly and often collectively, thereby shaping many events.'[7] Ethnicity is reinvented in such social activities within specific ethnic networks; as Kathleen Neils Conzen and others have argued, in these social settings 'symbols and slogans ... could unify the group despite differences.'[8] Our book is also instructed by Franca Iacovetta's recent *Gatekeepers: Reshaping Immigrant Lives in Cold War Canada*, especially its depiction of hegemonic middle-class culture; our focus on ethnic webs, however, emphasizes not the host society's agenda, but the immigrant responses to the new culture and the process by which immigrants created viable communities in strange cities.[9]

To interpret prairie diversity more fully we employ the notion of an imagined 'boundary zone' between the host society and immigrant group. This idea draws in part on Barth's insights on 'social boundary,' but it is also informed by post-colonial studies, especially the idea that the venue of relations between nations or cultures is a 'third space.' Such a space, writes Homi Bhabha, can be found especially in the city: 'it is to the city that the migrants, the minorities, the diaspora come to change the history of the nation ... It is the city which provides the space in which emergent identifications and new social movements of the people are played out.'[10] Such a focus rejects the 'binary logic through which identities are often constructed' and proposes 'a cultural hybridity that entertains difference without an assumed or imposed hierarchy.' This approach to cultural relations between seemingly distinct entities, the immigrant group and the host society, sees them as sharing a great deal rather than differing in almost every respect.[11]

Our book is a work of synthesis rather than a monograph based exclusively on original scholarship. It draws on a corpus of scholarly research, much of it in thesis and dissertation form, and on texts especially rich in ethnographic illustration. It also relies on the work of a number of research associates – Esyllt Jones, Peter Nunoda, Jennifer Rogalsky, Kenneth Sylvester, Janis Thiessen, and Hans Werner – with whom we formed an immigration history research group at the beginning of this project.[12] It finds its intellectual moorings in the lively international conversation addressing migration, ethnicity, and cultural diversity or multiculturalism and transnationalism in several scholarly disciplines. Though it employs theoretical concepts developed by other scholars – boundary, hybridization, identity, webs of significance, invented traditions – it is really not about theory. Nor is it the story of particular ethnic groups in detail, a comprehensive history of migration, or a systematic survey of the policies that shaped those migrations or the geographies that resulted from them. Rather, it presents a story about people meeting people. As history, it describes the fragmentation and even conflict that accompany all migrations, but it also documents the interconnectedness that has emerged in the cities of Canada's western interior. It recounts, first, the common experiences of migrants and their children, and, second, the process by which a new society took shape over the course of a full century. In short, it sketches a regional model of Canadian cultural diversity.

The book concentrates on the three largest prairie cities – Winnipeg, Calgary, and Edmonton – and refers in lesser detail to two others – Regina and Saskatoon. Today, these centres are similar in ambience and in the appearance of their streets, buildings, and public spaces. Two, Calgary and Edmonton, are home to about a million residents each; Winnipeg, nearly seven hundred thousand; and Regina and Saskatoon over two hundred thousand each. In a region of more than five million inhabitants, the major cities contain more than half the population and most of the area's governmental, business, medical, university, and communication institutions. They are rooted in plain or parkland and closely tied to resource-rich hinterlands. Of the five, only Regina is not located on the banks of a major river, a measure of the relation between modern Canada and a past associated with the Aboriginal–European fur trade. And only Calgary, founded on the edge of the foothills and within view of the Rocky Mountains, is not deeply enmeshed in the homestead images that dominated prairie iconography for much of the twentieth century. Railways fixed the cities' sites as pre-eminent within the agricultural regions they served. Air travel, television, and satellite increasingly integrated them into the wider world in the second half of the century. The societies of the two half-centuries are similar in that, during the development of both print-capitalist and screen-capitalist cultures, the people who guided these global changes resided outside the region, in the true metropolises of the world. These are smaller, or second-tier, 'big cities.'

In the decades between the 1890s and the 1920s, the Prairies took on international significance as a zone of agricultural settlement. The newcomers had left several dozen national communities, mainly but not only in Europe. They chose Canada because the frontier of open land in the United States closed in the 1890s, because changes in the international terms of trade favoured new farm regions, and because Canadian authorities sought immigrants aggressively. A number of Canadian departures in policy and social practice followed. These innovations included federal policies that supported the admission of Chinese immigrants to help build the railways and establish the mining industry, of Ukrainians, Russian Germans, Scandinavians, and Doukhobors to build farms, and of sojourners from southern Europe to lay streetcar tracks and sewer lines in the growing cities. The West's attractions for such immigrant groups then led governments, both provincial and federal, to introduce discriminatory policies. Between 1896 and the outbreak of the First World War, several laws were passed by the Canadian parliament that clearly established 'the principle that the absolute right of the state to admit and exclude new members was an essential feature of state sovereignty.'[13] Further policy changes in 1907 sharply reduced the number of Chinese, Japanese, and East Indians entering Canada, while orders-in-council in 1911 and 1919 signalled that neither African Americans nor members of such religious sects as Hutterites, Mennonites, and Doukhobors would be allowed to enter Canada without restriction.

Prairie preoccupations continued to play a major role in Canada's immigration policies through to the 1970s. After the First World War, again for purposes of western development, Ottawa reintroduced relatively open immigration in comparison to the policy of its closest competitor, the United States. The change inspired hundreds of thousands of eastern Europeans to come to the West during the 1920s but this movement was halted during the Depression of the 1930s. After the Second World War, labour requirements in western Canada's agricultural, mining, and logging industries prompted a significant increase in immigration,[14] though the *Immigration Act* of 1952 maintained the race-based philosophy of its predecessors. A prairie prime minister, John G. Diefenbaker, revised these principles a few years later by introducing a 'colour blind' immigration process. The germ of Pierre Elliott Trudeau's 1971 multiculturalism policy lay in pressure from the so-called other ethnic groups – mainly but not exclusively of the Prairies – who insisted that a royal commission on 'bilingualism and biculturalism' could not address adequately the cultural and linguistic character of the country. In recent decades the arrival in the prairie cities of visible minority immigrants from southern countries and of Aboriginal peoples from rural and northern reserves has ensured that race and ethnicity remained central concerns in discussions of public policy. In sum, the western prairie and its leading cities have been a forcing ground for Canada's discussions of multiculturalism for most of the twentieth century.

Foreign migration to prairie cities can be pictured in three distinct periods, running from 1900 to the 1930s, from 1940 to the 1960s, and from 1970 to the 1990s. The early-century immigrant wave was mainly European, mostly Britons, Ukrainians, Germans, Jews, and Americans, with smaller numbers of Scandinavians, other East Europeans, and

Italians. These immigrants shocked established Canadians, in part because the latter were just beginning to feel comfortable with the gov-
erning institutions they had established in the three prairie provinces.
The mid-century wave did not differ much in ethnic origin, drawing
especially upon British, Dutch, German, Polish, Ukrainian, and other
Europeans, but the migrants leaving wartorn countries and communist
regimes travelled for very different reasons from those of their turn-of-
the-century predecessors. Significantly, the largest single group of 'foreign' newcomers in prairie cities in the post-1945 generation came from
the prairie countryside. It consisted of British Canadians and Aboriginal
people, but also of second- and third-generation Canadians, that is, eastern and northern European-origin farm families who were uprooted by a
rural economic transformation. The urban society of the western interior
was more firmly established by this time, however, and the long-settled
were more confident about their ability to deal with the challenges of the
immigrants. The late-century wave was quite different again because it
originated in the less-developed countries of the so-called Global South
– Asia, South America, Africa, the Caribbean, and the Middle East. It
constituted a unique phase in the history of migration, not because of the
volume of arrivals – the number of foreign newcomers in relation to the
total population was in fact smaller than in early-century decades – but
because of their cultural backgrounds and the readiness of the urban
communities to integrate them.

The following pages demonstrate that no matter when immigrants arrived, their identities and loyalties were changeable.[15] Their evolving
sense of ethnicity defined the group, canalizing social life and enabling
leaders to mobilize followers for partisan, commercial, or social ends. In
the process, ethnicity was reinvented as an activity of the present more
than as an inheritance from the past.[16] Canadian leaders sought to establish Anglo-conformity in the opening decades of the twentieth century,
as historian Howard Palmer has argued convincingly. But a half-century
later, the leaders tentatively agreed that ethnic cultural diversity might
be a good thing. Despite the snail's pace of change, this recognition
only acknowledged what migrants and their children had been expecting from their earliest days in Canada. As Will Kymlicka suggests,
pluralism permits the nurturing of minority cultures in order to smooth
citizens' integration into the wider society and its economy: bilingual
education, group historical interpretation, and religious holidays do
not so much preserve cultures from change as they offer cultural resources used by immigrant groups while they integrate into Canadian

spaces. Canadians, writes Kymlicka, have 'made the possession of an ethnic identity an acceptable, even normal, part of life in the mainstream society.'[17]

Race and racism also figure in this story.[18] Racism surfaced in every decade, manifested in different ways and receiving various responses from the wider community. The views of historians David Roediger and others, who see race as a fluid cultural creation that may only symbolically employ colour to distinguish one group of privileged people against a less privileged group, are apt.[19] So, too, are those of historian Constance Backhouse, who argues that racism in Canada cannot be understood without recognizing the 'national mythology' that 'Canada is not a racist country, or at least is much less so than ... the United States.' Backhouse's ironic assertion is that a 'mythology of racelessness' and a 'stupefying innocence ... would appear to be twin pillars of the Canadian history of race.[20] The following pages support her critical view.

International observers sometimes refer to the 'Canadian model of diversity.' This book responds that immigrant–host interaction is as much a local as a national phenomenon.[21] The following sequence of case studies illustrates how prairie Canadians dealt with questions of diversity when challenges arose. It alerts readers to the process of cultural creation within the ethnic communities and, as established citizens responded, within the cities themselves. We recognize that the social experience of Canadian diversity interests the international community. In his *The Immigrant Threat,* Dutch scholar Leo Lucassen highlights Canadian and Australian policies of multiculturalism that, in his words, advance the idea that 'transnational identities and ethnic group consciousness are ... good things.' He contrasts this view with the rising European wariness of immigration.[22] We recognize that delegations of public representatives from overseas regularly arrive in Canada to investigate its research and best practices on the social and economic integration of migrants, and that many nation-states now debate whether the multicultural ideal can ever be achieved and even whether it is worth pursuing. We reply that Canada has devoted considerable energy to these issues and that its experiences do constitute valuable lessons in the development of cultural diversity. But what is the model's content, how did it develop, and can it be replicated? A history of immigrants and ethnic groups in the cities of the western interior of Canada contributes to the discussion of these important questions.

Part One
Early Century: Ethnic Webs and Boundary Zones, 1900–1930s

chapter one

The Ethnic 'Centre': Family, Religion, and Fraternity

Early-century immigrants largely were shut out from power, privilege, and wealth in the prairie city. But at the centre of the immigrant's story was a vital community. In a sense it was an ethnic ghetto, a gathering of people, but it was much more. It was a cultural creation, in the words of anthropologist Clifford Geertz, a 'web of meaning,' providing the vocabulary, symbols, and understandings by which life made sense and social action was ordered.[1] This cultural matrix intersected with social networks that linked the German, Ukrainian, Jewish, Italian, Chinese, and other immigrants to their own kind. Such relationships enabled immigrants to set root in Canada, devise strategies of survival, construct their 'counter-hegemonies,' and, quite simply, to adapt culturally. The host society may have offered an array of institutions – public schools, theatres, sports halls, and political parties – but the immigrants reached into their own cultural repertoire to build their own responses to this new world. Within their families, houses of worship, and ethnic clubs, newcomers drew on deeply rooted ethnic symbols and loyalties. Their very humanity was defined in the ideas that undergirded this network.

At the centre of these immigrant communities was the ethnic household, linked by kinship to other households and shaped by common understandings of generation and gender within. It did not matter whether it was a privileged German nuclear family, a suspect Italian sojourner community, or a male-dominated Chinese clan group; the kinship network was crucial in the lives of the immigrants. Interspersed among the households were community institutions. Religious practice provided the immigrants not only with a focal point of social interaction, but a world view, a cosmology that explained the costly migration, a belief system that ordered their worlds, and, oftentimes, a set of sacred

narratives that offered hope for the days beyond the difficult transition
to the new world. Alongside the places of worship were social clubs and
fraternities, some linked to religion and others founded on overtly secular
thinking. Most of these clubs offered mutual aid of some sort and oftentimes opportunities for entertainment, learning, and political action.

The social relationships and 'webs of significance' within the ethnic
household, religious centre, and club sustained the immigrants in the
new land. These were not simply transplanted associations from the old
world based on old loyalties and understandings. New ones arose in response to the social requirements of the new land, thus providing the
very tools by which the immigrant gained entry into the wider community. Outsiders might see signs of either assimilation or of persistence.
Arguably, it was neither. These newcomers used localized, reinvented
ethnic cultures as well as inherited social relations to guide their travels
through the labyrinth of the prairie city. If their own social organizations
stood outside the city's public world, they nevertheless provided the immigrants with a springboard into that world. The immigrants integrated
into the prairie city with the help of their own organizations, their own
ethnic vocabularies, and their own trusted relationships. Thus armed,
the immigrants entered the city gates.

Family

The family and kinship group lay at the root of the migration encounter
in the prairie cities.[2] Examples of the importance of family can be found
in all groups of immigrants, from the most easily integrated to the more
marginalized, and even to the most ostracized and profoundly uprooted.
The highly integrated English migrants to Winnipeg, argues A. Ross
McCormack, knew the family as the 'principal mediator of social identity
in … society.' The family served 'as a mechanism to reduce their sense of
dislocation and to facilitate their adaption' to the new world.[3] The family
was also the primary economic unit; not only was the husband the breadwinner, but women and children worked to bring in money for household expenses. In this way passage loans were repaid, houses were
purchased in tight markets, and households re-established. The world of
the more marginalized Italian immigrants to the Prairies was similarly
family oriented. Antonella Fanella writes that the early-century Calgary
Italian community consisted of a series of social ripples emanating from
the centre, which was the nuclear family, moving out next to the *parenti*
(the 'relatives') and then to the *paesani* (the 'townfolk'). This latter group

was trusted in a way that the *estranei* (the 'strangers') – and thus potential enemies – were not. But no social unit drew loyalty 'the same as what [was] owed to family.'[4]

Family was also crucial for the Chinese newcomers in prairie cities, whose domestic lives were disrupted severely by a head tax and by systemic racism. For the outsider looking in, ethnic institutions such as local chapters of the Chinese Benevolent Association were the most obvious type of adaptive mechanism. Even Saskatoon's tiny Chinese enclave had such a chapter and Regina was home to a chapter of the competing Toisan organization. But, as Harry Con has argued, interwoven in these associations were powerful kin groups. In Edmonton three clans – the Mah, the Wong, and the Gee – dominated the executive committee of the local Chinese Benevolent Association. In Winnipeg the clan named Lee from the county of Hok-san in China's Guangdong province had a monopoly on the city's eleven downtown Chinese-run laundries until 1910.[5] It is true that all the Lees were not closely related, but, as Con notes, 'in China all those who bore the same surname [were] regarded as being patrilineally related.' Within this understanding the Lees created the clan association Li Shi Kung Sho, showing how 'the surname group as whole took the place of the local clan.'[6]

The family, however, was a complex and changing social unit. It was not simply a nuclear constellation of father, mother, and children transplanted from the old world. American historian Tamara Hareven once described family history as having moved its focus from 'the family as a static unit … to the family as a process over the entire lives of its members.' During an individual's life, family relations came to mean different things, and, as Hareven saw it, the historian's task was to trace the changing meaning of family. Family history also included a study of 'the wider kinship group, … the family's interaction with the [everyday] worlds … and with processes such as migration … and urbanization.'[7] Family was no less dynamic in the life of the prairie immigrant. It seethed with gendered and generational conflict as inherited concepts of masculinity and femininity were tested, reaffirmed, and recast. It created social alliances with other social groups, helping immigrants access the resources of the wider host society. It intertwined itself in ethnic churches and clubs, finding in them the cultural artifacts to reinforce a stable identity. The family was central to the process of social integration.

Family members often responded as units to changing economic opportunities. Their remarkable geographic mobility was testimony to this impulse. Historian Arthur Grenke reports that 72 percent of Winnipeg

Germans of 1909 left the city within the immigrants' first five years.[8] Icelandic–Canadian novelist Laura Salverson moved frequently, following her father and then her husband during the first third of the twentieth century, living for a time in each of Edmonton, Calgary, Regina, Saskatoon, and Winnipeg, and in the latter on three different occasions.[9] When immigrant families were not moving physically, they were introducing other changes that might improve their economic prospects. One typical strategy was to change their ethnic label by changing their surname – from Caroline Czarnecki to Connie Kingston and from Steve Dziatkewich to Edward Dawson[10] – in the hope of improving the odds of getting work and getting on. Another was to join an ethnic network of 'home-based' enterprises. James Gray writes that 'when a Ukrainian went into construction business,' he 'trailed a small army of other Ukrainians behind him – a Ukrainian concrete-mixer, a Ukrainian plumber, a Ukrainian carpenter, a Ukrainian painter, a Ukrainian plasterer. It was the same with the Germans.'[11] And, he might have added, Icelanders, Poles, Jews, and Scots.

The work of building a household economy in the early prairie city is rarely described as easy. Indeed, published descriptions have a familiar negative ring. One prairie immigrant writer described 'ugly unimaginative houses' from which marched a 'dreary procession of plodding humanity bent upon its furtive scramble for bread' in a region 'where the one touch of beauty was the remote, incorruptible sky.'[12] Another pictured a prairie city filled with 'the beaten, haunted looks of men and women whose youthful lives had been blighted by servitude to machines.'[13] Even J.S. Woodsworth's colourful vignettes in his 1909 *Strangers Within Our Gates* pictured ordinary, vulnerable people in difficult times in Winnipeg. Usually all family members were required to pitch in to help. In the hard-working family of Ignace Lagkowski, Father was employed by the Street Railway Company, but Mother also went out to work, while the two youngest boys hawked newspapers and an older boy laboured in a factory.[14] At other times economic requirements fragmented the 'family' and members could only hope that further migration would put it together again. A.R. Ford, an Englishman bound for Winnipeg by train from the east, answered the question 'am I married?' in the affirmative, but with the quick aside that 'the wife and three kiddies are left in Old London … I hope soon to bring them out if I can only get a job … what a bitter pill it is to come so far and leave the wife and kiddies behind with scarcely any money, and not knowing what is ahead of you…'[15]

Sometimes signs of the importance of the family lay in the very antipathies it created. In these instances family was anything but the sacred underpinning of urban existence: family links created intense dislikes and forced members into difficult situations. Dirk Hoerder's richly textured *Creating Societies* documents such negative experiences. The Swedish sojourner Edwin Alm saw in the prospect of 'family' nothing but images of distress and repression; to avoid that distress in one instance in 1913, he helped send a young pregnant neighbour, the girlfriend of a visiting Swedish countryman, to the city of Saskatoon to seek an abortion.[16] In the case of sixteen-year-old Gus Romaniuk of Manitoba's rural Interlake district, 'family' was the repelling, destitute social unit that sent him to find work in the city of Winnipeg; here he was hired by two friendly Ukrainian women who 'lent him money so that he could buy some urban-type clothing.'[17] For Agatha Karpinski the idea of 'family' reminded her of her abusive father, who pressured her to leave her employer, the widow Mrs Scott, to marry against her will. Agatha was expected to marry a forty-year-old bachelor who 'looked like her grandfather' and tend not only to his domestic needs but those of his older brother as well. Young Agatha found safety from this pressure when Mrs Scott whisked her to Calgary, where she found work as a housekeeper for a Jewish family, became active in the Polish community, and established her own life in a strange but liberating city.[18] In these and other instances family did not serve the immigrants' best interests.

Family life often made for sharp intergenerational conflict. Parents may have thought that children could both embrace their own ethnic culture and enjoy the fruits of the new country, but children often did not. The heartache experienced by parents who felt rejected by their modernist children fills the literature. Children faced demands foreign to their parents. In John Marlyn's *Under the Ribs of Death*, fictional character Sandor Hunyadi is a bank worker who has changed his name to Alex Hunter, and nurtures 'patricidal' fantasies. He is ashamed that his father seems out of touch with capitalistic Winnipeg, 'talking about the brotherhood of man ... not the survival of the fittest, but mutual aid ... Mutual aid, Sandor thought, "he should come to school with me for only one day. The English gang would teach him mutual aid."'[19] In other accounts children bring home new and foreign ideas from the new urban environment. In Adele Wiseman's novel *The Sacrifice*, tailor Abraham is angered by his son Isaac's liberal education and admiration for Charles Darwin's theory of evolution: '"Who is the older anyway" ... himself or his son? To call his father old-fashioned because he refused to believe that he was descended from a monkey! ... He had threatened to throw Isaac and his atheistical books out of the house altogether.'[20]

Sometimes the accounts told of farm children who had tasted the culture of the urban middle class; in the prairie cities they had seen their Paris. The fictional Icelandic farmer in Gudrún H. Finnsdóttir's 1921 short story 'Fýkur i sporin' ('Lost Tracks') laments that his daughter rejects his life's work of securing a farm for her in their home district of Vik, Manitoba:

> It was in the city that she had become acquainted with this future [English doctor] husband of hers. Then when she had graduated and come home, there were constant visits from Winnipeg all summer. Every weekend Vik was full of young people, Icelandic and English, who came to ... relax in the country ... He saw that [daughter] Ragnhildur was enjoying herself, and he did not grudge her that, because there had not been much joy in Vik when she was growing up. Ingófur had often looked with amazement at his daughter in this group of strangers ... His little girl, the farmer's daughter, raised by him in isolation ... not only held her own, but also surpassed all others in beauty, intelligence and graciousness. And he was sincerely pleased and thankful ...[21]

And yet when he actually sees the daughter and doctor hold hands one night, he is 'overwhelmed by pain, disappointment, and anger ... Ragnhildur, she had forsaken him, she had let him down for the first time in her life, and for an Englishman – she, his only child.'[22]

As family elders opposed the forces of assimilation, they activated different measures to repel such changes. Oftentimes religion secured marriage bonds within the ethnic household. Among Winnipeg Italians, notes Brian Ross, 'Catholic attitudes concerning divorce [and] interfaith marriages ... also served to bind the community ... [for] any offenders were swiftly and effectively estranged from the congregation and community.'[23] But immigrant institutions and family also worked hand-in-glove to keep children within the ethnic fold. The French–Canadian community in Edmonton, for example, created a set of outreach programs for its youth. Members founded the theatre group le Cercle Jeanne d'Arc in 1913, after 'realizing the value of a dramatic association in terms of the preservation of the French language as well as the enjoyment to be extracted from it.'[24] This initiative in turn spawned several other Edmonton French groups.[25] Young men and women also were encouraged to find marriage partners through local ethnic associations. In Calgary, Polish youth organized a Polish-language entertainment society in 1931 and here, according to Krystyna Lukasiewicz, 'Saturday dances and amateur performances attracted large audiences.' In particular, the 'possibility of meeting single men ... attracted many women.'[26]

If youth-oriented programs instilled a love for the ethnic community and the possibility of marriage to fellow ethnic members, the strategies by which the immigrants pursued those goals could differ significantly. Frances Swyripa notes that Ukrainians shared a strongly felt common ethnicity and that their young people chose from a wide range of ethnically oriented institutions. In one example, Ukrainians in Saskatoon reached out to the youth with overtly nationalistic and religiously nuanced messages: the Petro Mohyla Institute, a *bursa*, or young women's residential school, begun in 1916, worked hard to educate young rural females within a milieu of Ukrainian nationalism. Once affiliated with the newly formed Ukrainian Greek Orthodox Church and its Archbishop Ivan Theodorovitch, the Mohylianky became a modern, democratic, and aggressive force for 'Ukrainian consciousness and activity.'[27] In a second example, Ukrainian children in Winnipeg were encouraged to accept Canadian ways in addition to Ukrainian customs: V.H. Koman, president of the Canadian Ukrainian Athletic Club, ascribed the club's 1925 founding to the belief that 'to ensure that our youth will want to be part of our' community, 'we have to offer them that which attracts them ... all aspects of sports,' and sports that deliberately copied the 'Dominion Day tradition of other sports clubs in the city.'[28] Evidently, families happily supported ventures that kept their children within ethnic cultures.

Gender

Family dynamics, of course, were generated by gender in fundamental ways. Tensions between women and men often resulted as the two sexes differed on ways to define meaning in life or to acquire status in the community. They practised different rituals, struck different social pacts, and negotiated different social ties and networks. Sometimes these differences simply reflected the divergent migration paths that women and men took. In their work on the global Italian diaspora, historians Donna Gabaccia and Franca Iacovetta speculate how gendered migration patterns produced different nationalisms as 'men underwent a process of "becoming Italians" abroad while women maintained regional and local loyalties at home.'[29] Often, old concepts of masculinity and femininity were at the root of these differences. Canadian historian Steven Maynard's suggestion that a pervasive 'appeal to manliness' in the late nineteenth and early twentieth centuries caused 'rugged men' to embrace 'rough work' as a 'challenge of danger' could describe many prairie immigrant workers.[30] Similarly, Joy Parr's description of middle-class immigrant craftsmen as having ethnically conditioned entrepreneurial 'self-control,' physical stamina, prudent planning, and spendthrift attitudes seemed typical of many prairie immigrants.[31] Numerous historical writings identify similar variances in gendered identities among men and women that drew on peasant pasts, Victorian middle-class culture, and a Canadian 'maternal feminism.'

Among urban immigrants in prairie Canada, gender was constantly being re-evaluated, often in ethnic contexts. The masculinity of immigrant men, for example, could be the subject of romantic indulgence or outright condemnation. At least one Icelandic woman in Winnipeg felt herself drawn to an Irishman not so much for his money or handsome looks, but for his 'Irish virtues and vices' that included 'irascibility, tenderness, imagination and a love of good literature that was quite sincere.' The way this woman saw it, Icelandic men shared the virtue of sincerity with the Irish men, but they had none of the Irish romantic characteristics.[32]

Members of the host society often viewed immigrant men in unflattering ways, putting them squarely outside 'normative' British–Canadian masculinity. No men were more maligned than Chinese males. In two court cases, in Saskatoon in 1912 and in Regina in 1924, Chinese men were charged with breaking a provincial law prohibiting their ownership of laundries and restaurants that employed white women. In Regina, Yee Clun, a married man and a prominent long-time Chinese resident of the city, bravely appealed his conviction on this charge. But Clun faced the strident racism of host-society women's groups, including the Regina Women's Labour League, which declared that Clun would make Regina the 'queer city of the west,' drawing 'an undesirable class of women into the city.' Meanwhile Regina's Local Council of Women argued that 'Chinatowns have an unsavoury moral reputation' and that 'white girls lose caste when they are employed by Chinese.'[33] Anglo–Canadian women's groups, according to Constance Backhouse, were driven by exaggerated reports 'of Chinese plural marriage and concubinage' and by claims that 'depicted Chinese men as addicts of opium and inveterate gamblers' who were thrown off balance morally by 'the pronounced sexual imbalance within the Asian-Canadian community ...'[34]

Other groups of immigrant men may not have been criticized as aggressively, but they did not escape unscathed. Winnipeg's J.S. Woodsworth argued that while the Italians were 'nominally Roman Catholics' and that the women in Italian communities 'occasionally attend church,' the

fact was that 'the men have escaped its influence' and embrace an 'absolute religious indifference.'[35]

Ethnic groups themselves created a hierarchy of maleness in which some men met the bar of respectable masculinity and others failed to do so. The test of success could vary significantly for the immigrant man in the prairie city. Frequently these urban newcomers were maligned as nothing more than defeated homesteaders. Edmonton, it was said, was flooded with Ukrainians whose 'homestead dream gradually vanished' during the 1920s.[36] In Winnipeg, failed Dutch farmers, recoiling from hard work and social isolation, embarked on vegetable peddling and succumbed to that rural fear of a descent into 'a working class proletariat.'[37] Winnipeg was home, too, to uprooted Icelandic farmers; one father who had lost all in his sheep-farming attempts in North Dakota arrived 'hopelessly beaten, outwardly humble and apologetic' but still holding 'forth upon the merits of country existence.' The story has it that he was taunted by his wife: '"I've not the least doubt you'd make a capital farmer, dear Lars – if whist and toddy were the tricks of the trade."'[38] For Adele Wiseman's character Isaac in *The Sacrifice*, factory labour spelled a terrible 'impotence' and sterility: 'It was not as in the old country ... [where] a tailor was a tailor, from the first snippet to the last button. Here he couldn't call himself a tailor. If he could have made ... something – out of his hands, something whole. But from the first day ...he was on pockets. Sometimes, for a variation, it was belt facings – but mostly pockets.'[39]

Immigrant men knew that it was chiefly in British–Canadian commerce that a respectable masculinity could be expressed. Fictional character Sandor Hunyadi's only reservation about his newly chosen name Alex Hunter was that 'it was too soft'; he acknowledged his fear later when he was moved to sympathy for a fellow immigrant by 'something soft within him that he ha[d] tried again and again to crush.' He blamed the softness – this troubled masculinity – on his 'father's blood in his veins, carrying this weakness ...'[40] The capitalistic city demanded a fundamental review of male character.

Immigrant women, too, reconsidered traditional roles. Sometimes they found themselves with enhanced status as managers of households in new lands, and other times as uprooted mothers engaged in a frantic search for meaning. McCormack's description of the British–Canadian family places women as its 'foundation stone.' In this capacity the woman of the house was central to 'her husband's and children's emotional adjustment,' for in Canada the home was 'the focus for the maintenance of British aesthetic cultural forms such as idiom, diet and values.'[41] Further status was earned when these same women earned supplemental income for their households, providing room and board for single males, thus insulating their countrymen from an alien society and providing loved ones with additional financial resources to withstand a capricious economy.

Tamara Palmer's survey of prairie fiction captures a quite different immigrant woman's world from the one observed by McCormack. Palmer argues that unlike rural novels, which often present 'the life-affirming character' of women refusing to be 'defeated by [an] uprooting,' urban fiction does not 'shift to matriarchal values … as a means of resolving the immigrant and ethnic dilemma.' She concludes that in novels about prairie cities there are no ethnic 'matriarchs whose nurturing vision ultimately effects a physical and social victory. Rather, the immigrant generation is portrayed as hopelessly uprooted, its wisdom and experience useless, even a liability, in the Canadian urban landscape.'[42]

Perhaps McCormack's perspective is too laudatory and Palmer's too dismissive. It is undeniable that immigrant women in the cities were buffeted by new challenges. They were tested by the new society, empowered by transplanted old-world mythologies, and especially circumscribed by middle-class values. Adele Wiseman's *The Sacrifice* juxtaposes two women. Quiet Sarah seems exhausted and overly dependent on husband Abraham. He watches her with paternalistic sympathy; her 'eyes distant and dream-haunted,' a woman who 'needs the present, the immediate satisfaction of life.' He sees her 'rooted in the earth, like a tree, like a flower,' and in self-congratulatory patriarchism he observes her lift 'her face to receive the gift of the wind [as] suddenly he sweeps across the earth and stoops to blow the dust. Then she comes to life; she seizes it … and works with it the miracle of creation.' But there is another woman: Sarah's counterpart, landlord Mrs Plopler, is different, an inveterate gossip possessed of endless energy. She lectures her husband and intimidates the corner grocer. She also extends her womanly friendship to weary Sarah: 'a moment ago Mrs. Plopler had been weeping with Sarah, watering a wound that was far deeper than she could understand.'[43] Here, a strong woman and a weak woman represent different aspects of the reality of immigrant life.

Immigration tested women in new ways. The women in Marlyn's *Under the Ribs of Death* are not free to negotiate their own paths into the new society; their men restrict the range of possible responses. Young Sandor, with his newly honed middle-class perspective, renders the women in his life as ghosts of an ethnic past. He is threatened by their mythological old-world powers. He arrives home in his ethnic enclave wearing his business attire, but he feels no power because he cannot shake 'their eyes upon him and the instant disapproval of the women who [sit] facing him in a long straight line against the wall ... a collective grimace.' Those women who display power he dismisses as beasts and mutations of old-world culture. The assertive Fraulein Kleinholtz possessed 'a man's desire to master' and other women remind Sandor 'of the female demons in old Hungarian peasant tales ... half woman, half monster, rising not from the floor, but from the depths below.' His only affection is directed to his mother, albeit, it seems, as an object coloured by his new middle-class understandings: 'in the center of the kitchen with baby in her lap' she appeared to him a 'stranger,' surprisingly beautiful but looking 'so tired.'[44]

Each urban woman's everyday world was a mix of old and new cultures. No doubt her role was altered by a new social reality, at least for those women from rural backgrounds: the daytime absence of the man from the house. As a consequence the man possessed a new power in the household derived from his role as primary breadwinner. Still, during the first part of the century, the immigrant woman could often maintain her peasant-based status as a household producer and custodian of folklore. By tradition and necessity, women's tasks included a combination of food production and household-based, income-generating activities. Until city bylaws prohibited the keeping of animals, many immigrant women turned their urban lots into miniature farms. German women in Winnipeg's Elmwood district found inexpensive land and kept chicken flocks, cabbage gardens, and perhaps a cow, while their men took lunch buckets to work in Winnipeg's mills, factories, and construction sites.[45] Polish women in Depression-era Edmonton and Calgary supported their families and unemployed husbands 'by sewing and doing house cleaning jobs,' but, as one woman recalled, 'there were nine children in our family,' and so 'mother kept chickens, cows and pigs' and 'prepared her own sausages and meat preserves for the winter.'[46] The requirements of these early-century immigrant households dictated that women were economic producers.

Until the first great wave of immigration subsided with the First World War, immigrant women were also the first hosts of newcomers. Myrna Kostash suggests that 'the boarding house in Edmonton or Vegreville, owned by a Ukrainian, operated by his Ukrainian wife and specializing in (crowded) accommodation for single men recently arrived from the Ukraine or the farm may have been the first example of independent Ukrainian business in Alberta.'[47] Turning the home into a boarding house could provide a real measure of economic independence. Woodsworth reviewed the story of Ladowska, a mother of two girls who had left her husband, 'who was cruel to her.' She 'can do better alone,' wrote Woodsworth, because 'she works by day and keeps two or three roomers.' He also told the story of Widow Machterlincks, who 'rented her house in which there are five rooms,' and which sheltered 'two families as tenants and between 15 and 20 men boarders,' thus enabling her to build up a little estate of 'several [city] lots.'[48]

Young immigrant women found in domestic service yet another old-world tradition adapted to urban life. The practice was common in western Canadian cities. Wsevolod W. Isajiw writes that 'there was hardly a Ukrainian settlement in the West from which girls and young women did not go to work in the cities.' He notes that by the 1920s 'Ukrainian girls could be found in most Winnipeg restaurants, though seldom in the most expensive ones.'[49] Although domestics in the city undoubtedly were exploited, their new urban roles often seemed liberating.[50] According to Krystyna Lukasiewicz's study, back-breaking homestead work and the prospect of large families 'pushed' young Polish women to migrate to Edmonton. The assurance of economic 'influence' as married farm producers did not counter their mothers' harsh experiences on the rural frontier. True, employment 'in private homes, hospitals and nursing homes' was 'poorly paid and low [in] status,' but 'even such jobs ... were considered better than the drudgery of farm work.'[51] The daughters of immigrant farmers sang the cities' praises.

Similar expressions came from young women sent to the cities to pay their families' travel debts incurred under the Railway Agreement of 1925. Marlene Epp and Frieda Esau-Klippenstein each have described the lives of young Dutch–Russian Mennonite women in Winnipeg, tucked away in church-supported, paternalistic Mädchenheimen, the 'homes away from home.' Despite regimented lives, controlled ultimately by rural church elders, the girls testified to a variety of life-enhancing sentiments. They expressed feelings of worthiness for 'doing what we could'; they cheered their social freedom on the weekly Maids' Day Off on Thursdays; they proudly showed off new middle-class skills and etiquette that made it 'easier for some of their families to settle in urban centers,' thereby 'opening ... the gate of the city.'[52] As they saw it, the sacrifice of urban domestic service away from their families allowed them to gain the skills of urban life, which they could pass on to their own children, enabling at least the second generation to become respected urban residents.[53]

Religion

If the family was the early-century immigrants' primary social network in the prairie city, the religious institution oftentimes offered the most crucial cultural matrix in urban life. Religion was especially important at a time when the vast majority of Canadians were attached to religious communities, mostly to those within the Judeo–Christian tradition. Certainly the social dimensions associated with religious communities were important: religion could provide supportive networks and infuse them with a familiar hierarchy, a power accepted by some, bitterly contested by others.

More crucial even than religion's social aspect was its cultural side. It could provide the mystery and understandings, and broad claims on truth, that took the immigrant through the steps of relocation.[54] It invited humans to build relationships with the divine. Paul Bramadat writes that non-Christian religions among immigrants in Canada usually embraced 'a view of the universe in which ... an unseen divine (or extra human force) or forces [were] at work' and in which a central goal was the cultivation of 'right relations with ... the divine entity or entities.'[55] Religion could also offer a divine explanation for the hard times of relocation. Especially within the Judeo–Christian traditions, religion stirred the immigrants to imagine the passage of historic time, to envisage a grand teleology that explained the vagaries of daily life, especially in a new and strange land. Historians of immigrant religion also depict it as adaptable, acquiring new symbols, imagining new religious spaces, and melding seemingly contradictory liturgical, pietistic, or millenarian strands into a larger synergistic system of thought.[56] Outsiders may have seen immigrants attend exotic-looking, even magnificent, buildings of worship; they may have heard gossip of strange religious conflicts and schisms around alien ideas. But it was the very familiarity of church, synagogue, and other buildings of worship and religious life that attracted the immigrants. The vocabulary could be compelling. In worship the newcomers could invoke the words and images of their forebears. In their gatherings they might grapple with the great questions of origins and destinies, and invariably they asked questions of right and wrong. Their meetings legitimized new community power structures, just or unjust. In some communities, they offered to explain or critique the marginalization of the minority group within the powerful host nation.

Religious centres in prairie Canada were especially complex sites of cultural exchange. Mainline Protestants – Anglicans, Methodists, Presbyterians, Baptists – were fewer here in proportion to the whole than elsewhere in Canada. Prairie people, as Anthony Rasporich has argued, seemed to have a special interest in popular religions; that is, in sectarianism, utopianism, and messianic fixations.[57] They could be anti-clerical, not a variation that was so much anti-religious as one that simply venerated ordinary members and heeded local understandings. The very complexity of religious activity in this polyethnic region – immigrant or majority cultures, liturgical or sectarian creeds, Christian or Jewish, western or eastern traditions – defied easy categorization. Prairie Canada was the site of a wide spectrum of religious practice, and at the local level many of these traditions engendered rigorous religious debate.

Asian religions and belief systems – borrowing selectively from a combination of Buddhist, Taoist, and Confucian practices – were central in the lives of Chinese immigrants. While none of the prairie cities is said to have possessed a free-standing Chinese religious temple in these early decades, Winnipeg and Calgary had distinctive Chinatowns and, despite their smaller Asian populations, even Regina, Saskatoon, and Edmonton had Chinese cemeteries, likely sites of visits on Chinese New Year or Qingming festivals.[58] Because of the practitioners' small numbers and religion's very close linkages to family, worship was usually outside the purview of the public eye. Still, as David Chuenyan Lai, Alison R. Marshall, and others have argued, religious discourse was fundamental to immigrant Chinese religion in Canada. Here was an ancient set of beliefs; the cosmos, seen as 'male Sky and female Earth (tiandi),' produced 'life energy (qi) from complementary opposing forces (yinyang)' and was 'understood on the model of the family.'[59] Thus 'in a traditional Chinese home of an eldest son … [there will be] an altar on which will be found … tablets with the names of the immediate deceased … of the male lineage' and oftentimes 'a statuette of a deity, usually related to the occupation of the family' and 'an image of Guanyin (… a deified woman) who is able to assist the dead, ensure progeny, and enhance the fortunes of merchants.'[60] Daily and monthly food offerings before the altar were central features. Because early Chinatowns were mainly 'bachelor societies,' many of these private rituals occurred within clan associations described above.

Chinese immigrants, of course, lived in a predominantly Christian society that did not view Asian practice as benign. In 1909 Winnipeg Protestant reformer J.S. Woodsworth displayed an overtly xenophobic tone in describing Chinese religion as centred on a 'god ... with long black beard' in 'dark recesses' behind the altar and bearing a 'malignant expression.' His text further described Chinese religion as 'a mixture and a puzzle, a marvel and a wonder, a mystery' carried into the streets on special occasions with sounds from 'outlandish fiddles and the boom- ing of the worshippers' drum ... [and] tongueless bells ... touched by the soft hammer ... [s]oft and liquid, ... heal[ing] the wounds of the harsh rasping of the other instruments.'[61] This description may well sug- gest the attraction religion held for the Asian immigrant in a strange land, but it also suggests just how strange the native-born Canadian con- sidered these religious practices. It was said that in Edmonton British Canadians enthusiastically 'defended' the Chinese when they became Christians, happily turning 'mission buildings into centers of Chinese community life' where Protestantism and the English language could be taught simultaneously.[62]

The importance of immigrant religious practice can be seen even in intra-community conflict within many newcomer communities. Religious traditions often promised inner serenity. As Orest Martynowych has writ- ten of Ukrainian worshippers in Winnipeg, they found a 'solace ... within the domed, candle-lit [basilicas], where the timeless liturgy celebrating Christ's sacrifice reassured the immigrants that their suffering was not in vain.'[63] However, this inner solace was often accompanied by social up- heaval. And that unrest revealed another dimension of religiousness. The religious institution held a whole spectrum of 'repertoires of contention.' Conflict within religious traditions, like other forms of social debate, was a 'learned cultural creation' used to express disapproval and manage conflict, dictating a 'limited set of routines' by which people made de- mands of other people.[64] In prairie cities, ordinary people could well con- front distant centres of religious power. Insisting on local priorities and understandings, the immigrant communities readily engaged in religious 'wars.' Criticism of the religious leadership was usually not directed at religious practice itself, but at leadership when it seemed insensitive to the needs of ordinary members. Myrna Kostash writes that Ukrainians could scowl at stories of oppressive priests, 'old country ... ragtags of folk- lore, stories about greed, lust, treachery and corruption.'[65]

Lay criticism shaped the very history of the prominent Ukrainian Greek Catholic Church in western Canada. Practising a centuries-old eastern Byzantine or Orthodox liturgy, and led by married priests, the church was at odds with the local French–Canadian leaders of the Roman Catholic Church. Nevertheless the Greek Catholics were expected to answer both to the Vatican in Rome and to the culturally distant French–Canadian archbishop located in Saint-Boniface, just east of Winnipeg. Rome forbade Ukrainian married clergy to migrate to North America and Roman Archbishop Langevin turned down a request for the establishment of a separate Ukrainian church. Ukrainian immigrants in Winnipeg thus were compelled to gather 'in private homes and chant ... mass with prayers as best they could.' In 1899 they rebelled, requested help from the Ukrainian Greek Catholic Church in the United States in forming a parish, and then set out to construct their own basilica. Other Ukrainian Catholics defected to the competing Russian Orthodox Church and even the Presbyterian-supported Independent Greek Church. Only after these brazen acts did the French–Canadian Archbishop Langevin write Metropolitan Sheptytsky, the head of the Greek Catholic Church in Galicia, to request Byzantine priests and nuns for western Canada. By 1912 the first Ukrainian Greek Catholic bishop, Nicetas Budka, arrived in Winnipeg to provide regional leadership.[66] Lay initiatives had secured ethnic religious leadership.

Religious conflict rarely could be predicted. The Jewish story in Winnipeg is a complicated tale of separations, near unions, amalgamations, contests, and peacemaking. Like the Ukrainians, early Jews in Winnipeg had taken the initiative when they found themselves in the 'distant west' without religious leadership. Living 'a great distance from the rest of the Jewish world,' writes Gerald Tulchinsky, prairie Jews were forced 'to do virtually everything for themselves,' acts that 'also infused them with an energy that made their efforts strikingly successful.'[67] Historian Arthur Chiel gives the specifics: Winnipeg Jews established a synagogue on Yom Kippur in 1879 when a group of men 'gathered in a house' and, in the absence of either a rabbi or a Torah scroll, 'prayed and fasted together as a group and experienced a measure of religious identity for the first time in their new setting.' But, given this relative informality, they also headed for a series of divisions. Only five years after their founding, in 1884, the small Winnipeg group separated into two opposing groups based on the cultural background of the devotees: the large Russian–Jewish Orthodox Sons of Israel and the small German–Jewish Reform Beth El group.

In time the Reform Jews worshipped at one synagogue, the Shaarey Zedek constructed in 1890, while the Orthodox created their own Rosh Pina, 'a traditional synagogue closely approximating the eastern European house of worship in its intimacy and informality.' The division sharpened in 1894 when the small Reform congregation sought sole legal recognition in Manitoba. To make matters even more complicated, in 1903 the more liberal segment of the Reform synagogue created a third house of worship in Winnipeg, the English-language Holy Blossom (although ten years later it reunited with the parent synagogue). Meanwhile the Orthodox synagogue was challenged by small dissident groups that created 'small synagogues,' which were 'self-contained and ruggedly independent' and more in tune with the 'immediate religious needs of their own generation.' By the 1930s, however, these mini Orthodox synagogues, out of step with the second generation and not able to win over new immigrants from Europe, suffered decline. After the Second World War the historic split between the Reform and Orthodox synagogues ended when 'both Shaarey Zedek and Rosh Pina affiliated with the United Synagogue of America, thus linking the congregations with a total membership of 1200 families, with the Conservative movement in America.'[68] The conflicts were rooted in intense religious commitment of the everyday, on the one hand, and competing strategies of integration into the wider society, on the other.

Religious conflict also involved theological debate. Esoteric perhaps to the outside observer, these ideas could engage members in everyday life. In his study of the Volksdeutsche Lutherans in prairie Canada, John Cobb has argued that their seemingly abstract historical teaching of 'justification by faith alone' had significant implications for the way they lived in the everyday, including acts of charity and neighbourliness.[69] Other theological teachings, however, could generate intense debate among German-speaking parishioners. Arthur Grenke explains that Black Sea German Catholics and Volga Lutherans had both come from the Russian Empire, but they held opposing views on the Holy Sacrament, the bread and wine said to represent the body of Christ. The ceremony of consuming these physical elements, Christianity's most sacred ritual, promised a spiritual union with God and a sense of religious well-being in the everyday. Ironically, controversy surrounding this ritual seemed to make it all the more compelling. The Catholic belief in the idea of transubstantiation – that the substance of the sacrament literally turned into the body of Christ – was summarily dismissed by the Lutherans, just as their own symbolic ideas were derided as 'lukewarm' by the Catholics. And each of the groups seemed comforted to know that they were right and the others wrong. The belief differences helped to cast German immigrants as two ethno-religious groups: German Catholics and German Lutherans.

But conflict could reside even within these subgroups. Lutherans in western Canada, represented by the competing Missouri and Ohio synods, differed sharply on the question of 'election.' This was the process by which a person came to have 'faith' and thus attain 'salvation'; that is, forgiveness of sin and promise of eternal life. Missouri Lutheran congregations claimed that God chose the immigrant even before birth in an act of 'predestination'; Ohio-linked churches believed that the immigrant chose God in an act of 'free will.' Biblical texts could be summoned to prove one position or another. In the everyday life, devotees insisted that their own view was 'true.' It alone generated religious solace, the best answers to universal questions, the strongest support for a moralistic code of conduct. Lay people could well see in religious doctrine not something esoteric, but the very cultural undergirding of everyday life.[70]

Ethnic Association

Like the religious centre, the secular ethnic club reflected ordinary immigrant concerns. The two institutions shared other qualities. Both witnessed ongoing conflict, encouraged individual participation, and registered remarkable growth. In other ways they also seemed intertwined. Many religious institutions served immigrant communities by working closely with secular mutual aid societies, but at least some ethnic institutions gained strength by denouncing religion as hypocritical, superstitious, and self serving. Together the religious institutions and the ethnic association provided an inclusive offering of ethnic services, meeting most new needs of urban existence. Both represented ethnic webs of solidarity and trust.

The linkage of worship site and ethnic club was everywhere apparent. Cultural and linguistic persistence was an interest of many religious organizations. In Edmonton numerous French-language societies such as the St Jean Baptiste Society had ties to the early Roman Catholic churches: their role was to defend culture, to seek *la survivance* of the French language. They were organized by an awareness that in western Canada they were members of a minority group, and must be prepared to battle for their cultural interests in the school language legislation in Manitoba and the Autonomy bills that created Alberta and Saskatchewan in 1905.[71] Many other groups linked religion and mutual aid. Among Italians in Winnipeg the Rome Mutual Benefit Society was founded in 1911 to assist the large numbers of Italian railway workers. Brian Ross writes that they were 'time-honoured, religious-communal traditions ... bred in the mountain and valley *campanio* of Italy but maintained and nurtured in the streets of Winnipeg's "Banana Crescent."'[72]

Other societies were founded on secular and even anti-religious grounds. Jewish and Ukrainian communities spawned several rigorously anti-religious ethnic institutions. The Winnipeg chapter of the Jewish workingmen's Arbeiter Ring was committed, as Rosaline Usiskin writes, to 'fight against sickness, premature death and capitalism.' An early member of the Arbeiter Ring in Winnipeg noted that it 'had acquired great influence among the young people because the ideals of freedom, internationalism, brotherhood and working class unity had captured everyone's imagination.' Passionately held progressive ideologies created subgroups of radicals, including the Revolutionary Marxists, the Socialist Territorialists or Zionists, and the Anarchists. Each of these Jewish groups funded mutual aid societies, sought to alleviate suffering from Jewish pogroms in Russia, voiced class solidarity with workers, and organized local forums with internationally renowned speakers. In the end, concludes Usiskin, 'a new culture was being created, a vigorous secular culture, for and by the Jewish immigrant worker.'[73]

Linking the Jewish community to radicalism were visits to prairie cities by anarchists such as the internationally renowned Emma Goldman, a daughter of Orthodox Jews. In 1907 she stayed in Calgary for two days and gave her standard speech on 'labour agitation, the emancipation of women and class differences.' Later in 1927, exiled from the United States, she visited Edmonton for a month, a sojourn supported by institutions such as the Edmonton Jewish Women's League, the Socialist Party, and the Edmonton District Labour Council.[74]

Strikingly similar ideas and institutions emanated from radical Ukrainians. Orest Martynowych explains that as early as 1899 in Winnipeg the secularist International Reading Room had pre-empted even the first Ukrainian parish. And by 1906, just before its collapse, the Taras Shevchenko Educational Society's 130 members had 'rejected clerical tutelage and debated the relative merits of socialism, nationalism and anarchism.' In the decade that followed secular organizations succeeded in winning the loyalties of more than 10 percent of the Ukrainian population. Repeatedly 'religion and the nature of man were topics that both socialists and nationalists addressed.' The aim of the conveners was clear: 'to persuade immigrants that the social order was not some immutable divine creation but the result of human greed and ambition.' Eventually the labour activists created a focal point of Ukrainian secularism in the imposing Ukrainian Labour Temple, constructed in Winnipeg's North End in 1919, 'a secular cathedral *par excellence.*'[75]

The dynamism within the ethnic institution is also apparent in the variety of such institutions. Grenke's study of Winnipeg Germans argues that their ethnic associations were so elaborate that members could well 'remain within the confines of the associations for all the primary relations and most of their secondary relations throughout … their life cycle.'[76] The first successful German club in Winnipeg, the Sherman House of 1884, helped new arrivals find employment in, and information on, the Canadian West, and to communicate with the Department of the Interior. The German Society, founded in 1892, helped rekindle old-world ties with its library of two hundred books, its international subscriptions to German-language newspapers, and its traditional carnivalesque celebrations, the Fasching and the Maskenball. Then, reflecting the heterogeneity of the immigrants, the Reichsdeutsche immigrants began their own society in 1904; the Swiss Germans, their own Helvetia Club in 1905; the Austria–Hungary Germans, a separate club in 1906; the Volksdeutsche of Russia, theirs in 1908; and the Hungarian Germans, their own Banat some time later. Despite these separations, the Germans united for specific events: the 1894 inter-German Musick Kapelle enthusiastically played for immigrants as they arrived at the Canadian Pacific Railway station; the 1906 Turnverein organized the immigrants to play Old Country sports; the 1909 Thalia club discussed art and presented plays. Specific labour unions were tied into American–German unions; workers at the *Der Nordwesten* newspaper, for example, joined the Deutsch–Amerikanische Typographia No. 23, and German builders signed up for a German-language carpenter's guild based in the United States. In 1913 when depression hit Canada, Winnipeg Germans organized a Deutsche Unterstuetzungsverein to provide aid to unemployed countrymen. Only the dismissal of things German during the war weakened these institutions.

Conclusion

What the outside observer saw as a border, prohibiting the immigrant from fully integrating into early prairie urban society, was in fact the demarcation of a staging ground for integration. Family circle, religious centre, and ethnic club were sites where immigrants nurtured their social contacts, cultural expressions, and symbolic worlds. In kinship networks, families spoke their own old-world languages, passed on folklore, sustained their aging elders, and addressed their young. These networks also provided them with the emotional and financial resources to enter the wider world. The lives of women and men were shaped by inherited ideas about gender, ideas that were severely tested in the new world. Intergenerational conflicts signalled that within the ethnic circle was a spirited debate on the best strategy for participating in that society.

Similar patterns can be observed in the community's institutions. Places of worship provided both social resources and spiritual vocabulary to help establish a sense of order in a new world. These social and cultural realities may have appeared to be transplanted from an old-world base, but oftentimes they were new-world creations born within conflict, shaped by ordinary members and local understandings. Ethnic clubs, too, were creations of the act of immigration; oftentimes taking a decidedly secular tack, they provided services to strengthen a community in a new world. The story of the immigrant to prairie cities has a strong social and cultural component, one that marks the genesis of kinship networks, cultural webs, and social institutions drawing immigrants together in a new land.

chapter two

Patterns of Conflict and Adjustment in Winnipeg

Newcomers used their ethnicity as a staging ground from which they could enter the wider community and to which they could retreat. The factors that distinguished their ethnic practices might include distinct ways of speaking or distinct types of clothing, and certainly distinct networks of friends. Ethnicity as staging ground was a strategy based on difference. It placed great store on the markers separating the various newcomer communities as well as on the differences between one's group and the host society. But there were many occasions in daily life when immigrants encountered members of other ethnic communities or, indeed, established Canadians. In these moments the two parties negotiated what scholars have described as 'the social processes of exclusion and incorporation.' They came into conflict, in other words, and they learned to cooperate. An outsider might describe the negotiation as a story about a city's ethnic pockets, about the barriers encircling each group, and about the boundary zones where the encounters took place.[1]

The imagined boundary zones are elusive targets. One might think of them as places where barriers between groups are being raised or lowered. Fredrik Barth, the Norwegian anthropologist, in his discussions of the boundaries between ethnic groups, suggests that the distinguishing characteristics between migrant ethnic group and host society – the factors that determined the height of the barriers – might include history, language, economy, and such symbolic markers as holiday celebrations, clothing or jewellery styles, and foods. In his hypothesis, different groups came to rely on different distinguishing characteristics. The 'social processes of exclusion and incorporation' operated simultaneously, encouraging some cross-cultural contacts and forbidding others, but what was forbidden and what was an appropriate matter for negotiation might differ from group to group.[2]

Important similarities of experience that affected immigrants and established Canadians alike are often described as 'assimilative pressures.' To use such language is not to claim there was a linear progression from 'immigrant' to 'Canadian' as was proposed by the first generation of migration studies, the so-called Chicago school, in the 1920s and 1930s. Rather, as Russell Kazal, Jan Lucassen, and Leo Lucassen have argued, immigrants and their descendants move toward a condition in which they no longer 'regard themselves as different from the native-born population and are no longer perceived as such.'[3] They might still embrace their old-world heritage and even regard their ancestral heritage as primordial but, by becoming residents of a regional city and citizens of Canada, they acquire other identities that are important in specific contexts. Paradoxically, established residents embark on a similar journey but in the opposite direction. As teachers, they come to know their students and to admire their abilities; as shopkeepers, they readily recognize a customer's courtesy and honesty; and, as politicians, they acknowledge a supporter's partisan loyalties. It is this aspect of *mutual* accommodation in boundary zones that makes the prairie story significant.

Memoirs of Exclusion

This chapter focuses specifically on Winnipeg, which received the largest percentage of the tens of thousands of immigrants who arrived in prairie cities in the opening decades of the twentieth century. At the site surrounding the forks of the Red and Assiniboine rivers, the clay gumbo of a former lake bottom was gouged out and hauled away as citizens built entire neighbourhoods, dozens of schools and apartment buildings, miles of streetcar tracks, and multi-storey factories and warehouses that were necessary to maintain one of the world's next great granaries, the Canadian prairies. New arrivals and established Canadians bounced and jostled against each other until they eventually found more or less stable resting places, but the process was a complicated one. Language, faith, and respect for national memories created barriers that distinguished one group's members from all others.

With nearly fifty thousand inhabitants, Winnipeg was the only 'big' city on the Prairies at the turn of the twentieth century. It exploded in numbers and influence during the next decade, and grew more slowly during the First World War, reaching a population of about two hundred thousand in 1921. Two decades later, in 1941, the capital region counted nearly three hundred thousand residents, larger than the other four major prairie cities combined. Manitoba's capital was the hub of prairie transportation, the focus of prairie-wide commerce and trade, and a junior manufacturing and financial centre in Canada.

Nearly half of Winnipeg's residents in 1921 were immigrants and, as late as the Second World War, one-third had been born in another country. This ratio was comparable to that in Calgary and Edmonton, and was matched in several other Canadian cities, notably Vancouver and Victoria in the west (also about 50 percent in 1921) and Toronto and Hamilton in central Canada (just under 40 percent).[4] The proportion of immigrants in the community's population, however, was only one measure of its character.

More important than the newcomers' status as immigrants was their place of origin. Public life in Winnipeg was British in tone. Though they remained convinced of their differences, the English (roughly 88,000), Scots (52,000), and Irish (32,000) constituted about 60 percent of the capital district's population in 1936 (172,000 of 288,000 people). Each was larger than the next most populous ethnic groups. Looked at from outside their charmed circle, these people were 'British' and, as such, constituted the established order. They were 'normal' in a world where the norm, the typical or average citizen, was otherwise very hard to define. They could behave as if they alone determined the rules of social intercourse. The British spoke the only truly acceptable public language, had grown up with the monarch, recognized the structures of parliamentary government and the old-line political parties, and shared an easy familiarity with English-speaking Canada's leading symbols, whether authors, songs, military heroes, or faces on postage stamps. If challenged, members of each British group might say stiffly that they were not the model of the modern Canadian and that someone else – Scottish Ontarians or home counties English or Labour Party Glaswegians – owned the title. Nonetheless, every Briton could claim that he or she was closer to the preferred model of citizenship than other residents of the city.

It was the presence of this British 60 percent and the fact of another 40 percent – the 'not British' – that made Winnipeg both interesting and difficult. One guide to the city's diversity was the wide range of languages spoken. The proportion of Winnipeg residents who spoke only English was strikingly low: 54 percent in 1931, when Calgary's was 69 percent. An even more telling index was the census report on residents' ethnic origin, determined by one's father's line. About 26,000 Ukrainians resided in the capital region in 1936, 17,000 Jews, 17,000 Germans, and

15,000 French, mostly French-speaking, Canadian-origin residents of the adjacent town of Saint-Boniface. There were also 12,000 Poles and 10,500 Scandinavians, many of whom were Icelanders. Each of these six non-British communities supported active cultural and athletic movements, weekly newspapers, specialty stores with distinctive foods, and consciously ethnic or religious political representation. Another eight groups in the Winnipeg region were much smaller but, with at least one thousand residents each, the Italians, Dutch, Belgians, Hungarians, Austrians, Russians, and Czechs/Slovaks were still large enough to be noticed, and so were the 760 'Chinese and Japanese' – a census category that distinguished mostly Chinese men. Each of these seventeen groups, small and large, was a consciously 'national' community, struggling for survival, a degree of acceptance, and some respect.

Yet another index of difference was religion. The Anglican, United, and Presbyterian churches accounted for more than half the total population in the capital region. The Catholic proportion, Roman and Greek Catholic together, was just under 25 percent in the late 1930s (Roman about fifty thousand, Greek just under twenty thousand). The Roman Catholic Church had its own city within the capital region, the French-speaking Saint-Boniface, and a rural empire that stretched across the prairies. Add to these deeply entrenched, historically rooted faiths several others, including substantial numbers of Jews and Lutherans, each just under twenty thousand, about 6 percent in each case of the capital region population. Together, the census reports on faith, language, and national group illustrated how cosmopolitan Winnipeg was during the opening decades of the century.[5]

If family, faith, and club provided a web of security for new arrivals, they also defined the boundaries of ethnic groups. Such boundaries, and such definitions, were aspects of each person's 'imagined community,' the identity they assumed and projected to others. Four memoirs written by sometime residents of the Manitoba capital region, each the product of careful reflection, each depicting society in the opening decades of the twentieth century, cast light on the imaginative process by which exclusions and distinctions were determined. What makes these authors unique is that three of the four were members of charter groups. John Tooth was English-born, an immigrant carpenter and jack of all trades whose memoir records the outlook of a member of the working class. Gabrielle Roy, a French–Canadian resident of Saint-Boniface, Winnipeg's twin city just across the Red River from Portage and Main, though not at all an 'immigrant,' recognized that her parents were migrants to a province increasingly dominated by the English language. Adele Wiseman, the child of Jewish immigrants from Ukraine, grew up in Winnipeg and, after graduation from university, embarked on a writing career that included striking pieces on the city's fabled North End. The Rev Charles W. Gordon was also born in Canada, in a small settlement in Glengarry County in eastern Ontario, the child of an immigrant Scots father and second-generation Scots–Canadian mother. A Presbyterian clergyman, he became famous for adventure novels written in Winnipeg around the turn of the twentieth century, but it is his view of his Scottish inheritance that illuminates the city and the immigrant experience. All four writers believed the sources of their distinctiveness were clear and irreducible.

As John Tooth understood, immigrants differed from the Canadian-born simply because they were immigrants. No matter their country of origin or status therein, whether from the so-called Mother Country or from a less powerful state, and whether departing in comfortable circumstances or as a consequence of poverty or pogrom, most would feel until the end of their days a 'phantom limb,' as if a part of themselves had been amputated. This phantom represented some of the basic elements of life, including the clearest sense of home, childhood, and place they would ever know. In the eyes of the Canadian-born, by contrast, the immigrant would forever be seen as someone who might possess divided loyalties.

Mr Tooth's memoir, written in the 1970s, pivots on his decision to leave England in 1910, a decision that shaped the rest of his life.[6] He hadn't wanted to emigrate but when he was twenty-one he experienced disappointments at work that convinced him to try his luck abroad for a few years. Possessing sound schooling and carpentry credentials, he integrated comfortably into Winnipeg society. Yet only at the end of his memoir did he write, for the first and only time, 'we Canadians.'[7] If he never acknowledged a handicap on account of his birthplace, Mr Tooth recognized that his immigrant status constituted a central aspect of his being.

Gabrielle Roy's memoir speaks to the role of language in perceptions of power in the community.[8] Writing in her native French, Roy opened her life story with a brief chapter that was designed as a child's version of an odyssey. In this case, the journey was a bargain-hunting expedition she had taken with her mother but it quickly assumed the aspect of an adventure into the unknown, one that ended with their safe return home. During the odyssey, there were risks to be faced along Winnipeg's main shopping street, Portage Avenue, a thoroughfare

so inordinately broad it could swallow a throng of thousands without showing it. We'd still be speaking French, of course, but perhaps less audibly,
particularly after two or three passersby turned around and stared at us.
The humiliation of having someone turn to stare when I was speaking
French in a Winnipeg street was something I'd felt so often as a child that I
no longer realized it was humiliation. Besides, I'd often turned around myself to stare at some immigrant whose soft Slavic voice or Scandinavian accent I'd heard. I got so used to it eventually that I suppose I thought of it as
natural for us all to feel more or less like foreigners on someone else's
ground. That is, until I came around to thinking that if everyone was a for-
eigner, then none of us was.[9]

After Roy's travels abroad and her decision to settle permanently in
Quebec, language ceased to be a preoccupation in her life except when
she recalled those moments of youthful embarrassment. Roy's contem-
poraries in French-speaking Manitoba saw things differently. The kind of
humiliation Roy described might be outlived, as she said, but the comfortable survival of one's mother tongue was not so easily assured. The
loss of its official status – indeed, its legal suppression – remained a griev-
ance for Franco–Manitobans. Language, or, to be more precise, first languages other than English, erected barriers among Winnipeg residents.
    Adele Wiseman, novelist and essayist, grew up in one of the Jewish
neighbourhoods in Winnipeg's North End. She understood that the city
was ruled by Christians. Her essay on markets in the North End, a story
that mirrors immigrant experience everywhere, begins: 'When we were
strangers in the land we made our own welcome and warmed ourselves
with our own laughter and created our own belonging.'[10] How she interpreted these words – particularly who could be included in the 'we' and
'our' – was a measure of her social life and an index to her estimates of
others. Outsiders could not be counted on because, by definition, they
didn't respond to the loyalties that were one's own. Wiseman appreciat-
ed that religious differences were profound: 'Was our way of killing food
better than "their" way? Well I should say so. Mostly they just grabbed a
chicken by the neck and whirled it round and round to break its neck,
poor little thing. Or sometimes they chopped its head off, so there was a
red gushy stump left. But even if they only put a bullet in it, it was a pretty
messy, unholy way to kill, without even a prayer or anything.'[11]What mattered was not so much how the chicken departed but that faith itself, as
expressed in the method of its slaughter, constituted a barrier among
Winnipeg's peoples.

National memory was another barrier among groups. Immigrants were arriving at a moment when talk of nationalism and national identity was rife in Europe. Reaching beyond just the upper layers of society, national sentiments coloured the dreams of ordinary citizens who could now claim membership in an extended community of belonging. They carried these affiliations with them in the form of poems by Taras Shevchenko, portraits of the Kaiser or the Prince of Wales, or songs about the Danube, the Don, or the Clyde. The best-selling writings of Rev Charles Gordon, published under the pen name Ralph Connor, illustrated the power of such sentiments. After graduating from the University of Toronto with a theology degree, Gordon joined his brother and three friends in a year of post-graduate study in Edinburgh. At the end of his life, Gordon reflected on his decision to travel to Scotland: 'To the question, what makes a man what he is? the answer is origins and environment, his race and his road. As we stepped out of the Caledonian Station [in Edinburgh] I knew where we were. We were back among our origins – more Scottish than Canadian.'[12]

In his autobiography, Gordon remembered fondly 'the ancient relics and sacred spots' that they visited in Edinburgh Castle. Then, he recalled, they stood on the castle parapet to take in

one of the most glorious views in all the world. To the south the Pentlands, east the Lammermuirs with the Berrick Law and the Bass Rock in the far distance, north the Forth with the Fife shore beyond, and then our guide turned our eyes northwest and stood in silent and rapt reverence.

... [our gaze] came to rest at last at the far horizon at a dim waving line of soft blue mountains.

Glancing at our guide's face we forbore speech for some moments. We knew that something beyond the common lay before us. At length my brother said quietly.

'Uncle Charles – those mountains – they can't be – '

'Sir,' said the old gentleman, a quiver of emotion in his voice, 'there they are. The Highlands of Scotland.'

Something leaped up within me and took me by the throat. The Highlands! Cradle of my race! Land of song and story! The Home of my father and mother! My eyes could see but dimly, but not for the distance. Not one of us spoke.[13]

Excessive and romantic, perhaps, but Gordon's language was not hollow. He believed that his own life and character were rooted in a place, a history, and a people. In this passage, place names evoked reverence, images of parents and home dropped onto the page almost unbidden, and national memory – an exclusive possession available in this case only to Scots – raised a barrier dividing his kind from all others. Members of every national group could have written similar statements and all of them, viewing the world from their Winnipeg islands, could see similar reasons for the boundary lines they respected.

The four memoirs differ in theme and plot but in all of them there is a powerful undercurrent concerning social boundaries and social barriers. Writing in their closing years, and reflecting on long lives and rich experiences, Tooth, Roy, Wiseman, and Gordon illustrate how people's awareness of such social and cultural divides pervaded the early-century city. For Tooth, the height of the barrier was determined by birthplace; for Roy, language; for Wiseman, faith; for Gordon, national memory. In their estimation the barriers between the various peoples appeared to be firm. They assumed that such fences would not be breached in the near future. They lived with the conviction that culturally distinct communities separated by high barriers were simply facts of life. Even as they wrote, however, the exclusions were being challenged. Activities were being launched in the boundary zones that treated newcomers and established residents as members of a single community.

Schools and Incorporation

City dwellers shopped in the same stores, used the same currency to evaluate purchases, and shared the same excitement accompanying fairs and concerts and spectator sports. In the crowds listening to radio broadcasts outside the *Free Press* building on Carlton Street – a boxing match from New York, the sixtieth anniversary of Confederation from Ottawa – they learned about their new neighbours while rubbing shoulders with them. The differences that had seemed so prominent in their first days and months in Winnipeg slowly faded. Though they still talked about the world around them as if it were subdivided into compartments by unbreachable barriers, they actually lived in neighbourhoods and a city where casual exchanges were frequent and often as innocent as a glance or a murmur of acknowledgement.

Schools occupied a prominent place in the boundary zones between migrants and established citizens. For students, schools were sites of urgent encounters with peers of varying backgrounds. For teachers, they were demanding workplaces where 'difference' and the 'civic ideal' battled for attention. For policy makers in government, they represented crucial opportunities and thorny responsibilities. And they also taught lessons to parents, who might listen with interest to stories about teachers and their children's classmates.

Early-century Winnipeg schools were crowded, turbulent places. When classes commenced in Norquay School in September 1906, Miss Harper's grade one class contained fifty-six aspiring students, twenty-six boys and thirty girls, ranging in age from six to fourteen years. Attendance during the term was poor, newcomers were numerous, and the dropout rate was very high; no fewer than eighty-eight children's names were recorded on her roll-call sheet by the end of that first term. Miss Conklin in grade two had an equally difficult task because the average daily attendance in her classroom (those who actually attended school) was well over forty students. Some years later, this same school was remembered vividly by two of its students. Joe Wilder, child of Romanian Jews, said it was dominated by Ukrainians and Poles; he hated it. Larry Zolf, also Jewish, described it as 'a really bad school ... where no one spoke English, or if they did, they spoke it with a thick Ukrainian accent.'[14] This was the context in which Adele Wiseman situated her 'book-molesting childhood':

> My gentile schoolmates usually found me rather likeable as long as we had not yet played the 'What are you?' game. What are you? English? Scotch? French? German? Polish? Icelandic? Ukrainian? I could have got away with Ukrainian, for a while at least, on the technicality that my parents came from the Ukraine. But I wouldn't. And because of my pigtails, I could have pretended to 'Dutch, I'll bet you're Dutch!'
>
> 'No, I'm Jewish,' I'd have to steel myself to say, finally, and watch myself turn into an instant monster in their eyes.[15]

To be English and Protestant was no guarantee of safe passage in the schoolyard. British–Canadian students whose families were poor, such as James Gray, often moved between the north and south ends of the city and came to know the differences well. Born in Winnipeg in 1906, Gray attended a dozen schools in the years between 1911 and 1923. He knew intimately the difference between the exclusively British atmosphere of the south end and the polyglot character of the north. The north end kids of European heritage, he wrote in his memoir *The Boy from Winnipeg*, beat up the weak, carried lice in their hair, taught their classmates very rude words in many languages, and had a better time on their numerous holidays. They also taught him 'how to survive in a school year as a minority of one, the skinny, half-sickly kid all the tough little "hunky" kids could beat up.' Moreover, they led him to conclude in retrospect that 'in the North End, where the struggle for existence became exceedingly sharp with the collapse of the boom in 1913, the kids were physically and probably mentally tougher than they were in the Anglo-Saxon communities.'[16]

Student life was not simply a case of pitched battles and crushed hopes. Children also saw positive models whom they wished to emulate. Most of their teachers, in a ratio of about nine to one, were young women, almost exclusively of British–Canadian heritage in the early decades of the century. Asked about these teachers, Sybil Shack, one of the former students, recalls that the girls in her group were 'uniformly inspired by the women.' She said: 'They were so kind to us. We must have been hard to put up with, because we admired them so much that we wanted to be close to them. We walked around at recess hanging onto their skirts and sleeves. We stood as close to them as we could get when we went up to the desk to get our spelling marked. We wanted so badly to please them. Most of them were very good to us. We wanted to be like them and we were ashamed of our parents and grandparents.' Another student endured a scolding because, rather than reveal to her 'beautiful teacher' that her parents could not read English or sign their names, she tore up her report card and threw it away.[17]

Some teachers, including some of the senior administrators in the system, saw their work as part of an unrelenting cultural battle. The story of Annie Okir illustrated their concerns. Annie and her brother, Reggie, aged ten, whose family spoke 'Bohemian' (probably Polish, but perhaps Czech), wanted to attend Strathcona School. However, their parents were receiving pressure from church authorities to send them to Polish school 'for confirmation.' These confirmation classes were essential if the family were to be accepted in their community, Strathcona principal W.J. Sisler wrote in his diary, because 'the church offers no facilities to them outside of the parochial school for learning the catechism. A week ago Annie was held up to ridicule at the church because she could not answer a certain question. The Sister told her that was because she went to the Public School.'[18] By dint of persistent visiting and serious attempts to understand the newcomers and their concerns, Sisler won the respect of parents and church authorities alike and, in the case of Annie, he did not give in. In September 1920 he noted in his diary: 'Took Annie Akir [Okir] and Reggie Langhammer to St. Joseph's Catholic School. They will stay for a year to learn catechism.' One may infer that Sisler and the priest reached a compromise: the children would stay one year in the church school and then return to the public school.[19]

The struggles within the schools could be intense and they could alien-ate children from parents. In his memoir *Peaceful Invasion* Sisler ex-plained why school soccer teams, one of the joys of his life, constituted 'a potent factor in creating good-will among children of the many racial groups and differing religious beliefs ... A boy got his place on the school team because of ability to play the game and to co-operate with others ... The interest aroused in winning or attempting to win a game and the honour of the school were uppermost in the minds of all members of a team.' Sisler recognized that parents might be dubious about soccer: 'Some thought the games would be hard on the player's boots; others wanted the boys to pile wood, dig the garden or run errands after four o'clock and on Saturdays. The good players always found a way to get to the games.'[20] His complacent, male-centred comment might seem rela-tively innocent but it offers a context for the story he told about two boys who were forbidden by their parents to ride a streetcar or do any work 'with their hands' on Saturday, then the customary day for school sports in Winnipeg. Sisler intervened on their behalf, assuring the parents that the boys could walk to the games. He also 'pointed out to their father that soccer was played with the feet and using the hands was contrary to the rules ...' The father then dropped his objections. A Jewish teacher of the next generation, the child of immigrants and one who was probably a contemporary of these boys, placed Sisler's joking defence in another light: 'The story may be amusing but to me it is significant, because the parents of those children valued the Sabbath and obviously the teachers had no idea of what they were doing to separate the children from their parents.'[21] To incorporate the child into his Winnipeg, Sisler might have replied, he was willing to place additional stress on relationships within the family.

The makers of education policy saw the world from Sisler's vantage point. In the Canadian system provinces controlled education policy and had to tackle the thorny issues of denominational schools and language of instruction. In Manitoba debates about education arose partly out of concerns that multilingual schools could not integrate the thousands of children arriving from eastern and southern Europe. They also arose, as Sisler's notebook illustrated, from the cultural struggle between Roman Catholics and Protestants that had propelled Manitoba into an infamous 'schools question' (1889 to 1897). Roman Catholics won part of that battle, a defence of their constitutional right to maintain denomination-al schools, in the Laurier–Greenway compromise of 1897. But Protestants won the war because the compromise acknowledged that a single, pub-licly funded, 'non-denominational' school system was constitutionally permissible. Catholic parents would have to pay for their own system – after they paid provincial taxes to sustain the province's schools – with their voluntary donations.[22] This legal circumstance goes some distance to explain the problems with which the priests in the vicinity of W.J. Sisler's Strathcona School were trying to deal: Roman Catholic schools were handicapped in the struggle to keep and educate their children. And the keen assimilationist drive of public school leaders constituted part of the story of school policy.

A second aspect of this story has often been misunderstood because it has been confused with the religious conflict. It concerns the language of instruction in all schools, a related but different issue. In order to appease the French, and perhaps to acknowledge the challenge raised by German-speaking Mennonites who remained outside the public system, the 1897 compromise opened the possibility that lessons might be taught in a language other than English: 'where ten of the pupils speak the French language (or any language other than English) as their native language, the teaching of such pupils shall be conducted in French (or such other language) and English upon the bi-lingual system.'[23]

Nobody knew what a 'bilingual system' might look like but it began to take shape in 1904 when the first 'normal school' for French-language teacher training opened. A year later, Ukrainian and Polish teacher training commenced and, within a decade, over one hundred rural school districts reported offering instruction in Ukrainian or Polish.[24] Winnipeg, as the metropolis of the West, presented a more complicated educational puzzle. As early as 1901, just a few years after the new wave of European immigrants began, a Presbyterian delegation led by Rev Charles W. Gordon visited Premier Rodmond Roblin, seeking the establishment of public schools for Ukrainian children in Winnipeg. Another delegation presented a similar case in 1902. However, by 1905 many British Canadians accepted the assertion of a young Methodist minister, J.S. Woodsworth, who was then working in a church mission house in Winnipeg's immigrant district: 'If Canada is to become in any real sense a nation, if our people are to become one people, we must have one language. Hence the necessity of national schools where the teaching of English – our national language – is compulsory. The public school is the most important factor in transforming the foreigners into Canadians.'[25] In other words a bilingual system might have worked in rural Manitoba, where districts seemed likely to be isolated for decades to come, but they would not work in a big city where people of many backgrounds were growing up together and required a common language just to get along.

The challenge of these classrooms was immense. British–Canadian teachers rejected the unilingual system as impossible in urban neighbourhoods where a dozen languages might be spoken. They tried translators in the classroom but found this approach to be expensive, time-consuming, and ineffective. They then turned to what W.J. Sisler called 'the direct method,' of which he was a leading exponent: 'As to the value of bilingual teaching, I am absolutely opposed to it so far as children are concerned. They should learn English as they learn their mother tongue, through actions, objects, pictures and the association of the proper words with ideas presented by them.'[26]

Language in the schools preoccupied an increasing number of Manitobans as the years passed. The provincial association of school trustees, dominated by English-language districts, voted for a unilingual English system in 1911 and the Manitoba Education Association passed a similar resolution in 1912. The influential *Manitoba Free Press* took up the cudgels and between 1911 and 1914 published no fewer than sixty-four articles and one hundred editorials on the subject, all of them critical of multilingual schools (that is, those teaching in languages other than English at least for some hours of the day), all of them favouring compulsory enrolment to the age of fourteen, and all advocating the use of English as the sole language of instruction. In the view of *Free Press* editor John Dafoe, immigrant children who failed to become fluent in English would be unable to relate to the wider community. He argued that church leaders such as the Greek Catholic Bishop Nicetas Budka were undermining civil society:

> Bishop Budka entered the Brandon [Normal] School, an institution maintained by public funds, and told the students that they were 'acting as pioneers in developing the Canadian-Ukrainian outlook' ... Imagine a foreign born bishop, who has been in this country barely three years, visiting a Canadian public institution for training of students and, in a foreign language, telling the assembled students, the majority of whom have been born in Canada, that their business in life is to develop a hyphenated Canadian outlook ... We take the liberty of telling Bishop Budka that any member of his race, or any other non-English speaking nationality in Canada, who is not prepared for himself and his children to become Canadians is not wanted in Canada. The Ukraine is the proper place for Ukrainians. If there is such a country as Canada-Ukraine, we do not know of it. Hyphens should be left at the port of embarkation to be applied for when the immigrant returns for good to the land of his fathers.[27]

Premier Rodmond Roblin's Conservative government, which relied on the support of the Catholic hierarchy and the votes of European immigrants in rural districts, tried to refute such arguments. As late as 1914, the annual report of the Department of Education suggested that the 'language problem' would disappear with time. But the August 1914 British declaration of war against Germany and the Austro–Hungarian empire, homelands of the immigrants and languages most criticized by British Manitobans, fused the political issues into a single target. All of a sudden, bilingual lessons, French-language texts, the Catholic Church's role in political discussion, and 'Canadianizing' immigrant children became part of a single partisan debate. To make matters worse for the Conservative administration, and providentially for the Liberals, this debate coincided with a scandal involving outrageous payments for the new legislative building and a report from a *Free Press* spy in the Conservative party concerning Roblin's vote-buying practices. Voters defeated the Conservative government in 1915. The new Liberal administration, led by T.C. Norris, then passed a compulsory schools attendance act and made English the sole language of instruction in the schools.

The Norris government policies represented a decisive shift in Manitoba's integration strategies and in the cultural experience of immigrants and their families. The province had rejected one version of a plural and multicultural future, a version in which immigrant groups might retain a very large proportion of their birth cultures, including state-supported separate schooling in their own languages. British-origin Manitobans had never contemplated this social model seriously but it had been envisaged by leaders in the immigrant communities. The province was also suppressing the French–English linguistic duality that had been at the heart of Confederation and had survived in Manitoba, despite several severe blows in 1890. Winnipeg's experience had shaped Manitoba's language policy. What Sisler called the 'direct' method of handling language in the schools became the rule in Winnipeg in the first decade of the twentieth century and then was extended to the rest of the province in 1916.[28] Whether, as a result of these policy changes, the province had accepted the social ideal of Anglo-conformity and the melting pot remained to be seen.

It is too easy to say that homogeneity was the inevitable result of public education and it is just as misleading to say that ethnic groups' resistance carried on without pause. The character of Winnipeg, where nearly half the province's students lived, was shaped by the language decisions of 1916 and by the contests between public and parochial schools. It would also be shaped by the everyday activities of schoolteachers and daily life in schoolyards. Schools were far from being the only vehicle of incorporation in the boundary zones but they were influential.

Incorporation through Party Politics

Recognition of common political interests developed in Winnipeg between 1900 and 1940 and is integral to the history of immigrant incorporation. In the electoral and political processes of that long generation, Winnipeggers listened to debates among political parties, participated in strikes of city-wide import, and voted in elections. In the process, they began to accept ownership of community institutions by adopting new loyalties, supporting new parties, and creating new views of the world.

When the immigrants arrived, control of governments – urban, provincial, and national – rested with those who already lived in the province, notably those British Canadians to whom much of the wealth, political power, and cultural authority belonged. The leaders of the Protestant churches, the military, the mainstream press, business, and unions were British Canadians. Their habits of authority encompassed women's activities because teaching and nursing as well as voluntary agencies such as the Margaret Scott Mission and the Victorian Order of Nurses were controlled by British Canadians. The same people also figured uniquely in the social circles of the wealthy, where debutantes 'came out' and leading matrons poured tea, each event catalogued on the social pages of the newspapers.

Immigrants could not vote as a matter of right in civic and provincial elections at the beginning of the century. In 1906 in the city of Winnipeg property qualifications restricted the franchise to fewer than eight thousand of the city's one hundred thousand residents;[29] almost all the eight thousand were British Canadian. In the provincial sphere, the new Roblin government introduced a literacy test in 1901 denying the franchise to a resident who was not 'a British subject by birth who has ... resided in some portion of ... Canada for at least seven years preceding the date of registration ... unless such person is able to read any selected portion of "The Manitoba Act" in ... English, French, German, Icelandic or any Scandinavian language.'[30] Premier Roblin explained frankly that he feared newcomers from central and eastern Europe might undermine the political system. The illiterate among them should not have the vote, he said, because 'they take no interest in the affairs of this country and are incapable of learning about them.'[31]

The irony is that, having been excluded from provincial politics in 1901, Ukrainian Canadians were soon being courted by Roblin's election agents. Many responded favourably, particularly because of Roblin's new-found interest in Ukrainian-language schools. In 1904 the premier re-vised his racist franchise legislation. Perhaps as a result many Ukrainian Canadians gravitated to the Conservatives, even as reformers in their ranks entered the Liberal party and the very radical joined Canada's Social Democratic Party, one-fifth of whose five thousand members re-portedly were residents of Winnipeg's North End.[32] With the aid of the Conservative machine, Ukrainian Canadians ran unsuccessfully for seats on Winnipeg city council as early as 1907 and 1908, and in 1911 Theodore Stefanyk was elected for a one-year term. The development of ethnic elec-toral machines, political clubs, and party-sponsored newspapers illustrat-ed how partisan politics were creating a two-way conversation between newcomers and longer settled citizens.

Almost all owners, managers, professionals, and other white-collar workers lived in the southern districts of the city during the first half of the twentieth century. Most were British in national origin. Almost all the lowest-paid wage labourers – the so-called unskilled labourers who lacked official craft papers – clustered in the North End, Elmwood, and several suburbs. They were overwhelmingly East European in origin. 'Skilled' blue-collar workers, who often possessed trades credentials, were distrib-uted across the city, though concentrated in less wealthy neighbour-hoods, and were overwhelmingly British or northwestern European. A student of these patterns suggests that 'living conditions ranged from the clean, spacious surroundings of the South End to the overcrowded, often unsanitary, housing characteristic of Wards 4 and 5 (Weston, the north part of the central business district, and the North End).' He con-cludes that, 'taken together, the combination of class and ethnic segrega-tion produced a social geography marked by vast differences in life chances.'[33]

Workers and their families were always conscious of money and, in its absence, of insecurity. John Tooth's memoir is dotted with moments when he could not find work and his family faced shortages: '1931 was a bad year for everyone. I believe I made $950.00 in the whole of that year, wasn't much to feed six children on, but then others had less ... Somehow we struggled through that year ... I recall my last paycheck just before Christmas was for $4.50. That was I believe the leanest Christmas the Tooth family endured, but nobody grumbled and Mother as optimistic as ever was sure things would soon improve.' He saw this anxiety as normal, an unpleasant but necessary part of life, and he accepted such worries because everyone had to do so. Only in the 1950s did the stress fade: 'I worked for the Maintenance dept of the Winnipeg School Board for eight years 1951 to 1959 [aged 62 to 70], and I believe it was the first time in my whole career I had the feeling of real security. For years I had had the feeling, what is going to happen on Friday night, will the axe fall again. I am sure there are very few people in our community who ever realize what a very real dread that is to many of the hourly paid workers.'[34] In Mr Tooth's Winnipeg, these 'hourly paid workers' lived in certain districts and held jobs at certain wage levels. And they slowly learned to attach ethnic and class implications to the lessons he articulated. Within a few years, income, housing, and ethnicity were linked in a single category – class – in people's consciousness.

The social and income differences became more significant in the fall of 1918 as the First World War ended and the worldwide influenza epidemic reached the city. The next few months were marked by extraordinary unrest. Inflation raised prices. The flu killed hundreds of citizens and reinforced the city's north–south divide.[35] Soldiers returning from the Front sought jobs and a resumption of once-familiar routines. As war industries demobilized, union leaders began to fear an unemployment crisis. The emergence of radical political alternatives in Russia and many other European countries gave new energy to political radicals. Two groups of Winnipeg workers who were expected to set the pattern for others – the machinists and the building trades workers – then triggered strikes in April of 1919. To support them, and to challenge the balance of power between capital and labour, the city's labour council called a city-wide walkout. For six weeks in May and June, in what is known as the Winnipeg General Strike, thirty thousand unionized and non-union workers – and their families – shut down the city economy in the hope that they could force employers to accept union demands.

So extreme was the confrontation that the city split in two. 'Class' became an inescapable force, shaping political discussions and voting patterns. The adoption of class identities meant that newly forged sentiments of solidarity cut across the cultural bonds associated with faith and language and national memory. South end divided from north; workers' families from middle-class families. The chasm that developed between the two political communities was profound and long lasting.

In the following decades, Winnipeggers again and again demonstrated their loyalty to those political representatives who reflected best their own class interests. In provincial elections, where a ten-member Winnipeg constituency conducted under a transferable, proportional, preferential ballot system permitted close scrutiny of these affiliations, residents of the North End consistently selected advocates of a 'Labour' or 'leftist' viewpoint and, when necessary, ignored differences of ethnicity and religion to do so. In the southern parts of the city, more conservative candidates received similarly uniform support.[36] The ideological loyalty of the voters put the lie to any suggestion that ethnicity alone dictated voter preference. The political choices made by Winnipeggers between the 1920s and 1940s transcended their ethnic and religious loyalties. This was adjustment of a particular sort: people in the North End united to support 'progressive' politics and to oppose South End 'conservative' choices, and vice versa.

Political scientist Nelson Wiseman and sociologist Wayne Taylor analysed Winnipeg voting patterns in a series of articles on elections held between the 1920s and 1950s. One of these studies, which focused on specific Winnipeg polls in Manitoba's 1945 general election, can be taken as illustrative of a political outlook that had evolved in the early-century decades. Fifteen distinct ballot counts were necessary in 1945 to discover the ten winners from among twenty candidates, a process conducted according to the preferential system. Wiseman and Taylor selected for special study two polls in which over 90 percent of the residents spoke English as a first language and two polls where Ukrainian and Yiddish predominated. In the former, located in a prosperous English-speaking district, they selected for special study a poll in which educational achievement was higher, professional–managerial occupations were prevalent, and average income was relatively high. In this favoured neighbourhood, the predominantly British–Canadian citizens 'voted overwhelmingly for Right candidates (90 per cent) ...' In the other English-speaking poll, which was situated in a working-class area where people earned lower incomes and had lower levels of formal education, and where a higher proportion of residents was born in Britain as opposed to being Canadian-born, citizens 'voted overwhelmingly for Left candidates (84 per cent).'[37] By placing the candidates on a rough ideological scale (Communists and social democrats on the left, Liberals and Conservatives on the right), Taylor and Wiseman's analysis demonstrated that, in the two English-speaking districts, the workers voted for the left-wing candidates, and the middle class voted for the right. English-speaking voters' adherence, measured by class indices, to a 'left' or 'right' group of candidates was the rule for 85 to 95 percent of the ballots in eleven of the thirteen counts.[38] It is an extraordinary demonstration of the power of class perceptions among British Canadians in Winnipeg society during the decades after the general strike.

Wiseman and Taylor undertook a comparable analysis of two North End polls. The first was a working-class area where, according to the census, income and educational levels were very low and 57 percent of the voters spoke Ukrainian. In this poll, two Ukrainian candidates, one from a 'conservative' old-line party and the other a Communist, received very strong support. In this neighbourhood, ethnic solidarity *did* matter. However, after one subtracts the votes for the Ukrainians, the remaining nine candidates on the left scale received over 40 percent of the vote, whereas the nine remaining candidates on the right received just under 4 percent. Similarly, in the other North End poll, wherein 47 percent of the voters spoke Yiddish, two Jewish candidates, both representing left-wing parties, received strong endorsements. After subtracting their votes, the eight remaining candidates on the left received 26 percent of the vote (an average of 3.25 percent each) and the ten on the right received 18 percent (an average of 1.8 percent each). It was not as strong an illustration as the others but it followed the same tendency.

In all four cases discussed by Wiseman and Taylor, ethnic, faith, and language considerations worked together with political ideology and neighbourhood loyalties to establish a clear division in Winnipeg society. Education and income correlated with voters' choices of left- or right-wing party representatives. The authors concluded that 'ethnicity is largely a confounding category which disguises class voting behaviour' in Winnipeg in the 1930s and 1940s.[39] In sum the events of 1919 had etched a nearly indelible pattern into city life. The pattern had been present in the geography of development during the preceding two decades but the general strike, the flu epidemic, and the political responses on all sides had reinforced people's awareness of social difference and generalized it across broadly defined neighbourhoods. The city's very structure – North End, West End, South End, Elmwood, Saint-Boniface, the suburbs – now represented authoritative generalizations that were imprinted clearly on people's imagined maps.

A widespread consciousness of classes – one's own and one's opponents – was expressed consistently after 1919 in national elections as well as in civic and provincial contests. Middle-class immigrants inclined to conservative choices in politics; working-class immigrants leaned to the left or progressive side. The class consciousness did not erase ethnic or religious differences but it did override them. And it elevated particular individuals, notably J.S. Woodsworth, soon to become the national leader of a Labour and then a Co-operative Commonwealth Federation group in the House of Commons (Canada's version of democratic socialism), to national recognition, thus enabling the left to secure access to the main communications media of the day. That A.A. Heaps, a Jew from north Winnipeg in the House of Commons, or Mary Dyma, a Ukrainian on the city school board, had models upon which to mould their own activity illustrated the hold of ideology and cross-cultural integration in this city.

The two patterns of behaviour and belief – the working-class progressive and the middle-class conservative – became powerful vehicles of immigrant adjustment and urban definition in the longer term. They offered explanations of ethnic and religious stereotypes, of income inequalities and social divisions. They presented a means by which to select likely recipients of one's vote. Most of all they constituted assurance that many others – perhaps of quite different religions and tongues and national origins – would be seeing these issues from the same perspective. John Tooth may not have mentioned Ukrainians or Poles or Jews in his memoir but he learned to see his community in ways that mirrored the lessons they were learning. He, like other British Canadians, began to recognize this identity of outlook and to vote with people whom he once regarded as aliens. By choosing sides, Winnipeggers were learning to emphasize a new community-based loyalty – class – that transcended older loyalties to language, faith, and nation of origin.

Conclusion

In the early-century decades, residents of Winnipeg discovered important, locally rooted reasons to lower the barriers among groups. They continued for some time to think in terms of ethnic exclusion and difference, as the four memoirs make clear. But the stories of the school pupils, teachers, and administrators demonstrate that their relationships with established Canadians and their experience with institutions of the host society also caused them to change their views, sometimes in spite of themselves. Important acts of citizenship, including political debate and voting, encouraged them to cross the barriers erected by ethnic belonging. Their class and party loyalties created two metaphorical Winnipegs, north and south, each divided into two ideological camps, socialist and capitalist, each camp united by the need to elect civic, school, provincial, and federal governments.

Part Two
**Mid-Century: Urban Cross-Currents
and Adaptation, 1940s–1960s**

chapter three

Ethnic Cross-Currents in Mid-Century Alberta and Saskatchewan

Immigrant culture in the mid-century prairie city differed significantly from that of the early-century decades. To a large extent it reflected a cultural mix from two distinctive groups of newcomers. On the one hand were the urbanized and highly educated European refugees of the Second World War and Eastern bloc communism. On the other hand were the children and grandchildren of the early-century immigrants; they were the second- and third-generation farm folk seeking economic survival in the post-war economy. They already knew Canada, its language and customs, and they were welcomed in the cities as participants in the new post war economy. The post-war refugees were welcomed not only for their economic contribution, but also as a way of legitimizing Canada's own remarkable military commitment during the war and its ongoing opposition to Eastern bloc communism. Both streams met kith and kin in the city from the early-century migrations. In many instances these earlier migrants had established an institutional footprint that marked a path for the post-war newcomers. Significantly, these two immigration streams interacted in a dynamic and vibrant way.

Once again a particular version of ethnic culture developed in the largest prairie centres. It was unlike the ethnicity found in the early-century prairie city, established in ethnic enclaves, reflecting local needs and old-world ways, and serving as a resource for selective integration into a British–Canadian capitalist world. Ethnic voices at mid-century more often came from the suburbs, indicating a broadened and more hybrid identity, one that combined elements of a second- and third-generation Nordic Euro–Canadianism with a transplanted sophistication of the post-war European newcomer. Ethnicity in this context seemed more pliable, symbolic, personal, and reinvented. It seemed especially adaptable to the quickly growing post-war prairie cities.

This mainstreaming of ethnic culture was apparent in the 'new' cities of Alberta and Saskatchewan. Unlike Winnipeg, these cities had not received large numbers of Germans, Jews, and Ukrainians, nor, outside of small pockets of Blacks and Jews, been home to ethnic enclaves in the early decades.[1] Not only were Alberta and Saskatchewan new jurisdictions – founded as provinces in 1905 and only fifty years old at mid-century – but their post-war cities were changing rapidly. Calgary, Edmonton, Regina, and Saskatoon each suffered significant stagnation during the Depression. With the strengthening economy of the Second World War and the economic takeoff of the 1950s, however, they began to grow quickly, especially benefiting from new discoveries of natural resources. Alberta's famed Leduc oil find in 1947 signalled its turn into Canada's 'Cinderella province,' shaped by big business and spinoff service industries.[2] In Saskatchewan potash and uranium extraction symbolized that province's change from a 'breadbasket' to a 'rich and diversified' economy.[3] The market-driven wealth in Alberta and progressive governments in Saskatchewan transformed both provinces into places that pushed cultural innovations, social welfare reform, and radical changes in medical service research and delivery.[4]

Two features in particular shaped the immigrant experience in the two provinces. First, the cities grew rapidly. In the decades immediately following the First World War the population growth rate in the prairie cities had dropped in comparison to most other cities in the country. By 1941 both the Alberta and Saskatchewan cities still lagged far behind the prairie giant of Winnipeg: while the old keystone city's population stood at 291,000, Edmonton had a population of 94,000, Calgary 88,000, Regina 58,000, and Saskatoon 43,000. This equation changed dramatically during and after the Second World War. During the 1950s, for example, Alberta grew by 42 percent, compared to Canada's 30 percent, and though it slowed during the 1960s, it kept pace with Canada's 22 percent growth rate. Saskatchewan as a whole grew more slowly, by only 11 percent during the 1950s and not at all during the 1960s, but its cities mushroomed in size. Winnipeg may have grown by 34 percent in the 1950s and 14 percent in the 1960s, but Regina increased by 37 percent and 24 percent, respectively, and Saskatoon by 79 percent and 32 percent, respectively. Even these strong growth rates were overshadowed by the phenomenal expansion of Alberta's main cities: both cities almost doubled in size during the 1950s, Edmonton growing by 95 percent and Calgary by 93 percent. During the 1960s the growth spurt continued as Edmonton increased its population by 46 percent and Calgary by 62 percent. Following these mid-century decades of demographic takeoff, Winnipeg's status as prairie giant was challenged. In 1961 it was still the largest city, its census area including 476,000 persons, but now Edmonton was not far behind with 338,000 people and Calgary with 279,000 people. Regina with 112,000 people and Saskatoon with 96,000 people were cities with significant economic and cultural strength.[5] Then, too, rapid growth in the new cities produced highly integrated urban spaces, with rates of ethnic segregation into distinctive enclaves less than 50 percent of that in the longer established cities such as Winnipeg and Toronto.[6]

The second feature of these four post-war cities was their increasingly polyethnic populations. It is true that by the beginning of this era these cities were host to ethnic and ethno-religious groups that seemed unusual in the Euro–Canadian cultural landscape of the West, marked by diverse symbols including Canada's first Muslim mosque built in Edmonton in 1938.[7] Still, by 1941 by far the largest cultural group in each of the Alberta and Saskatchewan cities – from 76 percent of Calgary's population to 62 percent of Regina's population – was 'British,' the amalgam of English, Scottish, and Irish residents. Moreover, the British–Canadian-dominated United Church – founded in 1925 by Methodists, Presbyterians, and Congregationalists – was the largest religious organization in each of the four cities, and the Anglicans the second largest in three of the four. During the 1940s and 1950s this ratio shifted profoundly. The proportion of British dropped in each of the cities by about 50 percent so that in 1961 they were in a minority in each of the cities, except Calgary. Germans in particular increased in number, by threefold in Regina, sevenfold in Saskatoon, and tenfold in both Edmonton and Calgary. Ukrainians, Dutch, Poles, and French each multiplied in size in all four cities.[8] Large percentage increases among the Hungarian and Italian populations occurred, too: by 1961 the Italians were the eighth largest group in Calgary and Edmonton; and the Hungarians the tenth largest in Calgary, Edmonton, and Saskatoon, and the eighth largest in Regina. The effect of these incoming eastern and southern Europeans was that the Roman Catholic Church became the second-largest denomination in each of the four cities, leaving the Anglican Church a distant third. The Chinese, benefiting from Canada's 1947 redefinition of citizenship and new family reunification laws, also grew in size, becoming the thirteenth largest group in Edmonton and the twelfth largest in Calgary; by 1961 the Chinese had grown to outnumber the Jews in Calgary, and rivalled them in Regina, Saskatoon, and Edmonton.[9]

Thus, although the post-war refugees themselves never constituted more than 4 percent to 7.5 percent of any one of the cities' populations, their numbers, combined with the internal migration of second- and third-generation ethnic farm families, transformed these four communities. The history of migration to these cities, then, was not only the story of two concurrent waves. It was also the story of the interaction of these two streams of migrants and their combined effect on the history of their urban communities. A creative tension developed as second- and third-generation rural folk met their countrymen, often urbanized modern Europeans. The interaction of these two waves constituted the dominant story of mid-century migration to the British–Canadian cities of Alberta and Saskatchewan.

The Great Disjuncture

Dislocated farm families constituted the single largest group of mid-century migrants to Edmonton, Calgary, Saskatoon, and Regina. Regional drought and global depression in the 1930s had pushed them toward the cities. That crisis, followed by the continent-wide, post-war economic phase, sometimes dubbed the Great Disjuncture, sent even more farm families to the cities after the Second World War. According to historians John Herd Thompson and Ian MacPherson, economic, technological, and political changes compelled farmers to become more businesslike. Technology, credit, and labour costs were all factored into making the life of the family farm more complex; farmers became preoccupied with 'cost-benefit analysis' and were encouraged to consider what was 'received in a year from [the] farm in return to labour and management.'[10] In the end, however, most found it impossible to make the costly adaptation, resulting in a massive migration to the cities.[11] During the 1930s the number of farm residents in Canada had fallen from 4.8 to 3.2 million, and it fell further to 1.4 million in 1971, about one-quarter of what it had been forty years earlier.[12] This influx of farm families into the cities constituted one of the most significant migrations in Canadian history.

The migration was never a simple affair. Immigrants followed the labour market and came to work in an increasingly diverse economy. They took on the rough work of installing the utilities and infrastructure of new suburbs; they managed the small businesses and the large corporate or state-run enterprises; they became the professionals and retailers servicing a consumption-driven urban population; they were the civil servants regulating the new economy. Sometimes potential migrants remained on the land until their households reached a breaking point and their families had to relocate in a moment of financial crisis. Sometimes they came to the city in the same fashion in which their parents had come to Canada, sending one family member ahead while those who remained made a valiant attempt to save the farm. Sometimes they came as 'temporary urban workers,' each visit lasting a little longer, until finally, as Dirk Hoerder has observed, they were 'worker-peasants returning to the farm but occasionally.' In the Polish Andreychuk family of Mundare, Alberta, for example, Frank, the father, and son John left home to work on the railways for short periods of time in and near Edmonton in an effort to subsidize the farm. Finally, however, it became impossible, and the Andreychuk family 'sold out and moved ... to Edmonton.'[13]

They may have entered the cities equipped with cultural values inherited from their parents, but they were bent on integration into the booming urban economies. Each group underwent the cultural fusion in different ways. Some of these paths mimicked British–Canadian values, finding in public education a quick route to middle-class life. For example, as Howard Palmer and Tamara Palmer once noted, Calgary's 'Icelanders' strong belief in education led many of the second and third generation to seek higher education' in the 1950s. Then, cashing in on their education, they became 'oil industry engineers, geologists and physicists as well as other professionals,' thus rising 'from a mainly working class group to a relatively wealthy and overwhelmingly professional population.'[14]

But the newcomers from the countryside with little education also seemed intent on assimilating into a middle-class suburban culture. In her study of young, second-generation Polish–Canadian farm women in post-Depression Edmonton and Calgary, Krystyna Lukasiewicz suggests that these women embraced the ideals of an urban middle-class milieu at the outset. Because they lacked formal education 'they were forced to join the lowest echelons of the female working class' in the city, working as 'domestic servants ... hotel and nursing home employees, cooks and saleswomen.' But as soon as they landed these dismal jobs the young women also plotted strategies to get out. As they saw it, their passport out of drudgery was marriage, and in part because of their experience with poverty among Poles, many of these women sought partners who were explicitly not Polish or Roman Catholic. The working-class homes they created with their new husbands emulated those of the middle class. One woman recalled with pride that 'my husband wouldn't let me work. He told me: "I married you and you are going to work for no one."' And then, when four, five, or six children came along, the mothers made the children's education a priority.

Significantly, Lukasiewicz argues, these young Polish women appropriated the mythology of upward mobility of their peasant parents and grandparents. Their views of middle-class ascendancy were interwoven with 'social values that prevailed at that time both in Poland and in Canada.' Indeed, their willingness to accept unpleasant jobs in order to ensure their children obtained a good education was driven by one overriding preoccupation: they realized that the '"desire to be somebody" that had motivated the movement of the peasants from Polish villages to the Alberta frontier' had not been realized, even by their own move to the cities. As a result, they dedicated themselves to the next generation. By accepting this fate, they were not yielding to British–Canadian dominance, but, rather, were challenging the entrenched hierarchy in prairie cities.[15]

It was a similar matter with the Jewish residents of these cities. They sought mobility, but not as unhyphenated Canadians. No doubt the Jewish people who had faced the anti-Semitism of the Saskatchewan Ku Klux Klan in the late 1920s and listened to the anti-Semitic language of the Social Credit Party of Alberta after it won power in 1935 often felt unwelcome in prairie cities.[16] Max Rubin observes that until the middle decades of the century, Calgary's 'Jews lived primarily in the east end of the city on either side of the railway tracks where housing was inexpensive and where most of the city's businesses were located.' By 1931 Calgary's Jewish population had grown but most Jews 'usually kept to themselves, most were still not that far removed from the pogroms of Europe and the anti-Semitism and economic barriers they had once confronted in their everyday lives.'[17] The Jewish population growth levelled off during these years, and only Edmonton experienced a noticeable rise in the number of Jews during the 1940s and 1950s.[18] Still, the Jews of the two new western provinces seemed to integrate well, organizing their ethnic institutions and living comfortably within the cities. Early-century radicalism had largely dissipated by the mid-1930s.

According to one Royal Canadian Mounted Police report for Saskatoon, 'the Jews of this city lacked the true proletarian outlook ... all consider[ing] themselves capitalists and potentially at least wealthy.'[19] A much-reported example of such material advancement was the career of Lena Anne Hanen of Calgary, a Jewish entrepreneur who organized a successful chain of forty women's dress stores, the Betty Shops, and operated them from 1950 to 1979.[20] But the upward mobility went beyond the story of individuals. By the time the Alberta cities took off in the 1950s, the older pockets of non-British immigrants had often dissipated and Jews had moved from the inner city to the suburbs. Significantly, they moved up Canada's 'vertical mosaic' as Jews. A move 'from Bridgeland in Calgary ... to more fashionable addresses in the Mount Royal or Britannia districts,' for example, was not only physical but 'psychological as well' for 'a better address ... told non-Jews that they had *arrived.*' In Edmonton, especially Reform Jews signalled the same upward mobility when they relocated westward towards the Glenora suburb, a former British stronghold and some distance from a synagogue.[21]

Japanese Canadians seemed especially bent on quiet assimilation into prairie suburbia. They may have been expelled from their British Columbia homes in 1942 and regarded as unassimilable and unworthy of citizenship by British–Canadian powers until 1947, but yet they strove for integration. In fact, as Aya Fujiwara has argued, the troubled 'war years marked the first time that the [second-generation] Japanese Nisei clearly claimed that Asians could also be part of Canada.' It was a complicated integration as the Japanese 'never accepted internment and property confiscation' as anything other than 'racist and undemocratic.' Thus their 'collective memory of the immigration ... did not have a celebratory side.' When they thought of multiculturalism they saw in it a 'solution for racism and a key for promoting an individual's fundamental human rights,' believing it 'was more a matter of harmonious coexistence and understanding between mainstream society and the Japanese community than a guarantee of collective rights.'[22]

A study by Elizabeth Macdonald details this strategy for integration in the tiny post-war Japanese community in Edmonton. It suggests that within a decade of arriving in the city from their exile on southern Alberta beet farms, these Nisei had become known for private home ownership, university education, nuclear family life, and geographical dispersion.[23] Outwardly they showed few signs of their inherited culture. In fact many now declared that their dispersion in Canada had a silver lining because it worked to end their insularity and clannishness. Few of the urban newcomers overtly practised Buddhism or Shintoism, spoke their ancestral language, recalled stories of Japan, or read Japanese–Canadian newspapers.[24] Their chief concern was that their children achieve the 'Canadian middle class ideal of individual achievement and responsibility in a society.'[25]

Still, it was clear that Edmonton Japanese residents' harmonious relationship with the wider society was not a case of cultural surrender.

Rather, life in the dispersed bungalows of Edmonton's suburbs echoed an earlier Japanese adjustment. Ethnic markers were subtle, perhaps, but they were important shaping mechanisms. Their modern homes displayed meaningful Japanese ornamentation. They claimed an identification with Buddhism or Shintoism. They spoke reverently of their Issei parents' sufferings. They claimed to think of Japan as a homeland. Many joined Edmonton's Japanese Community Club. Essential to their Sansei worlds, too, was the accustomed respect for authority (including ethics of etiquette, hard work, and conscientiousness), the traditional recognition that status required land ownership, the ancient religious appreciation for harmony, and the pronounced private commitment to maintaining an interest in family ancestors. These values guided the quiet discipline required for the recently maligned Japanese to integrate into middle-class suburbs.[26]

The avenue to middle-class respectability through the employment of ethnic symbols was most boldly taken by the larger groups. Ukrainians in places such as Saskatoon bore their ethnic badges proudly. But it was a particular kind of ethnic exhibition that was accompanied by signs of assimilation. One study has noted the manner in which many Saskatoon Ukrainians lived 'in the richer College Park, City Park, Grosvenor Park and Nutana districts' of the city, but converged 'on the ghetto for cultural activities which centred in churches and halls along 20th Street, on Avenue G, Avenue J, and Avenue M.'[27] Other studies have highlighted the public voice of the Ukrainians in Saskatchewan cities. Frances Swyripa has documented the founding in 1941 of the Ukrainian Museum of Canada in Saskatoon, meant to 'preserve "authentic" folk art and other artifacts from Ukraine,' but one that quickly 'evolved towards depicting the history of Ukrainian settlement in Canada as well,' a project that kept the museum alive.[28] Lesser projects, such as the one conducted by the Regina chapter of the Ukrainian Canadian Women's League, were also important; in 1952 it raised $47,500 for the construction of a local church campus, complete with a sanctuary, auditorium, kitchen, and rectory, all the while planning for a second Regina parish.[29] The Saskatoon museum as well as the Regina parish, however, were more than signs of the persistence of immigrant culture. Both revealed an ethnic reinvention. The previous generation's concern to maintain social boundaries and to support overseas Ukrainian national projects had shifted in orientation as the Ukrainian communities claimed their place in the Canadian mosaic. A strong and dynamic 'local' ethnicity among second- and third-generation Canadians was employed to secure social integration in urban Saskatchewan.

Supportive of this idea of ethnic invention is a 1969 analysis of Ukrainian linguistic assimilation in prairie cities. Zenon Pohorecky and Alexander Royick documented the striking resilience of spoken Ukrainian in places such as Saskatoon, Edmonton, and Winnipeg. Feeling the lack of full acceptance from Canada's majority cultures, Ukrainian newcomers in prairie cities maintained their spoken ancestral language. Indeed, between 1951 and 1961, as the number of speakers declined by 9 percent across Canada, the number who spoke Ukrainian on the Prairies rose. In Alberta, for example, Ukrainian speakers rose by 10 percent. As importantly, this study revealed that Ukrainians adopted English in such a way that it facilitated, rather than undermined, ethnic awareness. One explanation is that use of the English language in the city helped unite Ukrainians who had roots in a wide variety of rural communities: English 'ameliorated tensions between Ukrainians speaking different dialects' and helped 'democratis[e] the [various] dialects by subverting any alleged linguistic hierarchies.' Then, too, the anglicization of Ukrainian – that is, the liberal adoption of English words into the old lexicon – was not some kind of linguistic bastardization. Rather, it was a useful strategy by which newcomers could learn new words without mastering a completely new language, a new sound system, or a new grammar. Interspersed in spoken Ukrainian were words such as *shadop* ('shut up'), *horijop* ('hurry up'), *monki biznys* ('monkey business'), and *fiksymop* ('fix them up'). The authors conclude that the 'new earthy dimension of anglicized Ukrainian relieved tensions, because it established a joking relationship not only between English and Ukrainian but also between anglicized Ukrainians and the various Ukrainian dialects.'[30] The adaptation indicated that 'ethnicization' and 'assimilation' were not mutually exclusive terms. The second- and third-generation farm folk who came to the city at mid-century found a more welcoming social environment than their parents had in the early-century frontier. Ironically, their quick integration was linked to a repertoire of ethnically based cultural strategies.

The Post-War Newcomers

The Europeans who arrived as refugees and economic migrants in western Canada in the middle decades of the century were a disparate group. They included large numbers of Germans, Ukrainians, and Poles from eastern Europe, the Dutch from western Europe, new waves of southern Europeans such as the Italians and Greeks, refugees from the Warsaw Pact such as the Hungarians and Czechs, and smaller groups from a dozen different countries. The academic literature has depicted them as a group distinct from both the second- and third-generation farm families they met in the city and from the early-century migrants who preceded them to Canada. Unlike their predecessors, many mid-century immigrants came as urban professionals hoping to benefit from the booming resource-extraction economy in the West. With reference to Alberta, Howard Palmer and Tamara Palmer once noted that the mid-century 'wave of immigrants was smaller than the major wave in the pre-World War I era' but nonetheless had 'an important impact on the province.' Unlike the earlier wave, these immigrants headed straight for the booming mid-century cities. Few national groups diverged from this pattern. The tiny group of Romanian refugees who fled their country after it was declared a communist Peoples' Republic in 1946 included professionals and even some aristocrats, 'all of whom were sophisticated, well-educated people, often fluent in at least two ... languages ... unlike the earlier immigrants who had been farmers and labourers.' Similarly, the Estonians were mostly 'from middle class backgrounds' and included 'engineers, architects, veterinarians, medical doctors, dentists, clerks, tradesmen, army officers, lawyers and teachers'; indeed, they shared few cultural features with the second- and third-generation rural Estonian Canadians and integrated quickly into anglophone prairie Canada because of their educational achievements in the humanities and sciences.[31] Other statements of this sort describe most of the large immigrant groups: third-wave, city-savvy, professional Ukrainian immigrants who were contrasted with their left-wing peasant forerunners; German immigrants who, although acknowledged to include large numbers of blue-collar workers, were also known for their technical abilities and professional credentials.[32]

   This emphasis on the newcomers' sophistication is only half the story. In fact many post-war immigrants came as wage labourers and members of working-class communities, and many, too, originated in rural districts in eastern and southern Europe. They included the Polish immigrants who worked in Edmonton's packing plants and the Dutch who had once been small land-holding farmers.[33] David Aliaga's account of Italian immigrants to Calgary demonstrates that three-quarters of the Italian immigrants had been peasants in Europe. Of the remaining one-quarter, most were labourers and craftsmen who possessed a rudimentary education, having completed only a few years of *la quinta elementare*.[34] Most, too, came with very little money, the vast majority having possessed only one to five hectares of land in Italy. Many cited as their reasons for migration

'chronic unemployment, scarcity of land, and outright poverty.'[35] Not surprisingly many Italians accepted manual jobs, working mostly in construction, building the infrastructure of Calgary's expanding downtown office
district and of its growing suburbs. Specifically, many worked for 'the City
of Calgary in its road crews, fixing and erecting fences, doing landscaping
and working in general maintenance.'[36] So concentrated were the Italians
in these positions that workers often were not even compelled to learn
English; and both the bosses and the workers were *paesani*.

Unlike the immigrants of the early century, however, both the professional and working-class mid-century immigrants faced a rapidly expanding, increasingly open society. Just as the second-generation Jews and
Japanese in the prairie cities integrated quickly during the mid-century
decades, so, too, did the more marginalized post-war immigrants from
Europe. Several studies have noted that after only a few years, the Italian
working-class immigrants shed their old ways. According to a study by
Antonella Fanella these construction workers left their Italian bosses because they 'preferred Canadian companies where they were less likely to
be exploited.'[37] Howard Snider's 1966 study of post-war Italian immigrants in Edmonton found a high degree of integration, although 'men
are more involved in the Canadian social structure than women and …
young people are more involved … than older people.' The upward mobility among Italian youth after only ten to fifteen years in Canada was
especially noteworthy, and so, too, was their knowledge of Canadian opportunities and frequent contact with Canadian neighbours. By the mid-
1960s the most significant difference between early- and mid-century
Italian arrivals was that the newcomers' memories of Italy were more vivid;
the early-century immigrants had forgotten the old ways.[38]

This pattern was also revealed in Alan Thomas Rees-Powell's 1964
study contrasting two very different post-war immigrant groups: the
Dutch and the Italians. The former, consisting of northern European
Protestants, had a long history of favoured immigrant status, while the
latter, as southern European Catholics, were often deemed unsuitable
for Canada. It seemed the immigrants had become especially sensitive to
socially strange situations; that is, to the 'perceived dominant habits … of
an unfamiliar system.' It was testimony to post-war openness to Europeans
that 'the establishment of a *modus vivendi* by the immigrant,' an understanding of what is required for integration, was considered less difficult
in 1964 than in 1934, 1904, or 1864.[39] At a basic level the difference
between the favoured status of the Dutch and the 'new' immigrant status
of the Italians was readily apparent. Two-thirds of the Dutch who had

arrived in Edmonton between 1958 and 1964 revealed high levels of 'psychological integration,' whereas only one-quarter of the Italians exhibited this level.[40] In every other way, however, old stereotypes were defied as both groups experienced an increasingly open society. For example, on a 'psychological integration' index, the rates for the two groups converged after only six years in Canada: 77 percent for the Dutch and 66 percent for the Italians. And, surprisingly, the histories of these groups refuted a standard Weberian idea: the difference in 'economic integration' between the highly Protestant Dutch immigrants and the Catholic Italians was insignificant. Fifty percent of the recently arrived Dutch reported successful 'economic integration,' compared to 48 percent of the Italians, and similar ratios (80 percent for the Dutch and 81 percent for the Italians) were registered for those who had been in Canada for more than eight years.[41]

These post-war European newcomers were aided in their integration by an evolving ethnic identity. The changing nature of ethnic institutions, ethnic social networks, and ethnic culture was central to achievements in the prairie city. The Greeks in Calgary illustrate this process. At first glance it appeared they belonged to a tiny minority group with few established immigration networks and fewer community resources. And yet, as Donna Minions demonstrated, the Greeks achieved a smooth and harmonious mid-century integration. The Greek community in Calgary in 1942 consisted of only forty-seven households, and the occupants of most of these – sixty-four of a total of seventy-four people – were men, most of whom were single. Even though the Greek community was small and without organization, ethnicity did matter. At the centre of this small ethnic group was one individual, Demetrious Koumetrios, the colourful owner of four of the nineteen Greek businesses in the city. His ability to negotiate with the wider world was apparent from his public name: Jimmie Condon. His influence in the community and, indeed, his philanthropy were marked by the name of the first Greek Orthodox church built in Calgary in 1957, St Demetrious, in his honour.

Then, too, the most frequented ethnic site for these Greek immigrants was not an ethnic community hall but several Greek cafes. Immigrant Panos recalled that when he visited Calgary in 1956, he knew it was in his interest to visit George Andrianakos and his partner's Noble Cafe where fellow Greeks passed on word to him about work at Alberta Marble and Tile, a company owned by a Ukrainian Canadian. Immigrant Electra remembered that the Calgary Greeks also met 'over at Mel Melidonis', the Avenue Grill [where] Mel's second wife, [who] was Greek … put on big parties on the special days for all the Greeks.' Another immigrant reported that the idea for a Greek Orthodox church arose from conversations within the Greek soccer team and its supporters for the need of a strong 'Greek community.' As he recalled, the idea took hold at 'a party at Steve Meldon's restaurant.' These social hierarchies and social networks may have been informal, but they were no less ethnic, and they were significant in aiding the integration of newcomers.[42]

If there was an official site in which the Greeks in Calgary plotted their integration, it was their church. As one immigrant declared: in Calgary 'Greeks don't have their own neighbourhood ... like they do in Montreal'; thus, they 'have a harder time getting together with other Greeks ... Montreal has more Greeks, more Greek life style, and more fun.' And yet Calgary's small Greek Orthodox church, with only 250 adherents in 1961, played an important neighbourhood role. Despite segregation indices showing Calgary to be a very integrated community, the church attracted Greek families to its neighbourhood, resulting in 'a rather Greek neighbourhood,' filled with so many young families that up to thirty Greek children attended the local public school. The church also played a cultural role. It was the custodian, for example, of the Greeks' cultural repertoire, 'the prestige of Hellenic culture [that was] ... securely bound by religion and language.' As Greek immigrant Gabrielle noted, the church was also the 'place you gather to talk about Greek heritage.' Aside from a place 'to know about God and to hear about God,' it was a place to be Greek, for 'really to be Greek is to be Greek Orthodox.' Reflecting the importance of this cultural construction, the term *kinotis*, traditionally referring to the state-linked parish in the old country, evolved to mean 'spiritual community of overseas Greeks.'[43]

Poles in Calgary, as described by Kathryn-Anne Rhea Watts, also relied heavily on their church for social interaction. Although they did develop many ethnic institutions, one seemingly for each of several age groups – clubs for ex-combatants, university youth, senior citizens, soccer players, young mothers and children (Scouts) – the church had other social functions. First, immigrants attested that the Mass was a 'family affair' where children worshipped alongside their parents. Second, it was said that Mass provided 'a valuable opportunity for socializing and "catching up on the latest gossip."' The importance of this interaction could not be over-emphasized, said the immigrants, because 'gossip among friends [helped] bind ... the members of Calgary's Polish community.' Then, too, gossiping served to shape and discipline community action and to create an informal boundary, 'setting off Poles from non-Poles and community members from non-community members,' for gossiping was restricted to members of the group. Third, the very existence of the Polish parish in Calgary provided an arena in which upward mobility was given cultural meaning: within the parish immigrants could 'overcome the inferiority complex of poverty' and eventually show 'the local community that they were becoming wealthier.' The church thus played a crucial role as the generator of ethnic network, ethnic boundary, and ethnic status. In this way it served as the cultural underpinning of other Polish associations that were related to the Poles' everyday life. It turned identities into assets and advertised well-paying jobs. It extended informal lines of credit, established bungalow-building bees, offered temporary dwellings, provided rental discounts, ensured professional services in Polish, and provided travel services to Poland organized by knowledgeable people.[44]

Religion was also crucial in the lives of Calgary's Italians. As noted above, post-war Italians in Calgary integrated quickly. Antonella Fanella's work links integration to the rising importance of the church and a significantly new appreciation for religion. True, Italian immigrants derided religion in Italy; after all, 'the majority of the *contadini* were strongly anti-clerical.' They cited a corrupt priesthood and a religiousness that was steeped in fatalism, emphasizing relationships between the person and the saint that 'took the form of bargaining.' Upon arriving in the new land the Italians often did not find Catholic churches where they could communicate in Italian, and thus were shut out culturally and linguistically. But when the Calgary community finally, in 1963, received its first Italian priest, 'its first permanent Italian Scalabriniano father, Monsignor Angelo Sacchi,' the Italian–Canadian Parrochia di Sant' Andrea developed quickly in the renovated shell of an old Presbyterian church. Adherents flocked to the services. In fact, in comparison to pre-war Italian immigrants for whom religion was relatively unimportant, the post-war immigrants developed strong bonds with their new St Andrew's parish. Henceforth old life-cycle traditions that gave legitimacy to marriage, dignity to death, inclusion to birth and adolescence, were interwoven in church activities. Although the Calgary community discontinued *la processione* (the church-run festive parades of the Madonna), they practised the *festa dei santi* (festival of the patron saint). In time the church far outpaced in importance the old Italian community organizations, even the post-war amalgamation of the Associazione Italo-Canadese and Giovanni Caboto Loggia. Fanella concludes that 'it is ironic that the southern Italians who had been so religiously indifferent in Italy would grow attached to the church in Canada.' But then in Canada, the church had become linked to the very creation of an ethnic identity, providing fundamental spiritual resources to the immigrant worlds and creating the web of trusted relationships.[45]

The Meeting of Two Ethnic Strands

If the post-war climate in the Alberta and Saskatchewan cities created a much smoother culture of integration than was observed among early-century migrants, the presence of distinct waves of urban immigrants often created conflict within a particular ethnic group. This dynamic arose when groups with different rates of acculturation and disparate homeland experiences developed their strategies of integration. These differences could be class-bound, religious, or political in nature. Often the differences were so significant as to leave lasting divisions within the ethnic community. Those divisions were part of the process by which ethnicity evolved, mutated, or hybridized.

There were variations of conflict between immigrants of different immigrant waves. In post-war Saskatoon the pacifist Mennonites who had long emphasized avoidance of 'worldly' consumer and entertainment cultures divided along immigration lines on these questions. The most conservative were the so-called Kanadier, descendants of Mennonites who had arrived in Manitoba in the 1870s and whose rural-based leaders offered repeated warnings of evil worlds in the city. More accepting were the Russlaender Mennonites who had arrived from the Soviet Union in the 1920s and had accepted higher education, musical instruments, and even non-combatant wartime military service, insisting that 'brotherly and Christian love' must not prevent their youth from facing 'danger side by side with other fellow citizens.'[46] Still, in the post-war period the moderately progressive, albeit pious and patriarchal, Russlaender often found themselves in sharp conflict with the Fluechtlingen, or Displaced Person, Mennonites who often arrived as female-headed households, and had enjoyed the more secular lifestyles associated with Stalinist Russia and post-war refugee camps in Germany.[47]

In Edmonton, German immigrants cast an ethnic identity according to one of 'two types of Germans.' The Reichsdeutschen who arrived directly from Germany de-emphasized their German background and quickly assimilated into the English–Canadian mainstream, turning ethnicity into a highly personal identity that emphasized knowledge of birthplace. The Volksdeutschen from the Soviet Union treasured linguistic persistence for the simple reason that in eastern Europe they had been 'socially, linguistically and religiously isolated from their host countries' and had employed their ancestral language to fend off the majority Slavic culture.[48] In Calgary immigrants from Greece accused 'Eastern Greeks,' those from Toronto and Montreal, of questionable conduct. The Greeks from those cities were said to be aloof, keeping a 'little bit away' from the church, and when they did become involved in church, they were accused of opportunism, 'just us[ing] it,' and failing to become true *koumbaros*.[49] The charges varied, but they always served to set one wave of immigrants against another.

The most common intra-ethnic conflict, however, seems to have occurred between multi-generational farm folk who were venturing into the cities and first-generation refugee or economic migrants from Europe. For many rural immigrants, having been pushed to the political left by the economic difficulties of the Depression, the mid-century city was a site of conflict where they met their post-war countryfolk who had been pushed to the right by Soviet politics.

Such battles were apparent in the Hungarian community in Edmonton. As Steven Tötösy de Zepetnek has argued, intra-ethnic conflict was especially pronounced in the city's Hungarian Cultural Society.[50] Most of the early-century Hungarians in Alberta had been rural, having arrived as recruited sugar beet workers in 1914 and 1915 or as coal miners in the 1920s. In the mid-1930s these people, forced from their farms or laid off from their work as miners, began to arrive in large numbers in Edmonton. During the Second World War other Hungarians came to the city from the countryside. The immigrants gathered in search of ethnic comradeship. They considered joining a Toronto-based Hungarian trade union that 'wanted to expand all across Canada.' In 1944, however, some forty Hungarian families in Edmonton went their own way, forming the Hungarian Cultural Circle, later renamed the Hungarian Society. The society became a place in which to dance, speak Hungarian, and discuss the contents of the left-wing *Kanadai Magyar Munkás*, the 'Hungarian-language organ of the Communist Party of Canada.' Communist ideology became the political soul of the Hungarian Society.

The society seems to have been an orderly, dynamic, and relevant home for Edmonton Hungarians. But then the former farmers and miners of Edmonton came into contact with two post-war waves of Hungarian immigrants. The wartime refugees, numbering some eight hundred, included farmers, wage labourers, bureaucrats, professionals, and army officers. Their very presence in the local Hungarian club had the effect of depoliticizing the society. The 'leftist/socialist orientation of the active members of the society' was squelched and cultural activities, including nationalist Hungarian music and poetry, were emphasized. In a typical meeting in March 1953, the Hungarians celebrated 'the 1848 uprising against Habsburg domination.' The celebration was contained in a lengthy program that included three speeches, three Hungarian folk music recitations, six poetry readings, two religious pronouncements, a dramatic play, and two renditions of the Hungarian national anthem. Nationalism, not socialism, was the aim of the recast society.

If the original founders of the society believed that their compromise had brought unity to the Hungarian world in Edmonton, they were mistaken. In 1956 some thirty-six thousand Hungarian refugees arrived in Canada. In Edmonton the newcomers overwhelmed the tiny existing Hungarian community and also challenged the direction of the Hungarian Society. The society had expanded its services to assist the 1956 refugees with money, clothing, and household items, but this generosity did not stop the newcomers from trying to take over the governance of the society and precipitating a decade-long decline in its fortunes. The newly arrived refugees, mostly members of the middle class, opposed the depoliticization of the society, albeit not in the form of the leftist direction of its founders, but in the rightist direction of refugees from Soviet tyranny. The Cold War newcomers' argument was that 'during these times of political and ideological polarization ... the Society's *raison d'être* being cultural and nonpolitical' was mistaken. However, the society still predominantly consisted of left-leaning Hungarians who had come to Edmonton from the Alberta countryside in the 1930s or 1940s. The Soviet refugees were easily outmanoeuvred. In the end the newcomers turned against the society and instead allied with the Hungarian Veterans' Association. It was this 'politically conscious and strongly anti-Communist' organization, dominated by 1956 refugees, that eventually became 'an effective mouthpiece of the majority of Edmonton's Canadian-Hungarians.'[51]

The post-war newcomers were a disparate people, consisting of both a professional and a working class. They came from a wide variety of countries. But as with their cousins who had preceded them to Canada, the new immigrants from Europe discovered in the cities of Alberta and Saskatchewan a rapidly expanding economy and surprisingly open society. Informal ethnic networks and symbolic ethnicities were created in this context by even the most marginalized of the groups, thus ensuring that integration occurred within the security of an imagined tradition. Conflict for these new immigrants lay not so much between host society and immigrant as within the ethnic group. These tensions revealed fundamental differences between the descendants of the early-century immigrants and the mid-century refugees. This dynamic relationship suggested that integration was not conditioned only by the host society, but also by the pre-migration experiences of the newcomers. It suggested further an ethnicity in the making, one fusing different elements of the past with the exigencies of the present.

Conclusion

The two sources of mid-century urban ethnic revival in Alberta and Saskatchewan – the second- or third-generation Canadian farm family and the first-generation European refugee – thus shared several integration strategies. Each reflected the tenor of the time, the state of the economy, and the evolving regional identity of the Prairies. As in the rest of Canada, the 1950s marked a decade of religious intensity. Canadians sought a return to 'normalcy' centred in home and community, while traumatized refugees and indirect victims of war in Europe sought to reorder their lives. They strove for a state of equilibrium, cultivating the values and identities of their ethnicities, yet partaking of the promise of the post-Depression economy. The melding of ancient Japanese values with middle-class behaviour in Edmonton, the 'museumification' of Ukrainian contributions in Saskatoon, the amalgamation of Canadian and eastern European social practice among the Calgary Greeks, and the conflict between Canadian and Hungarian-derived political interests all suggested that ethnicity was a dynamic social force in the lives of the immigrants.

The mid-century process of integration was not achieved only in the context of a rapidly growing economy, however, but also of a newly defined prairie identity. It was in the mid-century decades that an old idea of the West as a distinctive, physically defined, wheat-growing region in Canada evolved into an identity based on inter-ethnic relations, a regional identity born of the mix of cultures in the early years of the century. The identity was also based in part on a new confidence that the West was a region of economic strength, no longer accepting without demur the economic leadership from Montreal or Toronto, but confident in the promise of its natural resources and in its socio-political leadership, including that of its native son, Prime Minister John Diefenbaker.

The new western identity was created by immigrants for immigrants. A 1981 study by David Millet suggests that the arrival of vast numbers of non-British immigrants at mid-century established a 'Canadian as opposed to a British identity' in the country. But within this Canadian identity were regionally determined versions of being 'Canadian.' In the West 'admission to the status of ... "real" Canadian ... [was] confined to the British, Dutch, Germans and Scandinavians, well into the 1950s.' Here, 'within the dominant group, the non-British held *equal* rank with those of British origin' so that while one might 'speak of "Anglo-conformity" in the East, it is more legitimate to speak of "Nordic-conformity" in the West.' The fact was that when 'a region such as western Canada did not have a large enough British-origin population to form a clearly dominant group, people of other origins were accorded equal status – provided they were white, and especially if within the white population they were racially Nordic, could learn English quickly and were Protestant by religion.' Here, non-British, Nordic immigrants 'felt they were making an alliance with those of British stock in order to produce a new country, rather than continuing a British heritage.'[52]

It is an interesting suggestion, but the findings above hint at an even broader, more fluid sense of a western-based Canadian nationalism in the making. Rapidly growing cities, an influx of immigrants from eastern and southern Europe, and their fusion with early-century migrants created an increasingly hybrid culture. Evidence suggests that by the 1960s non-Nordic newcomers were also beginning to feel ownership of Canada, an identity negotiated within the unique social and economic setting of the prairie city. Their own conformity to an incipient prairie Canadian culture occurred in spite of, and, indeed, with the aid of, a panoply of distinct (and not necessarily Nordic) ethnic symbols and resources. If this was a phenomenon in the four cities of the new provinces of Alberta and Saskatchewan, it was so, too, in the old prairie 'capital' of Winnipeg.

chapter four

Accommodation in Winnipeg

Winnipeg, the oldest and, at mid-century, still the largest prairie city, reflected the dramatic changes in prairie regional identity that occurred between the 1940s and 1960s. Like other prairie centres, it was affected by the exodus from rural districts and the influx of new arrivals from Europe. The newcomers' impact was not quite the same in Winnipeg as in the other cities, however, because Winnipeg citizens had been dealing with large-scale challenges of just this sort for a half-century. The new arrivals from Europe were joining larger communities of countrymen who knew Canada well. What is more, a new generation of Winnipeg civic leaders, whether Canadian or European in heritage, recognized the shortcomings of previous reception activities and were determined to smooth the newcomers' entry into the community. Both factors – the duration of an ethnic group's Canadian experience and the commitment of community leaders to improving integration strategies – underlined how the atmosphere in the city's boundary zones had changed between early and mid-century. The perceived barriers between groups had been lowered, established Canadians worked more closely with newcomers, and, increasingly, the children of earlier generations of immigrants assumed leadership roles in the community.

This chapter[1] takes three Winnipeg vantage points – that of one immigrant family, of several ethnic groups, and of the host society – to document changes in the boundary zones and, by extension, in the prairie regional experience. It begins with the family history of a young man who integrated very well into life in Winnipeg. In a series of interviews, Saul Cherniack contrasted his generation's experience with that of his parents, who arrived in the city in the first decade of the twentieth century. The chapter then considers the adjustment experiences of members of

several ethnic groups in Winnipeg as opposed to the other prairie centres, including Icelanders, Germans, Mennonites, and Japanese Canadians.
Finally, the chapter turns to the leaders of the host society, outlining the
role of several Winnipeg institutions that served the needs of newcomers.
Taken together, the view from these three vantage points demonstrates
that migrants and hosts increasingly considered the barriers separating
ethnic groups, and between newcomers and established British Canadians,
as permeable. The once impregnable fortress of British–Canadian culture was undermined by a new force: the notion of an evolving, plural
approach to questions of identity. A Canada-wide phenomenon, this idea
of Canadian pluralism assumed distinctive qualities in prairie cities, one
that relied on ethnic symbols and resources but also a determined commitment to bridge such barriers in order that all people might live comfortably in this society.

Saul Cherniack's Family History

Saul Cherniack's mother and father, both Russian Jews, both socialists,
migrated to Winnipeg during the first years of the twentieth century. His
father's father, who preceded them, 'started out as a street-cleaner, sweep-
ing in summer and cutting snow and ice to keep the streetcar tracks clear
in winter, and since he wouldn't work on the Sabbath, my father took his
place on Saturdays. Father, having been a watchmaker in Russia, then set
up shop as a watchmaker on Main Street.' Saul's father went to school at
St John's College, graduated with a BA in 1915, and then earned a degree
in law. He became an important figure in Winnipeg's Jewish community
during the next forty years.[2] Saul described his parents as having lived almost exclusively within Jewish circles:

> My parents made their home in Canada but were not entirely comfortable
> in the non-Jewish world. My father had an unduly respectful attitude for
> judges, including even friends such as [Justice] Samuel Freedman. He al-
> ways called him, 'milord,' not just his first name, as I would do. This was
> evidence, I think, of his respectful attitude to the legal system and those
> who made it work. My father was active in politics, but not so much at the
> provincial or federal level – for him, it was local politics. He was campaign
> manager for his good friend, A.A. Heaps, when he ran successfully for the
> House of Commons ... Father had a wide circle of Jewish political figures
> – ... but also non-Jews ... But he did not meet with non-Jews outside of

politics, where they had a commitment in common. Socially and culturally, his life was a Jewish life ...

And Saul's mother rarely contacted people of other groups in the city: 'Mother was less able to think of non-Jews as people who respected Jews. She was leery of others, probably because she lived her life completely as a Jewish person.'

Young Saul grew up in north Winnipeg, a part of both the Jewish community and the wider world represented by the public school. His parents were founders of the Jewish Radical School – a Yiddish-language, secular, socialist institution (one of three Yiddish schools, in addition to the one Jewish religious school, then operating in Winnipeg):

> I was in the first kindergarten class of the Jewish Radical School in 1921. And I attended classes in that school as a full-time student until Grade 4, and then an English-language public school from Grade 5, and St John's High School for grades 10 and 11. After school hours, I attended the Yiddish high school at the Radical School ... I attended [the Jewish Radical] primary school in the North End and can remember that, in grade three, I couldn't approach the school from College Avenue because I was in danger of being beaten up and was often called a 'dirty Jew.' We were dirty Jews to some people – this name-calling was not unusual at that time ... It wasn't just one way, either. In the Jewish colony along Dufferin, Jarvis, College, and Luxton streets, some Jews spoke of 'those Galicians' in the same way. Half the kids at Machray School were Jewish, and the other half were not part of my social life. There was one street I couldn't walk down, and another my sister couldn't walk down. I had few non-Jewish friends but there was a large Jewish community so this didn't matter. Even in high school my close friends were Jewish. Sports might have provided a bridge for some kids but I was no athlete. I can remember a play at Machray School in which the cast was half-Jewish, half not. And I can remember some non-Jews with whom I was friendly at St John's [English-language public] High and some more at the University of Manitoba.

This was Winnipeg in the early decades of the twentieth century, when the barriers between groups were high and the suspicions rife.

The 1930s, when Saul was a teenager, differed very little. Anti-Semitism became more prominent in public life and the Cherniacks encountered it on many occasions: 'I remember that Dad's law partner, Marcus Hyman, Independent Labour Party, brought in legislation to eliminate restrictive covenants in land deeds, and that he also got legislation passed to require the name of a publisher on pamphlets so defamatory propaganda could be traced to its source. This was in the 1930s, at the time that a local Nazi party was forming. My father told me that he had gone to a public meeting where Whitaker, the Nazi leader, said that Jews thought Gentiles were inferior. Father spoke out, said that Whitaker was a liar, and got thrown out of the meeting. He told this story with pride.'

When Saul began his legal studies, he ran into similar barriers at the University of Manitoba:

I went to the University of Manitoba for one year, 1933–34, and then articled and took law school for four years, doing my fifth-year articles with my father after the morning classes ended. At the university, our Jewish groups were aware of anti-Semitism. We were both [he and his future wife, Sybil] in the Menorah society and attended lectures and plays. One famous play was *Awake and Sing*, by Clifford Odets, about a New York Jewish family attempting to adapt to life in the general community and to participate in affairs of the world. We talked only among ourselves, as Jews, and not across religious or ethnic lines at the university. I talked to Professor Wardle in Biology, in 1934, who taught a Zoology class that was compulsory for pre-med students. He was on the Admissions Committee for the Medical School and he actually showed me lists of applicants in three categories – women and Jews were in groups separate from the main admission list – and told me how many could be admitted in each category. My sister, Mindel, got in on both the Jewish and the women's list ...

I married Sybil in 1938. She was born in the village of Blaine Lake, Saskatchewan, and at age twelve she moved in with family friends in Winnipeg to attend school. She lived in the West End and attended Mulvey Public School and Gordon Bell [English-language public] high school, where there were very few Jews. She was friendly with a wide range of people, very popular and outgoing, and was stunned to discover, when she moved over to the U of M, that her friends at the university were almost exclusively Jewish. Her Gordon Bell friends became distanced at university, were 'busy otherwise socially.' They weren't deliberately distant but new circles of friends formed. It troubled her, even was quite a shock. It wasn't a shock to me because I had already experienced that.

From 1935, amidst growing awareness of the fascist crisis in Europe, Winnipeg's political loyalties changed. Stalin's Popular Front decree was a part of this shift but so, too, was a growing willingness at home to look outside one's own political community for allies: 'Father was part of the founding of the Canadian Jewish Congress (a national association), in 1919. In the 1930s he thought its leadership was not fighting strongly and openly enough against the fascists. Father then became President of the Jewish Anti-Fascist League. That was the first time that Communists came into our office – 1935. It was then that father ended his anti-Communist phase and worked together with them in a coalition. The "respectable" Jewish community did not approve, but father was belligerent and determined to fight. Sam Freedman, who was president of the YMHA and who became a great man in our community, opposed joining a Winnipeg youth group because of the Communist presence in their ranks.'

It was in the late 1930s that Saul, now in his early twenties, moved into the wider community:

> Around the time of our marriage, Sybil and I became involved in the amateur Winnipeg New Theatre, which performed 'plays of social significance.' For perhaps the first time I really lived and worked with non-Jews, socially as well as in preparing for the performances. This was a great period in my life. We had four meetings a week, we attended rehearsals, raised money. We worked with people ranging from David Orlikow (later NDP MP), to Joe Zuken (later a Communist city councillor) and his brother Bill Ross (Communist Party leader). Because of our activity in the theatre and politics, I made close non-Jewish friends. Alistair Stewart, later a CCF Member of Parliament, was my first real friend outside Jewish circles – he married a Jewish girl. Sybil was membership chair of the theatre and we found support everywhere. We had common concerns. We thought politics were important. But it wasn't as if we felt 'a great need to reach out' to other ethnic groups. We just shared a point of view and thought politics should be part of theatre. One great friend from that time was Mel Stover, who told me that, as a child, he had shopped at a 'Jew store.' We won the Dominion Drama Festival in 1939 with a play by Albert Maltz. However, the Communist Party members and the non-Communists could not agree. After the Molotov-Ribbentrop pact, the CP won greater say in the theatre in 1940–41. The theatre group split up, and Sybil and I, along with others, quit.

The circumstances of the war affected residents of Winnipeg in ways that might not have been anticipated. Officials at every level were charged with ensuring that the war effort took precedence and that conflict between groups was avoided. As Cherniack recalled, 'Sybil collected donations for the war effort during the Second World War. She knew every house, from Salter to the Red River, from St John's to Cathedral. This area must have been half Jewish but there was respect for other cultures. But racism wasn't that strong by 1940 – though, socially, the groups lived apart.' The same applied in the armed forces, though anti-racism was even more emphatically enforced: '[in 1942] I took officer training (three months in Victoria, two months in Brandon), then an Artillery regiment for eight months in Wainwright, then studied Japanese in Vancouver for twelve months. There was nothing in my military experience that was anti-Semitic. We Jewish officers blended in with no problems at all. There was an anti-"Quebec French" element in my artillery unit. From sergeant and up in this unit, we were heading for active service. From corporal and below, everyone was conscripted – called Zombies, rudely.'

The acquisition of languages played a part in Cherniack's war experience and, to a remarkable degree, in shaping his life. He grew up in a bilingual environment: 'The language at home, at least until I was 15 or 16, was Yiddish. In Father's law office, when I went there, conversations normally took place in English. Our family took two newspapers, the Winnipeg *Tribune* and the *Israelite Press*, and New York Yiddish periodicals at home.' His schooling at the Radical School was usually in Yiddish. And, when he married, he ensured that his wife, who had grown up in a Saskatchewan farm town, and his two sons, born in 1943 and 1945, learned Yiddish as well. His bilingualism affected his fortunes in the Canadian army. After officer training and eight months with an artillery regiment in Wainwright, Alberta, he embarked on a new challenge: 'Among the qualifications for [Army] language school was knowing another language, and I had Yiddish.' He was dispatched to Vancouver for a year of language training: 'I spoke Japanese quite well by the end.'

Although the war ended before Saul could enter the Pacific theatre, he used his newly acquired skill when he returned to his Winnipeg law office: .

I subscribed to a Japanese-Canadian newspaper, the *New Canadian*, and read it to keep up the language. I saw a notice that the editor was looking for anyone with copies of Japanese-language plays, and I phoned to tell him of the dramatic passages in my textbooks. We met and became friendly socially and I then came in contact with Harold Hirose, an insurance man, who referred clients to me and invited me to speak at several banquets. I acted for many members of the Japanese community, especially when they bought homes. The Issei [first-generation immigrants] would not respond to me in Japanese but I talked often with Harold Hirose, who became their leader. The elders didn't want to speak Japanese in public and would depend on the Nisei [second-generation Japanese Canadians] to use English. This seemed to break the paternal authority of the elders, who could not speak for the community. Inter-marriage, or marriage out of the Japanese community, was frequent. I thought they might be rejecting their language and culture, perhaps because they were ashamed of the war waged by Japan. The Canadian government and many non-Japanese Canadians made them feel unwanted by their being exiled into provinces east of their British Columbia homes.

His work with Japanese Canadians marked the beginning of Cherniack's post-war contributions to the wider Winnipeg community. They also emphasized the continuing cultural barriers among ethnic groups.[3]

Cherniack believed the atmosphere of the city changed substantially after the war, despite the troubles visited upon Japanese Canadians. Though he continued to make his home in the North End, he observed, 'In the 1950s and 1960s a lot of Jews moved to the South End of the city, to River Heights. A non-Jewish client told me he moved to St Vital [east of the Red River] because he was concerned that his kids were losing their Jewish friends at Bar Mitzvah time … He felt that his own kids were not being included during these events because of the religious differences.' That Jews were responsible for social exclusion struck him as ironic. But his larger point was that the prejudice of earlier decades was much reduced: 'In the 1950s, people began to cross ethnic lines more, especially in business and law. But not socially. It was easier somehow to stay in our own community. It was not as if we kept them out or they kept us out, except in places like the Manitoba Club, the St Charles Club, and the Winnipeg Winter Club. In the late 1960s, Sam Freedman was the first Jew appointed to the High Court. He told me that he was the first judge not invited to join the Manitoba Club. When I was on school board, one of my fellow board members, a former army officer, asked me why I was a socialist. I told him – "because I'm a Jew." Minority experience goes together with being a democratic socialist in this society, in my opinion.' Cherniack may have concluded that the barriers between ethno-religious groups were lower than in the past but he did not suggest they had vanished. And, interestingly, he associated his adherence to a 'culturally Jewish' way of life with dissent against the established parties and prevailing economic order.

Saul Cherniack enjoyed a remarkable career in public affairs, winning election to the public school board, the metropolitan Winnipeg council, and the provincial legislative assembly, where he served as a cabinet minister. In retirement, he served for eight years on Canada's Security and Intelligence Review Committee, the independent body that reviews the work of the country's secret service. He had grown up in the divided world of Winnipeg's North End. He was very much aware of anti-Semitic people and anti-Jewish caveats. But, around the time of the Second World War, he began to make friends in the wider community. He experienced no anti-Semitism during his army career. After the war, the prejudice that moved him to accept responsibility for the wider community afflicted Japanese Canadians – for whom he provided many legal services – more than Jews. He put a premium on family ties and maintaining contact with relatives, even distant ones, rather than on Israel or the Winnipeg Jewish religious community. He became what he called a 'cultural' as opposed to a 'religious' Jew. And he chose socialism as his political loyalty, perhaps partly because of his family and ethno-religious heritage but also because of his North End neighbourhood experiences and his work with Japanese Canadians.

Cherniack's observations on his life are noteworthy for their differences from his father's outlook. As a second-generation Canadian, the son's world was much more open, much less restricted by Jews' own conventions or by anti-Jewish sentiments than was the father's. Like his father, Saul found his close friends and his social circle among Jews. But he was not a representative of Jews to the wider world, as his father had been. He concluded about his father's career: 'But he did not meet with non-Jews outside of politics, where they had a commitment in common.' His father actually endorsed this observation in a reminiscence delivered in Yiddish to a Jewish audience in 1969, near the end of his life. On that occasion, Joseph A. Cherniack emphasized to his listeners the importance of commitment to the Jewish community and suggested that Jews should see resistance to assimilation as a 'duty.' He added, in a phrase that spoke to the changes he had witnessed during his sixty-five years in the city, that his and his wife's 'greatest contribution is that our son and his wife are taking an important part in the life of the Jewish and non-Jewish community of Winnipeg.'⁴ Joseph Cherniack had never aspired to a role representing non-Jews. His son and daughter-in-law met such obligations with distinction.

In comparing the relative integration of the two Cherniack generations, it is important to remember that the mid-century experience of Saul and his family did not constitute assimilation to a British–Canadian norm. In a carefully phrased comment in which he contrasted their experiences, Saul recognized that he was more his father's son than might have been generally understood: 'Socially and culturally, … [my father's] life was a Jewish life. And, culturally, that's still true for me today, although in all other ways – socially, politically, and professionally – I am at ease in my country.' Saul Cherniack's adaptation was typical of what was happening in the boundary zones of Winnipeg and prairie Canada. He represented a dynamic, increasingly hybrid, but still ethnically conscious, generation. Despite continuing slights directed at their cultural group, he and his wife accepted their share of responsibility for the entire community.

Ethnocultural Groups' Experiences

Some ethnocultural groups in Winnipeg differed little in their mid-century experiences from those of their relatives in other prairie cities. They emphasized ethnic symbols and festivals, met in a variety of ethnically exclusive churches and clubs, and provided fraternal assistance to newcomers. Yet some other groups differed in a few specific ways, once again illustrating how an older, larger centre might house distinctive forces within the broader prairie story. The most important of these had to do with consciousness of a working-class perspective.

Some of the groups arriving in Winnipeg after the Second World War, whether from rural prairie backgrounds or directly from Europe, consciously planned to blend into the environment. Of these, the most evident in their determination to integrate without fuss were the Icelanders. As third- and fourth-generation Canadians, they joined the thousands of families who left rural Manitoba to seek a better future in the province's capital city. Known as 'Goolies' (probably from the International Order of Good Templars and its hall on Sargent Avenue, the main street of their West End neighbourhood), for decades they had accepted English-language schooling without demur. For an equally long time, their leaders had articulately opposed 'hyphenated Canadian' status. In a debate during the First World War, for example, when criticizing a legislator's defence of French as an official language, Icelandic–Canadian Member of the Legislative Assembly T.H. Johnston said: 'I want those who agree with [him] … to consider what would happen if all the nationalities represented in this province were to adopt that attitude. What kind of Manitoba would we have a hundred years from now? … We admit, and we all must admit, that there is only one nationality possible in the future, a Canadian nationality, and we claim the privilege of becoming merged in that, and the privilege of contributing towards that, whatever national characteristics we may possess.'[5] In their leisure time and without fanfare, members of their community sustained two Icelandic-language newspapers and a number of other periodicals, sponsored a summer festival in a nearby Icelandic village on Lake Winnipeg, and developed a privately funded chair at the University of Manitoba where Icelandic language and literature might be studied. These quiet ways permitted the maintenance of community awareness and of venues for cultural expression that were little noticed in the larger city.[6] Icelanders melted into the city and accepted community-wide responsibilities just as Saul Cherniack had done.

German immigrants who left war-ravaged eastern Europe after 1945 bore the stigma of German opposition to Canada in two world wars. And yet, as in the other two prairie provinces, they were able to integrate into the wider Winnipeg community with relative ease. These German-speaking newcomers became the counterparts of the groups in the Saskatchewan and Alberta cities that moved into the booming suburbs and quietly assimilated, reserving their expressions of ethnic attachment for private family and community moments. The role of Germans who had preceded them was crucial in their adaptation. Like the Icelanders, the Germans from eastern Europe were joining relatives and friends who had made their way in the city for several generations. Most of these long-settled German Winnipeggers denounced the military and political ambitions of their Wilhelmine and Nazi countrymen. According to historian Hans Werner, their positive outlook was built on deeper assumptions about race, faith, family, and work that had marked the friendly British–German relations in Winnipeg before 1914.[7] Post-1945 German immigrants could rely on these pioneers to show them the ropes. In a typical case the relatives of newcomer Walter Koberstein looked through newspaper advertisements with him, accompanied him 'to various work places, and helped him apply for a job.' Relatives could also point out 'homes in locations that capitalized on the advantages of living with others of the same cultural and linguistic origin.' But the strongest link between post-1945 and pre-war immigrants occurred within churches that encouraged the newcomers 'to reestablish connections with their religious heritage' and, through the formation of the Canadian Council of Churches for Refugee Relief, provided 'spiritual resources for their co-religionists ...'[8]

The established German Canadians exerted an ambiguous influence on the post-1945 newcomers. Those who arrived in the city decades earlier did not always welcome refugee family members from whom they had been separated by Stalin's terror and the Second World War. Their entrenched ideas about fidelity, masculinity, and women's roles were severely tested by the newcomers' wartime experiences. Their patriarchal assumptions were challenged, too, by newly arrived refugee women who had become heads of households by default. The long-settled Germans sometimes responded critically when men and women who had been separated from their spouses during the decades of turmoil sought new partners. Moreover, having long ago adjusted to the English language, the established German Canadians' interest in the retention of German seemed shallow to the newcomers. Thus, the post-1945 arrivals had to contemplate the prospect that their children would lose their birth language. Still, the established German-origin Canadians in Winnipeg offered visible proof that a good life was possible in Canada. The newcomers would find there was a price to be paid, in loss of language and culture, but even there the established German Canadians offered a measure of experience.

Hans Werner concludes that two 'imagined trajectories of experience' – what the ethnic Germans imagined they would encounter, and what longer-term Winnipeg residents imagined these newcomers could become – were crucial to Germans' accommodation. Those who arrived between the Second World War and the mid-1960s expected to enter an alien culture. They also expected a struggle to adapt in language and work. They responded delightedly to the freedom of worship and openness of civic identity in their adopted city and regarded the entire experience as representing more or less what they had hoped for when they made the decision to emigrate. In the view of their non-German Winnipeg hosts, whose community had been adapting to immigrants for at least fifty years, these newcomers belonged on a par with others. The established Winnipeggers assumed that German newcomers could deal with the job market and housing in just the way others had done. Thus, ethnic German immigrants to Winnipeg travelled a path parallel with the Icelanders: their integration was relatively smooth; they handled great changes with relative success; and they relied on previous generations of their countrymen who, in the process of aiding them, were expressing their sense of responsibility for the development of the entire community. At the same time, both generations – the newcomers by their adaptation; the long established by their acceptance of leadership roles – were contributing to the development of an increasingly hybrid prairie culture.

The experience of Japanese Canadians, who arrived in Winnipeg in the 1940s, differed considerably from that of Icelanders and eastern

Europe-origin Germans. Having been removed from their homes in coastal British Columbia in 1942 and dispatched to Manitoba, often as farm labourers, almost all the one thousand Japanese in the province moved to the city as quickly as possible. But they were not aided by previous generations of Japanese immigrants. What is more, they were the target of racist regulations that ensured they would be conscious of their ethnic differences for many years to come. And yet they, too, integrated quietly into the Winnipeg community as their fellows had done in the Alberta cities and as the Germans and Icelanders were doing around them. The one difference, perhaps, lay in the Japanese Canadians' commitment to changing Canadians' minds about what had transpired in 1942.

Japanese Canadians were less free to make choices about place of residence and place of work than their immigrant counterparts. Their employment options were limited between October 1942 and July 1943 by an extraordinary Winnipeg bylaw that set the minimum wage for Japanese Canadians at a higher level than was applied to other citizens, thus discouraging employers from hiring them. In the later war years, their selection of jobs was controlled by government officials. Thus, one young man who did not like his work at an abattoir found a job at a food-drying plant, but the authorities would not let him change workplaces. This same family's place of residence was subject to veto by an oversight committee that sought to ensure that Japanese Canadians did not cluster in any single part of the city. Both interventions imposed great hardships on the family. And, unlike other established Canadians, members of their community were denied an opportunity to participate in politics because they did not possess Canadian citizenship, which was granted by the Canadian government only in 1948. Such controls demonstrate that accommodation between established Winnipeg residents and newly arrived Japanese Canadians differed significantly from that experienced by Mennonite, German, and Icelander immigrants.[9]

The Japanese–Canadian response to restriction was also distinctive. In comparison to such Jews as J.A. Cherniack, who organized an anti-fascist group to oppose racist aggression in the 1930s, Japanese–Canadian leaders concluded that they could expect little support in the community and should not attempt to fight in their own defence. Instead, as historian Peter Nunoda has suggested, they chose to accept the officials' dispersal of their people across the city and to defend the government policy within their own community. As was the case in other prairie cities, they eventually melted into the suburbs. But, again, the Winnipeg story was slightly different. When Harold Hirose, Shinji Sato, Tom Mitani, and Ichiro Hirayama founded an organization to aid their fellows, they focused first on the poverty and living conditions on sugar beet farms and then on rescuing the four hundred individuals (four in ten Japanese-heritage Manitobans) who had initially chosen to be repatriated to Japan after the war but had then changed their minds. As leaders of the Japanese–Canadian community in Winnipeg, Hirose and his colleagues then turned to addressing wartime wrongs. The chief public campaign under their sponsorship, a campaign waged for over forty years, sought an apology from the federal government for the original relocation and dispossession. They did not fight, as a group, on behalf of other ethnic and religious minorities. They did not try to reshape Canadian institutions as a matter of general right, and they did not seek the leadership of the entire community. But one of their young followers, Arthur Miki, as president of the National Association of Japanese Canadians, did carry on their work. This 'redress' campaign culminated in 1988 with the federal government's official statement of apology and payment of compensation to the community as a whole and to the survivors of the 1942 resettlement. It was a national movement but it had a Winnipeg base.

Mennonites who migrated from South America and Mexico to Winnipeg in the post-war years differed from Icelanders and from ethnic Germans of eastern European origin as well as from the Japanese Canadians. And yet, ironically, given their church-based and quietist culture, they illustrated more clearly than these other groups how the history of Winnipeg could impinge directly upon newcomers. These Mennonites had followed a circuitous path to the city, having previously left eastern Europe or southern Manitoba, and having lived on tropical farm colonies for as few as ten or as many as forty or fifty years. Compared with the experience of either Germans or Icelanders, their experience in Winnipeg, given their distinctive heritage, was more religion based but also, and perhaps surprisingly, more class based. In her interviews with these immigrants, Janis Thiessen discovered that the Mexican and South American Mennonites relished the shopping and the bargains – the consumer opportunities – that Canada's wealth made available to them. One woman told her 'they couldn't get me out of Eaton's' (the large department store). But they were not as happy about the challenges their new environment posed to their church and to their view of themselves as independent actors in the world.[10] They experienced the class-driven nature of the city and their workplaces, and eventually integrated them into their distinctive view of the world.

The Mennonite home has often been perceived by scholars as the forum where immigrant families practised the 'old ways,' thereby communicating inherited cultural values to their children. In contrast, the urban workplace has been seen as a crucible wherein immigrants of other cultures learned the lessons of the new land. It is an easy step to assume that for these post-war Mennonite immigrants from Latin America, who were descended from several generations of farmers, the old ways would trump the new. Their forebears had responded to persecution and defended their faith by avoiding cities. One might expect that, like their predecessors, these immigrants would prefer to settle in rural areas and avoid the assimilative pressures – shop-floor conversation, supervisor's orders, union loyalties, slim pay packets – of industrial North America. After the Second World War, however, the promise of schooling for their children, of Canada's social safety net, and especially of family reunions after the horrors of war reconciled these newcomers to the prospect of industrial jobs in furniture making or the manufacture of housing components such as windows and doors. They relied especially on Mennonite-owned industries to provide them with workplaces where they could stand beside members of their own churches, speak Low German (Plautdietsch) freely, and relate to managers who shared their views. It was the factory workplace, in fact, that most influenced Mennonites' experience of accommodation in Winnipeg.

The very ethnic and religious loyalties that drew Mennonite workers to the factory in the first instance were soon supplemented by a class consciousness that separated employers from employees. This consciousness was expressed in the immigrants' complaints about mindless work, low wages, and aloof office managers. It was evident when they voiced fears that if they accepted a promotion, they would be distanced from friends on the shop floor. It drove their determination to ensure that such clock-driven discipline and drudgery would not be their children's fate, a goad that led to their emphasis on a child's high grades in school and on university degrees. One can taste the bitterness in the seemingly honourable title 'Mr. Chairman' that managers and workmates applied to an assiduous worker who had kept a careful record of the 239,608 chairs he had built over twenty-five years. And yet the Mennonite immigrant workers were not militant, not unionists, not outspoken rebels. Instead, they accepted the strictures and the consolations of a faith held in common with their managers and owners. As Janis Thiessen sees it, they acquired a view of work comparable to that described by Max Weber as 'labour-as-religious-calling.'[11] Religious solidarity – at work as well as at church –

blunted the potential for conflict implicit in their growing class consciousness. And their weak response to political participation – in many cases rejecting the vote and party membership – ensured that union or government intervention on their behalf did not take place.

Over time, as the companies 'became larger and more hierarchical,' class consciousness increased. The fact was that, in order to control the workplace, owners resorted not only to 'shared Mennonite ethnicity and employer paternalism,' but also to more formal industrial relations strategies. Their tactics included efficiency studies to promote shop-floor discipline and expanded benefit packages to increase workers' sense of commitment. Inevitably, as factory work processes became more carefully organized, professional evaluations distanced management from labour and ensured that the workplace would be less familial and democratic. Increasingly, 'immigrant workers defined themselves by their jobs and shopfloor status.' And, just as surely, 'immigrant owners fashioned a [distinct and separate] ethnic identity for themselves through consumption, church worship and choice of residential neighbourhood.'[12] For both groups – the shop-floor workers and the wealthier managers and owners – the ethnic and religious link across class lines became attenuated. Simultaneously, another link – class-based ethnicity – grew stronger. That this transition occurred among the agrarian and sectarian Mennonites is an indication not only of the strength of workplace culture but of the flexibility of their ethnicity. And, for the workers themselves, a sense of religious solidarity grew to match their working-class consciousness, a combination that blunted the potential for workplace conflict.

Class drew a new and socially significant boundary around the Mennonite workers' limited community. Within that border, religion continued to be a powerful force shaping their perspective. When they turned to contemplate the future, they dreamed of a time when their children would be able to maintain their inherited church-based outlook while escaping the limitations that working-class experience imposed. The Mennonites' experience of boundary zones between long settled and newly arrived was not identical to that of Icelandic, German, or Japanese Canadians. They constituted a distinct immigrant group, one for whom class and church were deeply intertwined, and as a result they encountered another version of Winnipeg's accommodation experience. But in a city where class had been burned into citizens' consciousness, these Mennonites became accustomed to thinking of themselves as members of a working class as well as of a church and an ethnic group.

Icelanders, Germans, Latin–American Mennonites, and Japanese Canadians consciously chose many of the strategies that shaped their community's development in Winnipeg. Each ethnic group responded differently to the city. Icelanders and Germans integrated smoothly and, indeed, were expected to do so by the wider community. Japanese Canadians held back, awaiting a more favourable moment to press for redress. Mennonite migrants who worked on the factory floor became working class to a degree that might have surprised their co-religionists in management; nonetheless, they retained aspects of their church's theology that undermined aggressive political or class-based initiatives. In these various ways, Winnipeg society in the generation after the Second World War differed from the early-century generation and, to a degree, from the other prairie cities. Measured by the tenor of the boundary zones, the sphere wherein migrant met longer settled citizens, the old barriers between groups were falling, many social exchanges were taking place across ethnic lines, many established citizens were assuming responsibility for the direction of the larger community, and a new prairie culture was taking shape.

Reception of Migrants: The Community's Vantage Point

To understand this city, one must come to terms not only with the vantage point of an individual or an immigrant group but also of those who saw themselves as part of the host society. What is surprising in Winnipeg is the self-styled hosts' increasing openness to newcomers in the post-war decades. Civic leaders created a number of institutions to receive and support new arrivals. And they developed a variety of strategies to ensure that city residents would receive these newcomers positively. In this, too, they anticipated developments in the other prairie cities and contributed to the emergence of an incipient prairie pluralism that constituted its own 'ethnicity in the making.'

Jennifer Rogalsky, in her history of Winnipeg's Citizenship Council, has explained that a reception service run by volunteers offered only a little support to immigrant families in the immediate post-war years. As the number of immigrants grew, so did the variety of services. The Citizenship Council and its descendant, the International Centre, provided leadership that has been cited as a model for immigrant settlement in Canada.[13] Recognizing that there had been mistakes in receiving immigrants in the past, and believing they could do a great deal to make 'these newcomers good Canadians in every sense,' the Winnipeg Welfare

Council directed its efforts into two distinct spheres: assisting the settlement of newcomers, and educating the wider community about the character and potential contributions of the migrants. Volunteers on the Refugees Committee provided newcomers with information on housing, jobs, and welfare services, and arranged for night classes in the English language. They also conducted programs at meetings of service clubs and church organizations about how established Canadians could and should support newcomers. The volunteers themselves belonged to no single ethnic group or faith, and espoused no single approach to social issues, but simply tried to serve the needs of the newcomers from the perspective of the religious communities and in the interest of the entire city.[14]

The Citizenship Committee became more energetic and coincidentally more immigrant-based in the next decade when it invited as many as forty of the national groups in the city to send representatives to its meetings. Its actual decision making was dominated by prominent citizens, most of them British Canadians.[15] It did not provide services but, rather, assumed that long-established agencies such as the YMCA and YWCA and the public schools would work directly with immigrant families. Committee members also lobbied for policy changes that would assist immigrants who were having difficulty adjusting to government's rules about welfare, family allowance, and pension payments. Mary Panaro, a one-time immigrant whose family had known hardship when it arrived before the First World War, led a group examining the impact on newcomers of such government regulations. Another group prepared a directory, published in four languages, to explain the city's health and welfare services to newcomers. Yet another subcommittee set up a program of home visits through which the Volunteer Bureau might familiarize immigrants with 'Canadian customs and habits' by means of concerts, tours, and visits to Canadian homes. The volunteers were very active in 1956–7 in response to the arrival of refugees fleeing the uprising against Soviet domination of Hungary. To meet the demands of the thirteen hundred Hungarian newcomers, they worked with Winnipeg churches to provide 'clothing, housing, furnishings and assistance in accessing medical services and employment.' In short, this city-wide, centralized, volunteer-based agency organized many reception services for immigrants in the decade after the Second World War.[16]

An obvious flaw in this volunteer work was its class and ethnic bias. No doubt these mainly British, mainly middle-class citizens were well intentioned, but they must have made mistakes that belittled their clients and betrayed their own lesser estimates of other cultures. Nonetheless, what stands out in retrospect is the willingness of these volunteers to transfer power over the institutions they were creating to the recipients. Similarly, the Citizenship Council survived in the 1960s because relatively recent immigrants became involved in its programs. These volunteers understood the needs of newcomers and, as well-connected members of society, also knew how to get things done.[17]

When refugees from the Czech uprising of 1968 arrived in the city, the council provided a clearing house for services. It also offered afternoon English classes for adult women. When the classes met, the teachers acquiesced to a student request that lessons should address survival skills and the vocabulary of the street rather than adhere to the former curriculum of Greek myths in English translation. Recognizing that such a service conflicted with women's family obligations, the council provided babysitters, the first step in developing a daycare program. The council leader, Sonja Roeder, herself a post-war immigrant, then decided that the council needed its own physical space and in 1969 won the support of Winnipeg's populist and self-declared ethnic Mayor Stephen Juba. He arranged the lease of a large building for one dollar per year and the waiving of city taxes. Roeder attracted a host of prominent citizens, including the mayor and the police chief, as volunteer labourers on the renovation of this International Centre. Italian, Hungarian, and Filipino volunteers each provided furnishings and decoration for one room, thereby creating a multinational setting. Rather than just a coordinator of services, as it had been between 1946 and the early 1960s, the Citizenship Council had grown into a settlement agency and an ally of government.[18]

The Refugees Committee (1946 to 1948), New Canadians Committee (1948 to 1951), Citizenship Committee (1951 to 1957), Citizenship Council (1957 to 1969), and International Centre (1969 to the present) constituted meeting places for migrants and long-standing Winnipeggers. In each of these incarnations, volunteers mobilized community support in response to the needs of newcomers. These were local activities, built in the first instance on volunteer labour, later expanded with the aid of government grants. The centres were eventually taken over by the migrants themselves and became vehicles for education as well as settlement services.

A second aspect of the Welfare Council's work with post-war immigrants was to address the wider community's recognition of these newcomers. As a volunteer explained, they wanted to give newcomers 'some grasp of what we mean by Canadian Citizenship and democratic freedom, of the way in which citizens can and do take responsibility for all matters connected with the running of their government ...' In 1950 the Citizenship Committee organized a Cultural Folk Festival, to be followed in the next few years by Citizenship Days where new immigrants who were receiving citizenship certificates were given a formal public welcome. In 1952 the renamed Citizenship Council's now annual event was attended by eight hundred people. The 1953 event featured a pageant of flags of all nations and the 1954 version included a choir, speakers, and a tableau spectacle representing prairie history. This version was filmed by Associated Screen News for broadcast as part of its newsreel package in movie houses across the country. The 1955 ceremony was chaired by Canada's Governor General Vincent Massey, who travelled to the city to welcome all those who had received their citizenship in the previous year, including Winnipeg's Canadian-born who were reaching the voting age of twenty-one. The organizers encouraged public participation, inviting the symphony orchestra, school classes, members of the Canadian Legion, and armed service personnel. In the ceremony, according to the *Winnipeg Free Press*, new Canadians and 'Canadian babies' were placed on an 'equal footing.'[19] The process itself declared that the city attached importance to treating newcomer and native-born as equals and acknowledged the homespun truth that a public welcome was a memorable moment in any individual's life.

The federal Progressive Conservative government of John Diefenbaker introduced national citizenship courts in 1961 as a means of formalizing the grant of citizenship. The first court meeting in Winnipeg was, according to a Citizenship Council member, 'a very cold, cut and dry thing. People were lined up all around the wall. That was it.' Volunteers responded by offering to organize a reception and guest speaker for the next session and to attend the event to welcome the new Canadians. This became the pattern, and women's church auxiliaries became the sponsors. The citizenship court ceremonies became a highlight of many lives, similar in some respects to other ceremonies marking life passages such as baptisms, graduations, marriages, and funerals. The power of such acts of recognition also struck the Winnipeg hosts, as in the case of the volunteer who recalled 'a little old lady' with tears running down her face during the ceremony. Describing the moment in an interview years later, the volunteer host wondered once again if the newcomers' formal renunciation of home had been a difficult step. As this recollection suggests, the combination of the citizenship court and the welcome ceremony engraved the idea of a two-way relationship in the minds of newcomers and volunteers alike. For both, it marked a sense of completion and a new beginning. More than a one-dimensional event addressed exclusively to the newcomer, it entailed established Canadians' recognition of the immigrants' presence and rights as citizens.[20]

Winnipeg's self-styled hosts carried out their roles with varying degrees of sensitivity. Whatever the degree of gatekeeping or paternalism they represented, however, many of these volunteers perceived that the relationship with new arrivals was reciprocal. In short order, they relinquished the operation of service agencies to newcomers who could, in turn, meet the needs of the next generation with understanding. The International Centre and the citizenship ceremony came to represent victories for immigrants, rather than top-down impositions by distant and controlling hosts.

Conclusion

This polyethnic culture was an urban development, not a prairie-wide phenomenon that affected town and country alike. City life demanded that immigrants adapt. A royal commission investigating Manitoba society in 1946 was told by Ukrainian leaders, men who rarely agreed on anything because they represented bitterly opposed nationalist and communist factions, that integration was an inescapable fact of city life. In the rural areas, they testified, 'There are antagonisms in the local communities which act to reinforce the desire of the Ukrainians to maintain their own culture.'[21] Their statements placed Winnipeg's role in the ethnic patchwork of Manitoba in sharp relief.

The hybrid culture was also more evidently a Winnipeg story than a phenomenon equally represented in all prairie cities. The Icelanders' and Germans' experience most closely resembled the simultaneous melting and retention of ethnic identities that took place in the other prairie metropolises. The Japanese campaign for redress illustrated the greater possibility of ethnic tenacity in Winnipeg in the righting of an historic wrong. And the development of an ambiguous Mennonite class and religious consciousness suggested that the Manitoba capital was closer to international metropolitan and factory stresses than were the Saskatchewan and Alberta centres.

The community-wide reception activities in Winnipeg at mid-century were more extensive than those in other prairie centres because of both the greater size of the Manitoba capital's problems and the greater duration of its experience with such issues. They resembled most closely the institutions emerging in Toronto in these decades. Franca Iacovetta has suggested that Toronto's hundreds of thousands of immigrants were made to 'conform to "Canadian ways"' by the gatekeepers who controlled so much of Canada.[22] Her emphasis on the social control exercised by the hosts, as opposed to the agency of the newcomers, does not fully capture the Winnipeg reality. Instead, the Cherniack family history and the Icelandic and German group histories suggest that community leadership often came from within the ethnic communities themselves. The lowering of barriers in Winnipeg after 1945 was hastened by the development of a creative tension between two generations and between two types of new urban dweller: the city-bound, rural, ethnic migrants; and the Canada-bound who had fled from Europe. These various groups fused, aided by well-meaning British Canadians imbued with a newly developed pluralist idealism. An increasingly hybrid culture permitted newcomers to assume ownership of the community all the more quickly. Their version of prairie society was created with, and in spite of, distinct ethnicities, and represented a Winnipeg variant of Canadian pluralism. Thus, Saul Cherniack's contributions in so many different spheres bore witness to the community's new-found openness. He may have remained 'culturally Jewish' but he was also, as he said, 'socially, politically, and professionally ... at ease in my country.' His career illustrated the strengths of the new prairie identity and the qualities of its pluralism.

Part Three
**Late Century: Globalization and the Prairie
Newcomer, 1970s–1990s**

chapter five

The Global South in Calgary and Edmonton

The last third of the twentieth century marked a rather sudden trans-formation in Canada's prairie city. Some changes seemed to link those regional cities more indelibly to the wider nation. As elsewhere in Canada, and now aided oftentimes by provincial legislation, a new mes-sage of multicultural inclusion and a government-funded social safety net bolstered a sense of welcome to all, a common cultural citizenship across the land. This culture was propelled by the technological innova-tion of inexpensive air transportation and electronic ties of affordable long-distance telephone links, television, and, later, the Internet. In this milieu old ideas of periphery and centre were challenged, and the inter-ior and its people seemed more closely tied to other sections of Canada, and indeed to the wider world.

Ironically, these very innovations, when set within the context of a ris-ing global economy, also had the effect of decoupling the prairie cities from other Canadian points. Certainly the economy of the western in-terior, connected by rail to the ports and trading on such commodities as wheat, had been linked to the wider world since the birth of modern Canada. But after the 1960s federal neo-liberal policies and free trade agreements, and oil and mineral production, increased those trans-national ties and loosened the historic link between the prairie cities and those of the eastern and western metropolises. In particular, oil gave Alberta's cities a sense of confidence and even swagger, separating them in new ways not only from Ottawa, Toronto, and Vancouver, but also from neighbouring prairie cities, the old multicultural giant of Winnipeg, and the once confident frontier outpost cities of Saskatoon and Regina. A number of other social and cultural consequences ap-peared, as well. Residents outside the cities, Aboriginal Canadians from the North especially, entered the cities just as forces of globalization dampened the historic flow of European immigrants and replaced them with rapidly ascending, confident, oftentimes professional newcomers from the Global South. The consequences affected the history of racism, of family relations, and of transnational linkages.

Perhaps the most immediate consequence was the sudden and very visible presence of immigrants from Asia, Latin America, the Caribbean, the Middle East, and Africa in the boom cities of Calgary and Edmonton. Growth in the cities was seemingly boundless. Having tripled in population during the 1950s and 1960s, they tripled again by 2000 as each approached the one-million-resident mark. Calgary became the 'head office' centre in the West, Edmonton the capital of one of Canada's richest provinces; together they constituted Canada's fourth metropolitan presence and a force to be reckoned with in corporate and political circles. Both possessed busy international airports, National Hockey League teams, a dynamic skyscraper-dominated urban core, and a series of spacious and well-planned suburbs. Both showed the riches of Canada's oil patch. They were never, of course, quite as self-confident as the press made them out to be. The fact was that a resource-driven economy was unstable. And the issue of wealth sharing with the rest of Canada threatened to undercut what Alberta now considered its birthright: oil. Still, economic growth and diversification occurred. New economic sectors developed, the foundation was laid for an array of small service-oriented businesses, and Albertans ventured overseas to invest in other resources.[1]

The late-century cities of Alberta were also cities of labour-market immigration. They 'received a disproportionate share of people, largely because economic conditions in the province were generally far better than elsewhere in Canada.'[2] By 1967 the Alberta cities were drawing more immigrants than the provinces of Manitoba and Saskatchewan combined: fifteen thousand in Alberta compared to eleven thousand in Manitoba and Saskatchewan. And in 1976 the two cities each took in almost 50 percent more immigrants than did Winnipeg: 6000 each compared to Winnipeg's 4500.[3] In the year of 1996, Calgary and Edmonton were among the top ten immigrant-receiving cities in Canada, with only Toronto and Vancouver possessing more immigrants per capita. By that year, too, Alberta's two largest cities attracted 86 percent of the province's immigrants. Twenty percent of these cities' total populations now consisted of immigrants.[4] In 1997 Mayor Al Duerr summed up the new Alberta urban culture: 'Calgary is still referred to as a Cowtown, or just a bunch of oilmen and ranchers. We're sort of discounted. The reality is very different.'⁵ It was a sentiment shared by immigrants themselves. The daughter of ninety-six-year-old Filipino Canadian Francesca Punsalan told the *Calgary Herald* in 1996 of her mother's arrival in Calgary sixteen years earlier: 'Ima [mother] didn't like Toronto at all, "too crowded" she says ... We had heard ... that the economy was good because of the oil boom ... [Mother] has grown to love Canada ... She even likes the winter here.'⁶ Tens of thousands of immigrants seemed to agree.

This immigration flow was significant for more than its volume. It also changed the cities' social composition. Although the number of Calgary's foreign-born declined during the course of the century (the proportion dropping from 48 percent of its population in 1921 to 21 percent in 1971), during the same time its immigrant cohort became more noticeable than it had been in earlier decades. The majority of late-century immigrants were 'visible minority' newcomers from the so-called Third World or Global South who were also socially confident and upwardly mobile. In actual numbers these 'visible minority' immigrants in Calgary were not numerous and the city was still very much a Euro–Canadian place. The 1971 census, for example, recorded the presence of 7900 Asians, compared to 225,000 British, 110,000 western Europeans, and 32,000 eastern Europeans. Data for spoken language within their households showed that although 40 percent of Calgarians spoke a language other than English, it was still a European language, in the descending order of German, Italian, French, Ukrainian, Dutch, and Polish.⁷ By 1989 Calgary had undergone a radical transformation. In that year by far the largest single group of immigrants, 22 percent, was ethnic Chinese, although originating in three different locations: Hong Kong, mainland China, and Vietnam. They were accompanied by noticeable percentages of other Southeast Asians, primarily Filipinos (7 percent), East Indians (5 percent), and Brunesians (3 percent). In addition good-sized communities of Lebanese, West Indians, Koreans, and Latin Americans became established in Calgary. So great was the surge of immigrants from the Global South that by 1981 nearly 10 percent of the people of Edmonton and Calgary hailed from Asia, Africa, and South America.⁸ By 2006 a significantly larger percentage of Albertans had been born in Asia than in Europe, many more in Central and South America and the Caribbean than in the United States.⁹

The new immigrants changed the very nature of the ethnic community in the cities. Their social webs intertwined seamlessly with many of the host society's institutions, especially in comparison to early-century realities when immigrants often were confined to ethnic ghettos and linguistic pockets. The immigrants who qualified to enter Canada under the celebrated 'points system' – that is, professionals or skilled workers – and the 'family class' immigrants they sponsored usually moved to the suburbs within days or weeks of arriving in Canada.[10] And, because these immigrant professionals came to Canada able to speak English, their economic and social integration into suburbia was remarkably rapid. In the suburbs of Edmonton and Calgary they could set up their homes alongside the children of early- or mid-century European immigrants. They spent their professional earnings not only on middle-class consumer goods, but also on ethnic institutions that became a central feature of the late-century urban cultural landscape. Significantly, too, both the federal and provincial governments made multiculturalism an official policy, and extended settlement services and a social safety net to the newcomers.

If the immigrants integrated relatively quickly, they did so without being directly assimilated. In contrast to early-century immigrants, they seemed at once willing to be labelled 'ethnic' and yet poised to accept positions of influence and power. When the immigrants felt they were being excluded from the Alberta dream of upward mobility, they seemed more ready than early-century immigrants to publicly 'name' systemic discrimination – racism in particular – counter public expressions of xenophobia, and rigorously demand the end of 'underemployment.' Their very presence spurred Alberta's urban society to advocate and then celebrate multiculturalism. This eagerness was especially apparent when immigrants achieved middle-class status and underwrote the cities' claim to be cosmopolitan and cultured.[11]

Edmonton and Calgary seemingly entered what David Harvey and others have dubbed the 'condition of postmodernity,' pluralistic, flexible, and open.[12] Unlike the urban immigrants of the early-century decades, here was no great divide in which particularists were pitted against pluralists, communitarians against individualists, pre-moderns against moderns. Rather, a cultural mixing resulted in a multi-stranded, multi-layered, and intersecting series of ethnic webs. Over time the immigrants' community had become less an ethnic base from which to negotiate an entry into the wider society than an ethnic kaleidoscope of cultural exchange shared by all who chose, or were compelled, to participate.

Urban Networks and Cultural Need

In the 1960s sociologist Raymond Breton introduced the concept of 'institutional completeness' to explain the survival of immigrant cultures in

Canadian cities.[13] He observed that immigrants built networks of ethnic institutions that were so 'complete' there was no need for the immigrants to patronize the stores and social agencies of the host society. This well-established phenomenon, observed in early-century cities, could also be seen in late-century prairie cities. A close look at these sites in Calgary and Edmonton, though, indicates that it might be more correct to say that the mid-century Alberta cities offered an 'holistic' rather than 'complete' set of services. Ethnic institutions served the late century's immigrants' most profound cultural, and even political, needs. But they did not necessarily provide for all physical (retail, financial, professional) needs or their social needs, the focus of which, by late century, had transferred from ethnic mutual aid society to state-supported social safety net. What the ethnic institution now offered was not a set of services per se, but a wider cultural context wherein one's most sensitive needs could be met.

Studies of late-century Latin American, Asian, and African communities in Calgary all shed light on this new kind of immigrant network. A 1994 study of Latin Americans in Calgary by Bat-Ami Klejner suggested that 'friends and neighbours are something that almost every immigrant misses.' All immigrants 'struggle to form a social network [of fellow Latinos] to aid in the settlement process as an important part of their acculturation experience.'[14] Importantly, the 'aid' in an age of state-funded social safety nets was usually not financial or material, but cultural. It was based on the need for immigrants to relate on a deep and meaningful level with other people during the process of integration. A 1997 study of Africans in Calgary by Ransford Kwabena Danso noted that in the context of 'the absence of social and kinship support, ethnic associations are most indispensable.' The reason is simple: the 'Africans come from communities that are extremely informal and relaxed, where interpersonal relations are easy.'[15] Other late-century studies of Southeast Asian societies argued that the ethnic organizations found their moorings in the old need for community.[16] In fact, the ethnic institutions took over the function of the ethnic enclave, as few Southeast Asians 'work for each other, none shop exclusively at South Asian stores and there is nothing remotely approaching a South Asian neighbourhood anywhere in the province.'[17] The institutions met only some of the social requirements of daily life, but they were reliable, widely distributed, and well funded. They met the requirements needed for cultural holism; indeed, for gestalt or a sense of well-being.

Observers of the coming of Asian, South American, and African immigrants to Alberta have commented on the remarkable speed with which a comprehensive set of well-programmed ethnic institutions was created. It easily overshadowed the network of ethnic clubs in the early decades. Paul Lin's 1977 study counted 190 ethnic associations in Calgary alone, including ethnic churches, with specific foci on immigrants from particular countries.[18] Patricia Marie Hackney's 1979 study examined 177 ethnic organizations in both Calgary and Edmonton, and found that they represented thirty-nine different national groups. Moreover, the services they offered were remarkably diverse and 'included craft guilds, music societies, language schools, religious associations, social clubs, youth groups, women's associations, student groups and athletic associations.'[19] They also came in different sizes: the senior citizens' Chinese Oi Kwan Foundation had twelve members, the Arab Canadian umbrella group in Alberta had two thousand,[20] and the Calgary Multicultural Centre had 'more than 100 ethnic organizations and upwards of 30,000 individuals' in 1988.[21]

The associations were especially impressive in their ability to bring together, even invent, immigrant groupings. Lin's 1977 study of Chinese organizations in Calgary emphasized this achievement in light of the fact that 'the Chinese community in Chinatown is [so] ... fragmented ... by political and social ideologies' that 'settlement services ... are provided by the churches – the Chinese Pentecostal Church and the Chinese United Church, both in Chinatown.'[22] Danso's 1997 study of African organizations in Calgary highlighted the process by which separate organizations of the Eritrean, Ethiopian, Ghanaian, and Nigerian Canadian associations came together to create an umbrella organization, the African Community Association of Calgary, known locally as the ACAC.[23] Many other such umbrella groups were founded. Edmonton's Sunni Pakistanis, for example, joined third-generation Lebanese Canadians in using the Al-Rashid mosque founded in 1938. When the Pakistanis became the dominant Muslim cohort in the city, they in turn welcomed Muslims from Egypt, Palestine, and India to use the mosque. Similarly Alberta's loosely linked Hindus overcame their inherited differences and in 'an imaginative fashion' both the Hindu Society of Calgary and the Hindu Society of Alberta offered 'devotional practices and ... the celebration of ... *Holi* and *Diwali*' to disparate groupings of Hindus.[24]

The ethnic organizations seemed especially rigorous and flexible in devising programs for different age groups in new settings. Certainly early-century ethnic organizations had emphasized education, and specifically ethnic language classes for children, but late-century organizations also targeted a vast array of other demographic groups.[25] A multi-faceted concern for the elderly, for example, was revealed by the

Chinese in Calgary, whose numerous institutions included the Calgary
Chinese Elderly Citizens' Association, the Chinese Friendship Groups at
the Chinese Culture Centre, the Cantonese Opera, and even the Mahjong
'league' at the Chinese seniors' building.[26] Other ethnic organizations
assisted young professionals; during the oil patch's recession years in the
mid-1980s, for example, the India Canada Association of Calgary and
the Council of Indian Societies of Edmonton went out of their way to
address the underemployment of highly trained East Indians.[27] The
rights of 'illegally overworked and underpaid' wage labourers was the
specific concern of Calgary's Society for Immigrant Workers when it was
founded in 1988.[28]

Overall, these ethnic institutions seemed to pursue contradictory
goals. On the one hand, they promised to replicate the community-
centred culture of the immigrants' homelands; on the other, they openly
spoke about integration into Canadian middle-class society. Examples
from an old medium, the ethnic newspaper, illustrate the immigrants'
bifurcated agenda. When the *Canadian Chinese Times* of Calgary launched
a new, freely distributed, Chinese-language paper in 1982, it reported on
the happenings in Chinatown. But its central purpose was also to assist in
the immigrants' integration. The newspaper promised that its front page
would feature 'local news ... often condensed and translated from *The
Herald* and *The Sun,*' the cities' main daily newspapers. Further, the newspaper promised to 'help newcomers deal with immigration and citizenship laws, job vacancies and community services.'[29]

A similar pattern can be seen in the ambitious agenda of the much
smaller, and more radical, West Indian black community in Edmonton.
In 1972 it organized the Afro-Canadian Society with the communitar
ian hope that 'if we could just get together in one organization we
could do a lot more than in the past.' But the organization wanted
more than close ethnic relationships. In 1976, with only forty members, the society claimed no less an objective than to enrich the culture
of Edmonton, as well as to protect the rights of its members in their
new homes. The society's president Barry Thompson reported that his
social group hoped to 'offer Edmonton a lot in the way of culture like
the Ukrainians and the Scandinavians,' a culture exhibiting more 'than
Harry Belafonte songs.'[30] And, above music and athletics, the society
boldly offered its members 'human rights representation.' It would
hold Alberta to its promise of a life that 'is much better and fairer' than
in the West Indies. Similar aims can be seen in 1984 when a West Indian
monthly community newspaper, *The Communicant,* was launched to

serve African Caribbeans and immigrants from west and east Africa. Spokesperson Esther Rodney announced the newspaper's goal was 'to bring people together in a positive way.' By distributing four thousand issues to 'black food stores, barbershops and seamstresses' and reporting on 'education, religion, careers, travel, fashion and community news' it would, she said, 'unite [the] province's black population.' But more importantly, this so-called politically militant paper also announced that it would ensure that its readers were given 'a chance to live as human beings,' to find 'equal opportunity to serve' Alberta's urban society 'in the capacity [for which we] are best qualified ...'[31]

Like the Bengali, Hindu, Chinese, and other communities, the West Indians in Alberta developed ethnic institutions geared to the integration of immigrants in the new society. Such organizations played the role of a virtual ethnic web: they brought together immigrants spread over large areas of Calgary and Edmonton, and they served the need for ethnic cohesion and social integration. By doing so they accepted a kind of 'institutional completeness' within an imagined social network. More importantly, they reflected two basic features of life in the postmodern and kaleidoscopic city.

Upward Mobility and Residential Dispersal

A close look at the immigrants from the Global South reveals their powerful desire to achieve upward mobility and suburban life, no matter its residential dispersal. Most studies observe among these newcomers an intense hope for professional advancement and fulfillment. The immigrant population in the 1970s and 1980s, for example, was young. Of the 5900 immigrants arriving in Calgary in 1976, almost 30 percent were in their twenties and 18 percent in their thirties.[32] Many, too, were members of families with small children. In one representative immigrant group, more preschoolers could be counted than elementary, junior high, or high school students.[33] Studies from the 1970s also show that most immigrants came with skills and training, in either profession or trade. Alberta's newcomers 'included a very large percentage of highly trained professionals and skilled workers, including doctors, engineers and many other professionals.'[34] And changes in 1978 to the *Immigration Act* that privileged Canada's occupational demands over the immigrants' educational achievement brought in large numbers of skilled tradespeople.[35] Even amid reports of underemployment, Calgary's educated immigrants seemed to get on well. Hackney's 1979 case study of the West Indian Gujarati Mandal club in Calgary reveals that 68 percent of respondents

to a questionnaire possessed university education and another 16 percent had technical training. More significantly, 78 percent of the respondents claimed to have obtained 'employment in the area of their
education.'[36] Even the immigrants who were underemployed in years of
recession voiced optimism: 'Romanian university graduates and technicians ... will have to be "pioneers,"' wrote one Calgary compatriot, 'and
through our behaviour and achievements ... prove our professional
qualifications, ... a difficult job,' perhaps, 'but the rewards will accrue to
those that follow.'[37]

With bust following boom in the cyclical resource-extraction economy
of Alberta, immigrants hoping for rapid upward mobility often were vulnerable. Immigrants who came between 1975 and 1980, for example,
benefited from a strong economy but faced severe difficulties in the recession of the early 1980s.[38] Two different studies of Vietnamese refugees in Calgary and Edmonton outlined the pitfalls confronting the most
exposed immigrants. The first, a macro study by R. Montgomery of the
seventy-five hundred Vietnamese refugees who arrived in Alberta in
1979 and 1980, recorded their quick integration. Their unemployment
rate was only 8 percent in 1981. Unfortunately, because they found work
as quickly as they did, many of these refugees waived opportunities for
'language and vocation training,' making them vulnerable in the 'very
competitive labour market' of the early 1980s.[39] The major complaint
soon was that 'poor English language skills' and 'lack of experience'
were forcing many of these Indochinese newcomers into low-paying jobs
or unemployment; many others were compelled to seek financial support from extended family, friends, or state welfare.[40] A second study, by
Katherine A. MacRury in 1979, which examined thirty-five recently arrived Vietnamese refugees who had once been in the South Vietnamese
army, recorded a different reality. These newcomers were in fact underemployed because, despite their high levels of education, they were unable to find jobs linked to their training. As significant as any physical
deprivation was a cultural shortcoming. They spoke of the pain of being
unable to participate in the culture of Edmonton's middle class. Their
aims included 'helping' other people, 'improving English,' establishing
a sense of 'belonging,' cultivating 'social relations,' and earning individual 'achievement.'[41] Only the volatile Alberta economy kept them from
achieving their dreams of full integration into middle-class culture.

Those who achieved the goal of middle-class status moved quickly to
the suburbs. In neither Edmonton nor Calgary could one find ethnic
enclaves per se. One could not even locate what scholars have labelled
the 'cultural proximity model,' a situation in which 'people of the same

ethnic origin of their own volition choose to congregate in particular localities so as to maximize the advantages associated with residential propinquity and maintenance of group norms and values.'[42] Indeed, both cities were among the least ethnically differentiated in Canada. Even where it appeared from colourful banners and business signs that an ethnic enclave existed, the façade was misleading. Calgary's highly visible Chinatown in the 1980s was home to relatively few Chinese immigrants.[43] In fact, the first-generation Calgary Chinese in the 1980s had an 'index dissimilarity' (ID) measurement of .500, only slightly higher than second-generation Italian immigrants with an ID of .455 and not substantially different from third- and fourth-generation Swedish Canadians with an ID of .306. Even the working-class black community of Calgary, numbering only 800 persons, was highly dispersed, registering an especially low ID of .364, spread out as they were in 132 of the city's 153 census tracts.[44]

Clearly, the Calgary economy produced the means for upward mobility and the 'points system' attracted immigrants who could leapfrog the traditional inner-city ethnic enclave. In fact, if immigrant groups congregated at all, they did so within a suburb and not an inner-city enclave. Kit Man Kitty Mok's account of Calgary's greater Forest Lawn suburb describes a small working-class neighbourhood of only eight thousand residents located near the Calgary International Airport. Forest Lawn possessed 'a highly mobile population of diverse ethnic groups and immigrants ... includ[ing] Chinese, Vietnamese, Arabic, Latin American and East Indian [groups].' Perhaps it had higher than average rates of crime, unemployment, and social assistance, but it also had a disproportionate number of ethnic associations and host-society service providers.[45] In 1990 twenty-one immigrant associations or host-society service providers were located within twenty square blocks, that is, between 8th and 26th avenues SE and 28th and 47th streets SE.[46] In that year, too, 52 percent of the city's Chinese, Vietnamese, and Filipino population was concentrated in Forest Lawn. Thus, in this unusual suburb, an ethnic concentration of sorts was apparent from the fact that 23 percent of residents claimed a mother tongue other than English or French, and that 5 percent spoke neither of Canada's official languages.'[47]

Similar patterns of ethnic suburbanization were apparent in Edmonton. Like the immigrants to Calgary, notes a 1985 study by Kenneth Fairbairn and Hafzia Khatun, those who came to Edmonton during the century's last decades represented a 'a youthful, married population, relatively affluent and in the full-nest stage of their life cycle; in short, a suburban-oriented group.'[48] This case study of the nine thousand South Asians – East

Indians, Pakistanis, Bangladeshians, Sri Lankans – identified the social characteristics of these newcomers. Their story was not one of upward mobility as much as outward mobility, a migration from initial inner-city, temporary, apartment housing to the suburbs. More than two-thirds of the household heads of this group of immigrants were professionals and managers and many others were students, technicians, and entrepreneurs.[49] They lived in attractive neighbourhoods of Edmonton: in 'the newer suburbs, the university residences and the apartment areas along the northern bank of the [North Saskatchewan] river.' South Asians in particular tended to live in the newest suburbs: Mill Woods, Blue Quill, Kaskitayo, and West Jasper. Most of these immigrants were geographically mobile – 100 percent had moved at least once within the city, 66 percent more than once, 56 percent more than twice. The moves were short in distance, averaging only 5.8 kilometres, and usually traced a simple trajectory from rented apartment or rented house to a privately owned house. Significantly, ethnicity was unimportant in this decision; 84 percent of the immigrants gave 'middle-class' reasons for moving: 'a shortage of dwelling space,' 'home ownership aspirations,' and 'proximity to ... work and schools.'[50]

Late-century immigrants in both Calgary and Edmonton made suburbia their home.[51] Their residential integration was due, first, to the rapid growth of the cities that coincided with the arrival of waves of immigrants from Asia, Latin America, and Africa. Second, the ubiquitous ethnic organization, coupled with inexpensive travel by car and bus, allowed for ethnic identities outside residential clusters.[52] Third, both cities, by international standards, were small, meaning that most immigrant groups lacked the critical mass to create meaningful ethnic enclaves.[53] Fourth, and most important, this immigrant wave tended to be professional and educated, bent on integration into a middle-class suburban society.[54] The late-century immigrants were certain of their ethnicity and of their middle-class status. The network of ethnic institutions they developed gave expression to the former; the dispersed suburban residences declared the latter. Evidently they had succeeded in simultaneously embracing a centripetal and a centrifugal social tendency: they found in their ethnic webs the resources to build links to, and intersect with, networks in the broader society.

Host-Society Responses

If the world of the Alberta urban immigrants revealed an inherent contradiction, so, too, did the world of the host society. The society could be very demanding of its newcomers and this reality was most clear in stark charges of systemic discrimination. True, some groups, such as the Chinese and Japanese, who had faced racial discrimination in the early decades of the century, now rarely reported widespread instances of racism.[55] But other groups continued to suffer forms of exclusion. Howard Palmer and Tamara Palmer argue in their study that between 1974 and 1977, immigrants from the Indian subcontinent who had often come via Fiji, East Africa, or the West Indies faced significant 'negative reaction.' Reports of vandalism and assault against the Indian populace were widespread and so, too, were reports of 'racial gang fights in Edmonton' between 'East Indians and a segment of the White Canadian population.'[56]

In her thesis, Yvette Y.L. Knott reported that in 1979 and 1980 the very idea of a large influx of Vietnamese refugees received a hostile response from many Albertans, including the Alberta government. Indeed, more than half the letters to Alberta newspapers in the summer and fall of 1979 responded negatively to the coming of the Vietnamese. These letters complained that 'large numbers of a foreign race would [undermine] the Euro-Canadian (white) majority' and that their coming would 'encourage other countries to dump ... refugees in Canada.' At the same time two July 1979 polls, one by the newspaper *The Albertan* and the other by CBC Edmonton, registered negative responses of 84 percent and 83 percent, respectively, to the question of whether Canada should 'take in large numbers of Vietnamese refugees.'[57] In a similar analysis, Cecille Depass observed negative expressions toward immigrants during Calgary's 1988 Winter Olympics. Most Calgarians may have 'caught the spirit of the Olympics by ... actively supporting amateurs such as the Jamaican bobsled team and the British skier, Eddy the Eagle,' but some did raise the spectre of a 'Third World invasion.' In one instance the province's Human Rights Commission censured a Calgary businessman for releasing a lapel pin depicting 'three men, an Asian, a Sikh and a Black holding hands and looking down on a far smaller white man.'[58] A similar reaction could be seen in a 1989 Calgary-originated petition that took issue with turban-wearing Sikh Canadians joining the Royal Canadian Mounted Police.[59]

These were the high-profile flashpoints of racism. More persistent were charges of systemic discrimination, most often seen in underemployment. Benson Morah's 1974 'Assimilation of Ugandan Asians in Calgary' argued that, although it might seem that the level of education was the 'most significant in assimilation,' in fact 'the application of that education' was vital for an 'immigrant's satisfaction with his occupational status.'⁶⁰ Were newcomers being excluded from the upper echelons of society? Depass's study on 'the changing colours of the south in the Canadian vertical mosaic' suggested that, although people who were part of visible minorities often became professionals or skilled technicians, 'very few reach the upper echelons of the organizational hierarchy.' It claimed there was evidence of increased upper-class suburban gatekeeping; in subtle ways well-heeled Calgarians guarded 'the points of entry to their respective organizations' and those who did lived 'in some of the upper middle class neighbourhoods such as Eagle Ridge, Edgemont, Hawkwood, Palliser and Pumphill.'⁶¹

Racism was an even more subtle phenomenon when it was directed against the Chinese immigrant community. As Hackney's 1979 study argued, permission may have been 'given to the alien to enter the host community,' but that entry did not entail 'access to major values of the host society.'⁶² The host society, she said, kept for itself the capacity for true virtue; immigrant actions always seemed to bear moral scrutiny. Racism was also intertwined with a variety of fears. Some Calgarians worried that the state-sponsored social safety net and state immigration services provided 'preferential treatment' to immigrant job hunters, and would ultimately lead to a 'foreign takeover' in the job market. Xenophobia was exploited by some politicians during the economic downturn in the 1980s. In fact, a focus on immigration became a 'decoy ... designed to draw attention from economic issues of rising inflation and unemployment.'⁶³

The most common form of discrimination, though, was levelled at immigrants not proficient in English. Latin American immigrants to Calgary, for example, although reporting high degrees of integration, spoke of the personal pain of belonging to a visible minority and of not speaking English well. Klejner's 1994 thesis reported the claim of one forty-two-year-old El Salvador woman that although she functioned in the city with confidence, 'at the beginning it was very hard' for 'everyone speaks English, nobody speaks Spanish ... Most of the time to avoid feeling embarrassed, I don't talk.' But learning the vocabulary of the host society, according to Klejner, was not a simple matter of acquiring new words: 'when immigrants go through the experience of living in another language their identities are challenged.' A thirty-seven-year-old male from Argentina testified: 'we studied English before coming [from] ... Argentina ... [but] I'm not "me" in English.' Then, too, accents were often associated in the media with questionable behaviour. One forty-year-old Guatemalan woman recounted how office relationships at the company for which she worked were shaped by Canadians who 'confus[ed] things with Miami Vice ... confus[ed] TV programs with reality ... unfortunately the propaganda on TV is terrible, about our culture, our people ... and how can you ask a Canadian to have a different idea if he ... only knows what he sees on TV.' Although many of the people interviewed in this study agreed that education could eventually challenge such stereotypes, they were also resigned to facing some form of exclusion in their lives. A twenty-seven-year-old woman from Paraguay claimed that 'being an immigrant does not go unnoticed, if it is not your skin colour it will be your accent. Every time you walk into a store and open your mouth you are an immigrant.'[64]

Racism was a subjective phenomenon, sometimes imagined, sometimes misinterpreted. But as these various studies indicate, the host society in the Alberta cities could set a high bar for acceptance. Long gone was the legal sanctioning of racism, but fear of immigrants and mistrust of their cultures remained a reality in Calgary and Edmonton.

In seeming contradiction to a fear of strangers in the Alberta cities was the remarkable humanitarian concern during the coming of the so-called Vietnamese Boat People. Though Yvette Knott encountered opposition to them in 1979, she also found Albertans who were 'positive and generous.'[65] This generosity came not from the general public or, initially, from government agencies, which were 'negative' or 'cool' to the idea of Southeast Asian refugees, but from individual sponsors, churches, and ethnic groups.[66]

A wide variety of ethnic, religious, and secular organizations became involved in the Vietnamese immigration. Between January and July 1979 two agencies in particular – the Catholic Family Services and the volunteer Calgary Immigrant Aid Society – worked hard to resettle refugees. Then in June 1979, as initial enthusiasm from charity groups waned, the Calgary Inter-faith Community Action Committee established a subcommittee dubbed Someone Cares; it spoke of airlifting eight thousand refugees to Calgary, although in the end it settled on promoting private sponsorships. Other organizations, including the Alberta Vocational Centre, the Calgary Public School Board, the Mount Royal College, and the YWCA, also participated in refugee settlement by organizing ESL classes. Ethnic institutions such as the Calgary Chinese Community distributed clothing and furniture from Chinatown's Ng Tower and organized the umbrella Calgary Chinese Community for Vietnamese Refugees committee. The small Vietnamese community, including Catholic, Buddhist, and secular societies, organized a visitation program for the refugees housed at the York Hotel. And throughout Calgary, families and community groups signed up for sponsorship through an umbrella group under the auspices of the Euro–Canadian churches. Of particular importance was the Mennonite Central Committee, which organized twenty-three groups, but agencies linked to the Anglican, Presbyterian, and Catholic churches were also important. In the end, it was said that more than five thousand Calgarians had become involved directly as private sponsors of the Vietnamese and Laotian newcomers.[67]

Many of these Euro–Canadian sponsors seemed motivated by a spirit of inclusiveness. They spoke of their 'moral obligation to act according to religious or humanitarian principles' and celebrated the virtue of 'spontaneous acts of compassion and goodwill.'[68] Indeed, Knott's study suggested that the response of individuals to the church and service-club initiatives was unprecedented. It marked a major shift in the mentality of individual Canadians who, until the Second World War, had usually left to church hierarchies and governments the task of refugee assistance.[69] Clearly, the heightened 'financial resources and leisure time' of many Albertans now had become coupled with the ethos of 'assistance to those less fortunate.'[70] There may have been negative responses from the public when the idea of bringing in the refugees first surfaced, but they had been countered by the outpouring of aid from thousands of individuals.

Numerous associations in Calgary now sought to help immigrants in general. By the 1970s the new immigrants could access a complex web of institutions that comprised Alberta's social safety net. In Calgary alone these included a disparate array of organizations with special programs for immigrants: the hospitals – Calgary General, Foothills, and Holy Cross; education facilities – the Alberta Vocational Centre, the Department of Advanced Education, and the YWCA; government agencies such as the Alberta Human Rights Commission, Alberta Social Services and Community Health, the Canadian Court of Citizenship, the City Social Services; and private organizations such as the Catholic Family Services, the Jewish Family Services, and the Advice, Information and Directory (AID). The organizations prepared to face a variety of pressing needs. Among the top eighteen needs identified in 1977 by these organizations, countering discrimination was in ninth place; fear of the new Canadian culture, twelfth; and addressing social alienation, thirteenth. At the top of the list in order of concern were language, basic skills, housing, furnishing, and jobs. The agencies took different approaches. The small Jewish Family Services matched 'Jewish immigrant youths with Canadian-born

Jewish youths so that the immigrant youths [could] join in the various youth activities.' The much larger Calgary Immigrant Aid Society had be-. come 'an agency to which most of the other agencies refer[ed] their immigrant clients when necessary.'[71] Some groups such as the Immigrant Aid Societies of the Catholic Family Service provided multi-faceted aid, including 'reception services at the airport, assistance in finding housing, provisions of used furniture and clothing, assistance in registering children for schools, help in filling out forms, help in applying for welfare assistance, family counselling, assistance in finding employment and financial loans.'[72] Together, the public and private concerns provided an unprecedented array of immigrant aid service.

Generosity among citizens' groups was apparent also in Edmonton, where the community volunteer Edmonton Immigrant Services Association, or EISA, was established in 1976.[73] David Bai's study noted that the EISA provided those services wrapped in an 'ideology of multiculturalism,' suggesting that ethnicity and Canadian citizenship were not opposing identities. Thus the EISA supported the new immigrants' struggle to cultivate and even to expand their homeland cultures in an Edmonton setting. The association set out to educate Canadians on the contributions of immigrant cultures to a 'unique Canadian identity.' To this end the EISA took over the historic McKay Avenue School (once the temporary site for the Alberta legislature) in 1984 and turned its main floor into a multicultural centre known as McKay House. It became a marked success, with up to '40 ethnocultural or community groups ... us[ing] the facility for everything from executive meetings, gala receptions and religious festivals, to on-going heritage language courses.' Overall, the growth of the EISA programs was rapid: its historian notes that by 'the end of 1986–87 fiscal year, EISA provided six services in settlement, five in citizenship and five in multiculturalism, for a total clientele of 31,413.' Finally, the EISA also worked in concert with community organizations, especially church-based groups such as the Edmonton Mennonite Society for the Assistance of Newcomers, St Barnabas Refugee Society, and Edmonton Catholic Social Services. This impulse followed the path of cultural developments in late-century Edmonton. The EISA, for one, benefited from the fact that Mennonites had adopted a 'liberation theology ideology' and a 'multicultural management team,' while the Catholics had begun to emulate 'secular, large scale ... voluntary organization[s].' Whatever the reasons for the EISA's expansion, it was clear that interwoven in a culture capable of racist language was a social presence bent on philanthropy and tolerance.[74]

Making a Multicultural Society

Perhaps it is true that local governments hesitated in supporting the coming of Southeast Asian refugees in 1979 and 1980. But evidence suggests that both the provincial and civic governments in Alberta delighted in a semblance of multiculturalism. Oftentimes it is Trudeau's Liberal government that is credited with introducing official multiculturalism policy in 1971. But the policy was not without western roots and wings. Among strong proponents of the policy was University of Calgary professor Howard Palmer, who had been an author of Volume Four of the 1969 federal Royal Commission on Bilingualism and Biculturalism report, a volume that 'recommended broadening the tolerance level of Canadians to minority groups through educational and broadcasting policies and specific support for "the arts and letters of cultural groups other than the British and French."'[75] Then, too, not only Ottawa but also the Alberta government adopted a multicultural policy in 1971. Indeed, as David Bai pointed out in 1982, it was a policy that explicitly 'recognized … cultural and linguistic diversity.' That policy established both the Alberta Cultural Heritage Council, an advisory group, and the Alberta Heritage Foundation, a granting agency. In 1988 the two agencies amalgamated with the recently launched Alberta Multicultural Commission. In the 1980s, too, the Alberta government took a proactive step to encourage immigration with the signing of the Canada–Alberta Immigration Agreement, a labour-market-driven memorandum that promised to help businesses import skilled workers, welcome immigrant entrepreneurs, and assist in family reunification.[76]

On the official level, Alberta and its cities favoured immigration. But ordinary citizens also seemed to be changing their attitudes to the arrivals from the Global South. A study of the *Calgary Herald* suggests that the old image of Nordic towns or WASP societies was beginning to be seen as a liability, while a new cosmopolitan and multicultural image was increasingly embraced as an asset. In the 1970s many Calgarians, and even the *Herald,* seemed wary of multiculturalism. In 1978 when the newspaper published statistics that indicated that 20 percent of Calgarians were immigrants, historian Howard Palmer declared that the word 'kaleidoscope' had now come to describe 'Calgary's constantly changing ethnic mix' and that 'immigration brings new elements of vitality and excitement.' His colleague at the University of Calgary, sociologist James Frideres, agreed but insisted that Calgary still had 'the feeling of being a WASP town' and that Calgarians were 'still unwilling to admit that the town is taking on more visible ethnic groups.'[77] A 1979 story in the *Calgary Herald* that applauded the assimilated Chinese Canadian seemed to agree. The newspaper highlighted the Chinese immigrants who were 'well represented in the professions, especially science and math-related fields.' It noted that oftentimes the newcomers had adopted 'Western names like George or Hugh' and cared less 'whether next year is the year of the horse or the rooster.' Many of these professionals, noted the paper, 'live in Huntington Hills,' although they were also 'dispersed throughout the city.'[78] It seemed Albertans were convincing themselves that immigrants could settle and yet not alter the cultural landscape.

Through the 1980s and 1990s the ethnic 'kaleidoscope' described by Palmer was claimed by Calgary and Edmonton as their own. The main urban daily newspapers and the weekly provincial papers began to represent immigrants as Alberta assets. No doubt the ethnic readership was sufficiently large and powerful to secure sympathetic coverage. But given the way in which the topic was interpreted by reporters, it seemed as if the host society was appropriating the stories of immigration as part of its own identity. Calgary and Edmonton suddenly needed to be ethnic.

Two stories published by the *Calgary Herald* in 1982 reflect a new stage in the development of this emerging ethos of urban multiculturalism. In May the newspaper ran the story of a sign war at Ruby's Restaurant in Chinatown. It reported that in an ironic act, proprietors Amy Wong and Domino Lau had been ordered by 'the city's senior sign inspector, Aileen Wilson, to take down the [English-only] sign [and] to put in Chinese characters or face a $50 a day fine.' Apparently Wong and Lau's sign had violated the 1976 Chinatown Design Brief, a bylaw meant to protect and strengthen the city's Chinatown. The Chinese-Canadian objected to the heavy-handed Anglo–Canadian inspector. They insisted that the 'English letters' had been imported from Hong Kong and that a 'Chinese tradition ... says bad luck will follow' owners who change a sign of an active business. Civic officials had arrived at a new point in the city's history. Calgary would have a multicultural face, whether its immigrants approved or not.[79] In another story, published in July 1982, the *Herald* announced the end of Ramadan and described an image of kneeling men and shrouded women. But the climax of the story was the boast that 'Calgary had just built a new mosque, the largest in Canada.' So grand was it that 'visitors from all over [had come] to see the mosque, from Toronto, from New York, from Tunisia,' and that they were 'all impressed.'[80] Calgary was now not only multicultural, it was so on an especially grand scale.

Conclusion

Trinidadian writer Sam Selvon, who migrated to Canada via the United Kingdom in 1978 at age fifty-five, wrote only one short story set in Canada. The story, 'Angus at the Races,' was an 'amusing and humorous' piece, according to critic Victor J. Ramraj. It depicted two West Indians happily visiting a Calgary racetrack. But what was 'missing' from this story, and present in many of Selvon's other pieces, was 'the harsh circumstance of the London immigrant's life and the bittersweet tone of the early stories.'[81] What was it about the Alberta city that drew such a positive response from Selvon's character? Perhaps it was that Calgary took its place as a relatively small and defined city within a continental interior, the very opposite of the urban, sprawling giants of London, New York, Paris, Toronto, and Vancouver, with their powerful but controversial ethnic enclaves. Perhaps Selvon himself had learned about the Alberta city's multicultural past, linked as it was to the coming of the post-war immigrants from all points of Europe and confirmed by the large influx of newcomers from Asia, Africa, and the Americas. Perhaps the host society's stumbling on the obstacles of xenophobia, discrimination, and underemployment could be forgiven because of the sweet aroma of its heritage festivals. Perhaps the fragmentation of urban culture caused not social dysfunction, but an energy welcomed by cities seeking international attention and approval.

No doubt the Alberta cities signalled that prairie urban culture at the end of the century had changed again. Fragmented identities and contradictory voices, amorphous urban structures and virtual enclaves, but all interwoven in new ways, these were the grist of late-century urban culture. Immigrant groups and subgroups not only created their own social networks in the city, they lent a multi-strand 'web of significance' to it. They asserted their dynamic ethnic identities through newly created cultural institutions, and yet strove to embrace the Alberta dream: field research indicated a deeply held belief among newcomers that they could gain entry into the middle class, including its public institutions, residential districts, social values, and consumer lifestyle. The host society could set a discriminating bar of acceptance, but it could also be tolerant, even appear generous. Its old-fashioned benevolence, once directed to members of very specific classes, was increasingly translated and redirected to a new, broader cosmopolitan identity. A pluralistic Alberta urban society certainly expressed itself in a series of boundaries and divisions, but also as a network of dynamic, intercultural relationships. By the end of the

century the Alberta cities had taken their inheritance of a Nordic–
Canadian, continental, pioneer society, and redefined it in part with the
cultures of Asia, South America, and Africa. These were the marks of late-
century urban ambition, opportunistic, perhaps, but also dynamic and
cosmopolitan. Old immigrant enclaves had been replaced by a dynamic
ethnic web integrated into the very identity of Edmonton and Calgary,
securing for them an image as plural, open, and cosmopolitan societies.

chapter six

Gender and Family
in Hybrid Households

In some ways, despite significant economic and demographic changes in the five prairie cities, life within the urban immigrant community changed little over the course of the century. Immigrants still found their bearing in the new land within their own social organizations. As noted in Chapter 5, for example, social networks that included social clubs and religious sites of worship remained significant into the last decades of the century. In fact some studies demonstrate that newcomers invigorated both inner-city and suburban social organizations. Others show how the role of religion remained crucial within a rapidly secularizing society, most apparent in the rise of an array of non-Christian religious buildings – a small mosque in Saskatoon in 1978, an impressive new Hindu mandir in Calgary in 1990.[1] In other instances Asian and Latin American newcomers lent a hand in reinvigorating older religious establishments, mainline Christian churches in particular.[2]

Family was not unlike these various social organisms. It was marked by continuity but underwent change as well. Certainly it remained a fundamentally important site for the integration of the immigrants in Canada's interior cities during the last third of the twentieth century. Despite Canada's points system, the number of immigrants selected in that individualizing process did not overtake the numbers of 'family class' immigrants. Of the 55,000 immigrants to Alberta between 1984 and 1988, 42 percent were admitted as 'family class' immigrants, 34 percent as 'independents' under Canada's points system, and 24 percent as refugees.[3] So significant were family-class migrants that neo-conservative critics lashed out at them, complaining that with 'neither limit on the numbers, nor assessment of literacy or skills,' these newcomers sabotaged excellence as a criterion for immigrant selection.[4] In the meantime more progressive ethnographic studies during these decades spoke of the immigrant family in positive terms. Some scholars argued that, given inexpensive travel and transnational ties, extended families attained new significance; grandparents, for one, could settle close to adult children in ways earlier immigrants simply could not.[5] Other studies emphasized that a nuclear, tightly knit, suburban, child-centred family acted as a social anchor in the kaleidoscopic city of a strange new land.[6]

If the importance of the immigrant family had not changed over the course of the century, the precise role played by it had. In the early decades the immigrant family was a dynamic and even conflict-ridden site, but it was also a haven in a world in flux. Family was the very locus of 'traditional' and 'primary' relationships, one that countered the individualizing tendencies of the urban, capitalist world.[7] Over time the nature of the family seemed to change from a site of protection to a matrix of adaptation. Christopher Lasch's 1979 book, bearing the ironic title *Haven in a Heartless World*, is instructive: he argued that although 'most of the writing on the modern family takes for granted the "isolation" of the nuclear family,' in fact 'the modern world intrudes at every point and obliterates its privacy.'[8] A more recent Canadian study of the family by R.W. Sandwell also reflects the late-century family in particular: she writes that historians 'have not only documented the persistence of a-liberal patterns within households but have identified the family itself as a "hot zone" where the new liberal order was both created and contested.'[9] Numerous works specifically on the late-century immigrant family concur; they suggest that the very heart of the household and ethnicity – childhood behaviour, eating habits, gender relations, dating practices, sexual codes of conduct, and household religion – shifted upon migration.[10] Even when it appeared that immigrant families 'barricaded' themselves behind ethnic practice, it seemed they were in fact adapting to new expectations in creative ways.

The late-century ethnic family also served as a crucible for social change in a wider sense. Old family practices were severely disrupted by the migration process and by the points system that Canada accepted in the 1970s. Still, in the prairie city as elsewhere, it is too simple to say that the family yielded to a culture of liberal individualism.[11] Rather, the ethnic family was a site of accommodation and adjustment in which inherited values and symbols fused with new cultural understandings offered by urban life in the new country. The late-century immigrant family became a hybridized social unit in a diasporic culture. If, as Lasch observed, the modern family was not a 'haven' from an encroaching wider world for the urban dweller, nor was it one for the late-century immigrant. The late-century immigrant family in Canada's interior cities was the very site of cultural change.

The Meaning of Family

Sociological studies of prairie cities in the 1970s and 1980s emphasize the family's central role in the process of immigration and integration. It seemed not to matter whether the immigrants were from Chile, China, Korea, India, Pakistan, Philippines, or Vietnam; family resources provided an important path into Canadian society for all newcomers. Moreover, the family's importance was shared by all classes of immigrants, including the professional, wage-labour, refugee, and even single female sojourner groups. Some differences did exist within these classes, however, as ethnicity and family dynamics intertwined in different ways, with different results.

Professional immigrants, usually arriving under the points system, most often were able to vault into a suburban, middle-class culture. It was a world anchored to a privately owned home and nuclear family. Often these immigrants had experienced urban and technologically advanced communities in Asia, South America, or Africa. In these continents they had constituted 'skilled, educated, resourceful and heavily anglicized middle classes.'[12]

Cecil Pereira's 1971 study of East Indians in Winnipeg shows how professional families moved immediately upon their arrival into the comfortable, west-side suburb of St James-Assiniboia. Here they made ownership of private homes a priority, no matter that it meant such a geographic dispersal that one could 'hardly find two [East Indian] families living on the same street.' And here they began their private lives within a 'primary group level of family and friends' and 'strong parent-child relationships.' In suburbia the newcomers could disregard and ignore their Canadian-born neighbours if they chose. Conversely, the telephone and the car allowed them to gather widely scattered East Indian friends into a virtual, temporal neighbourhood in short order. In this process they often discarded old taboos of shunning 'other castes,' knowing that in Canada one was 'able to gain prestige by achievement rather than by ascription.' They also knew that integration required informal social contacts with other educated East Indians, ones that could be made from within the family home. Indeed, the family residence – site of informal visiting, card playing, or common meals – surpassed the ethnic institution in importance. Family resources were even turned to helping other kinfolk find their place in Canada, perhaps by greeting them at Winnipeg's international airport or guiding them in their own search for residence and vocation. But the same families could also disregard the wider ethnic community when it suited them, and revert to their nuclear households where close parent–child links and an atmosphere of 'informality and sincerity' held sway. Here a 'familiar milieu' granted 'shelter and ego-support' and provided its adult members with the encouragement necessary if they were to negotiate the workaday secondary world of 'anonymity, individuality and independence.'[13]

Working-class families had a slightly different history. A 1979 study by Greg Teal points out that about half of Edmonton's 550 Koreans were working-class migrants, most of the men in steel construction industries and most of the women in the garment sector. Perhaps the Koreans were perceived as workers by their industrial sponsors in Edmonton or as members of the working class by union organizers, but in their everyday lives the newcomers' worlds centred on the family. Their life stories recounted their pasts as peasant families in Korea's countryside. They had been driven to the large cities by government policies that deflated farm commodity prices and then further compelled them to emigrate. In Edmonton, the Korean newcomers clustered close to their places of work. They settled as families in small neighbourhoods of walk-up apartments or inexpensive houses, and collaborated with immigrants of similar age. Eighty percent of the adults in this neighbourhood study were between twenty and forty years old, and a third of the children were preschoolers. As in the lives of their professional counterparts, these working-class immigrants often dismissed ethnic organizations. During the week they left their homes to labour alongside fellow Koreans in non-English-speaking environments with a single purpose: the sustenance and upward mobility of their families. Indeed, the women and men often survived dismal factory conditions with the singular belief that 'if they worked hard they too, or at least their children, could rise to the professional strata.' Incomes were also spent alleviating worries about the plight of extended families in the old homeland: at least 25 percent of the families had sponsored a grandmother in the city and 10 percent a grandfather. For the working-class immigrant, family was not only 'an important integrative mechanism,' it was so in its own unique way.[14]

Refugees faced a starkly different reality. Usually they came without much family, sometimes as individuals, most often as young nucleated families with fading hopes of ever again seeing their kin or their elderly parents. Indeed, the wider kin group was more often a focus of deep anxiety than a source of material or psychological aid. In this context the ethnic organization often served as a surrogate family or clan.

Two prominent examples in prairie Canada were the Chilean refugees of 1974–5 and the Vietnamese refugees of 1979–80. The Vietnamese newcomers had fled their homeland in rickety boats with such haste that they lost contact with most of their close relatives. In Canada they were haunted by the escape and 'anxious about the fate of their relatives in South Asia ... refugee camps.'[15] Young Vietnamese women in a 1987 study in Saskatoon spoke of happiness with life and of their satisfaction with strong support systems that developed among the women who shared this working experience. They also said that they were eager to find work. But in an understated way all 'indicated that they would be happier ... if their [extended] family was in Saskatoon.'[16]

The Chileans in Winnipeg recorded similar desires. As former political prisoners, many tortured before being exiled, the Chileans were burdened by the 'great and lasting concern for friends, relatives and former associates who had been left behind in the gaols ... of Augusto Pinochet.' The absence of strong kin networks hurt these groups. One Chilean refugee spoke of his first winter in Winnipeg in 1975–6: 'It was *rough* and *tough* for us. We didn't have any job. We didn't have any care. We didn't have any home. We were moving from one place to another because of the children, because of the regulations. We didn't know anything about the law, about the tenant and landlord agreements.' The refugees were forced to find state-funded assistance or organize quickly into 'loosely structured informal associations.'[17] These associations guided the newcomers into the retail, employment, and social-service sectors of society.

Unlike wealthier immigrants, refugee families displayed an exceptional interest in establishing close-knit, ethnically distinctive districts. A 1982 study of immigrant patterns in Winnipeg by Bernard Thraves showed that Portuguese and East Indian chain migrants, Filipino and West Indian professional migrants, and Chilean and Vietnamese political refugees had profoundly different residential patterns. The Filipino and West Indian professionals were much more dispersed, located as they were in almost two-thirds of Winnipeg's census tracts; the Chilean and Vietnamese refugee immigrants, on the other hand, were clustered in only a fifth of those tracts. Refugee groups, too, were disproportionately concentrated in inner-city neighbourhoods where they clustered in more affordable, low-status housing.[18] In the absence of extended

family, the ethnic association and the immigrant enclave held pronounced significance.

A study of a fourth class of immigrants, those who arrived as single individuals, also holds out the paradoxical lesson that family was excep-
tionally important within the immigrant community. During an era when
marriage rates plummeted in Western societies, they remained high
among these prairie newcomers.[19] Studies indicate the importance of
marriage among single female factory workers, who had replaced single
male sojourners as the largest category of single immigrants. Cleto
Buduhan's 1971 study of Filipino female workers in Winnipeg, for example, described a marriage-conditioned social hierarchy within the
tightly knit ethnic community. The lowest persons on this scale were single women over the age of thirty, pejoratively dubbed the *matanda na* or
'already old.' Then came the *dalaga/binata*, the more recently arrived
and more marriageable young women and men in their early twenties.
Higher up on the social ladder were the married *may asawa*, those having
embarked on a 'settled and quiet life' with 'no more problems.' The
birth of the first child catapulted these young married women from the
upstart *nanay* to the respected *aling*. The very highest status was achieved
when the young family purchased a house, 'the ultimate mark of wealth
and prestige,' of 'stability and freedom.'[20]

Other Winnipeg studies underscore this pattern. Bok-Nam Yoon's
1983 study of 250 newly arrived, Korean, female garment workers concluded that true womanhood for these newcomers was defined by becoming a 'housewife and mother.' Indeed, the very aim of a 'better future
for husband and children' had pushed them to leave their homeland
and travel the difficult path to Winnipeg.[21] Amory Yuk Mui Ong's 1987
examination of eight single Asian women in Winnipeg repeated this
idealized vision. Unlike the Vietnamese women refugees, these women
endured dead-end jobs. Separated from their families in south Asia,
numbed by 'feelings' of loneliness, insecurity, and anxiety, they spoke of
a profound sense of 'being lost between worlds' and 'being different.'
Their uniform answer to these problems was not return migration, the
search for a better job, or government assistance. Rather, and almost
without exception, they hoped to improve their lives by 'having a spouse.'
Indeed, marriage for these women was perceived as a means to 'resolve
all three – personal, economic and social – areas of difficulty at the same
time.' Evidently, the late-century immigrant found in neither the ethnic
institution nor the welfare state a match for family as site for 'familiarity,
shelter and ego support.'[22]

Gender and Integration

The family may have been centrally important to the immigrant, but it was not a haven of changelessness. Rather, it was the very site in which old cultural identities were tested and altered. Ideas about gender and gender relations were especially subject to change.

At first look, the changes seem easy to define. The image of the early-century, tenement-house woman is of one who laundered for neighbours and tended cabbage patches and chicken coops. The mid-century image is one of mothers in small, respectable bungalows who attended parent nights at school and baked ethnic specialties for the holidays.[23] The late-century working women presented yet another picture. They found placements for the children in daycare centres, and worked at the shopping mall or hotel as service workers or in offices or public institutions as professionals. Some studies have suggested that these women, no matter their job status, felt a special sense of well-being within the family structure. Nancy Foner, for example, writes that late-century New York immigrant women gained a 'sense of empowerment ... from earning a wage ... and having greater control' over it, a sense reinforced by North America's women's 'liberation culture.'[24] Gender definitions affected men in equal degrees. Men in the offices, laboratories, and service industries of the late-century prairie cities faced realities that differed from those of the men who worked in heavy industry and construction during the first two-thirds of the century. Again the change can be viewed as simple and unilinear. Following the formula of American historian Anthony Rotundo, one might say that in the advanced economy of the prairie city, masculinity became defined in the language of individual achievement, mixed with elements of publicly expressed passion and 'conspicuous consumption.'[25]

But was it this simple? And what did happen when these emerging gender identities were plugged into marriage and family life? One study of Greek–Canadian families identifies a weakened 'patriarchal orientation and an increasing emphasis on companionship' in the family.[26] Such a theme accords with conventional assumptions that migration disrupted the male-dominated, extended family. In this scenario immigrant women began to work outside the households and men came to rely more on their wives' social companionship. But such changes in gender relations were not consistent. Gender for these immigrants was often influenced by cultural inheritances. Their ideas reflected their personal histories, kinship lines, religion, national backgrounds, class, and language. The consequence could produce a truly hybridized gender. Daniel Coleman explains that Canadian immigrant male perspectives are 'born of the concussion of two or more cultural codes for masculinity'; indeed, 'out of conflict among a plurality of masculinities.'[27] Clearly women, too, were presented with a repertoire of gender constructions that included a diversity of femininities.

If the simple sum of the late-century immigrant experience was greater gender equality, the process of getting there was complex. The story of many late-century immigrant women in the prairie cities was anything but egalitarian. Some women spoke of lost status and diminished well-being within the wider society. Oftentimes, having moved from close-knit, kin-based societies, they possessed fewer social supports after immigration than before, jeopardizing their ability to negotiate their way in new cities.[28] Women could speak of a double jeopardy, in that they could be disadvantaged by both gender and race. The young Winnipeg Chinese woman who faced the derisive comment on the street shortly after her arrival in about 1980 – 'You Chink bitch, why don't you go home!' – knew she had two strikes against her, 'being a visible minority and ... being a woman.'[29]

But women could also face disadvantages within the very context of the immigrant household. A 1985 study of ninety-five Asians, Africans, and South Americans in Regina and Saskatoon by Angela Djao, Lily Tingley, and Roxana Ng notes the disadvantage that came to immigrant women with 'the loss of the family unit, the extended kinship network, the ... close community, and the emotional support that those groups used to provide.'[30] These women registered heightened loneliness, anger, and stress, but also vulnerability to male authority. Oftentimes these women learned English after their husbands – a practice they said was encouraged by discriminatory Canada Employment and Immigration policies – and thus became more dependent on the men and 'often felt excluded from social activities, ashamed or useless.'[31] A 1991 study by Kit Man Kitty Mok of Asian women in Calgary noted a similar isolation of female migrants from public worlds, leading to significant feelings of 'isolation.' Statistics revealed a stark reality: many women were able to speak a little English, but fewer than 40 percent could 'understand English in conversations ... [or] television or radio perfectly well'; about 80 percent reported that they alone did all the cooking, but only 15 percent did the grocery shopping on their own; 95 percent had used public health services, but only a small percentage utilized childcare centres.[32]

Immigration meant that many women, especially young mothers, felt secluded and disempowered in domestic worlds.

Reports of spousal abuse that appeared throughout these late-century decades underscore these studies of disadvantaged women. A 1977 examination of service agencies in Calgary indicated a severe problem with domestic strife among immigrant groups. Third on a long list of cited problems was 'authoritarian husbands resulting in physical abuse of wives and children,' and only eighth and ninth on the list were 'family problems' and 'loneliness.'[33] The 1985 Regina and Saskatoon study reported that about 20 percent of immigrant women said immigration itself had brought negative changes to their marriage: husbands and wives saw each other less frequently, women felt increased loneliness and unhappiness, oftentimes husbands drank excessively, and anger and antagonism now characterized their marriages.[34] A 1995 study of South Asian immigrant women of western Canada and Canada's Atlantic region concluded that 'patriarchal relations' were 'a major factor in South Asian women's lived experience of subordination, powerlessness, violence and other forms of oppression.'[35]

Other studies that attempt to explain increased male dislocation and violence provide further evidence of an endemic problem. The lack of traditional communal controls and uncertainty about appropriate male behaviour seem to have exacerbated abusive behaviour. A 1995 study by Helen Ralston linked domestic abuse among western Canadian immigrants to arranged marriages. Here young immigrant women, within uncertain and unfamiliar new cities, were compelled to 'agree ... to the man's control over gender relations in family and community.'[36] Tomoko Makabe's 1998 work on Sansei Japanese recalled that fathers who suffered racial abuse in the mid-century decades sometimes brought their frustrations home to their children. One son recalled that his father, a Winnipeg mechanic, harboured such 'hard feelings' about wartime internment's cutting short his education that the father experienced further frustration, expressed in repeatedly getting 'mad at everybody' at home.[37] Other scholars link a host of negative emotions to the condition of male underemployment during the 1990s. In Calgary immigrants noted that job-market restructuring often sent highly educated immigrant men to work in menial jobs. Here they saw their competitive advantage erode, faced the prospect of unemployment, and experienced significant frustration in 'ghettoised occupations.'[38] Oftentimes despondency was linked to underemployment. One immigrant man asserted that

'I could have been a Physical Education professor, but ... they don't recognize my degree ... and now ... I don't feel like studying for two years ...
I don't think it is something that will promise me any future.' Another
man, once a national soccer coach in his homeland, was said to have
faced many problems including severe depression when he found himself
in a dead-end job, 'peeling fish.'[39] These social dislocations also exacerbated domestic upheaval, including violence against women.

Despite these reports of problems at home, numerous ethnographies
of these late-century decades suggested a transition to greater degrees of
equality within marriage. In fact, some argued that even within middle-
class families in which husbands worked and women did not, egalitarian-
ism was enhanced in Canada. The reason was simple: migration from a
deeply patriarchal society and integration into a modern welfare state
provided women with greater influence over husbands and greater lati-
tude in the public arena. Muhammad Siddique's study showed that
Pakistani and East Indian women in Saskatoon in the 1970s (only a third
of whom were members of the workforce) reported the development of
'symbiotic unions' with both wife and husband participating 'together in
most of their activities' and seeking 'mutual solutions to patterns of adjustment.' Moreover, a new consciousness of ethnicity, and the association of married couples with ethnic institutions, encouraged men and
women to socialize together. Together, they took in ethnic movies and
'cultural programs, variety shows, religious and social gatherings' at the
Pakistan–Canada and India–Canada cultural associations. These new associations, coupled with a physical separation from old kinship networks,
were said to enhance the wife's status. Although not ending her dependency, separation from old-world kin groups shifted that dependency
from mother-in-law or sister-in-law to the husband himself. Unlike studies elsewhere, the Saskatchewan survey suggested that in this new dependency wives won 'a great deal of the husbands' confidence.'[40] Helen
Chan's 1980 work on immigrant women in ethnically disparate suburbia
went a step further, suggesting that these marriages were enhanced by
becoming 'based on the notion of romantic love.'[41]

Even immigrant women who did not work outside the homes reported
opportunities to engage the wider social world. Certainly, as Franca
Iacovetta and Joan Sangster have pointed out, the late-century Canadian
state employed an assortment of institutions to foist a middle-class familial culture onto the marginalized and the newcomers.[42] However, some
ethnographies also suggest that immigrant women could subvert these
institutions to serve their own ends. Public medicine, for one, served

those purposes explicitly, even for the most culturally conservative. A 1999 study of Saskatoon Arab women, for example, discovered that they worried about maintaining their spiritual, psychological, and physical health, and saw Canada's modern medical system as an important resource to that end. Despite reporting distress at having to expose their bodies to male doctors, these women combined remedies from their homelands with regular visits to Canadian physicians.[43] Even the very tasks of household management could increase the family 'interface with Canadian social and economic institutions.' One study of stay-at-home Vietnamese women notes that as husbands went off to work in the public domain, the wives had opportunities to learn 'how to do the vital things – how to take a bus, where to shop, how to enroll children in school, how to use the post office, the bank, and credit cards.' At the very least, these tasks catapulted the women into 'the vanguard of new cultural information,' altering their old, household-centred, private roles.[44]

A much greater degree of conjugal equality was registered by women who worked or studied in the public arena. These women often spoke in glowing terms of their opportunities to participate in that sphere. A first-generation Japanese–Canadian woman in Saskatoon said simply: 'I enjoy the freedom of being able to work' for it 'is not common for women in my country to work after they are married.'[45] And they spoke confidently about insisting on equality within the home. A young Nicaraguan wife and student in Calgary described a household that was re-examining old gender roles: 'the only problem I have [is] because [my husband] doesn't want to do anything (in the house) so he says that if he had known that I was going to change like this .,, [insisting that] he has to help ... I wouldn't have come' to Canada.[46]

For most women the last half of the century was a time of significant transition. Helen Chan's study comparing the Chinese women who came to Canada in the 1970s with the experience of those who had arrived during the 1950s is especially illuminating. The latter, who arrived shortly after the 1947 repeal of the *Chinese Exclusion Act*, often followed the male head of the household by a few years and were accompanied by their children. They in turn prepared the way for the new arrival of large numbers of Chinese wives and brides joining older, one-time-sojourner, male compatriots. Changes in immigration regulations after 1957 in particular brought hundreds of 'young mail order brides' from Hong Kong. Both groups of women were restricted in what they could do. They were expected to accept traditional forms of life, to assist the businesses of their Canadianized husbands, and give birth in what came to be known in their circles as the 'Canadian Chinese baby boom of the late 1950s.' Thus they re-established the patrilineal and patrilocal traditions of their homeland in which 'roles of the family members were … clearly and rigidly defined by age, sex, generation, folkways and mores.' In fact, it was the 'exalted' role of the mother to teach her daughters subservience to men, 'to her husband … and to her son after the death of her husband,' and to ensure the general subservience of any daughter-in-law 'to all members of the family.'[47]

Within a decade or two, however, these Chinese families began to speak about the ideal of egalitarian marriage. By the 1970s and 1980s these once strongly patriarchal families lauded the importance of female participation and even leadership in family-owned laundries, grocery stores, and restaurants.[48] Wing-sam Chow's study of Chinese women in Winnipeg claims that husbands were grateful for their wives' contribution to the household economy. One man noted that his wife's full-time job 'at a garment factory' allowed the couple to own 'part of the commercial block, a residential house for themselves and a station wagon' and to sponsor 'his father, brother and sister to visit them from far off Hong Kong.' By the early 1980s a number of women even provided leadership in family businesses. There was 'Mrs. Huang,' whose 'small and brightly lighted restaurant' not only boasted the city's only 'Cantonese deep-fried pastries,' but provided the social basis for the support of Huang's 'two university student sons who worked at the restaurant.' 'Miss Yeng,' a graduate from a local university who accepted the 1973 amnesty for illegal immigrants, was said to have opened a restaurant in a downtown hotel, followed by a restaurant in her own building in the suburbs. Eventually, she used her business earnings to sponsor her younger brother, and adopted the argument of 'job creation' to help her father qualify as an immigrant.[49]

Late-century immigrant women demonstrated their independence, too, in organizing female social networks and institutions. Reflecting a continued reality over time, Bok-Nam Yoon's study of single Korean women in Winnipeg in the early 1980s emphasized the role of religion in meeting the newcomers' primary social needs. These young women countered the feeling of being 'strangers' in Canada by creating close-knit residential groups in downtown apartments, and then by joining ethnic churches. Within six months of arriving in Canada, almost three-quarters of these women had become regular attendees at one of two Korean churches. Significantly, even 'those with no religion in Korea' attended church in Winnipeg. The reason for this adherence seems to have been social in nature. Two central Korean churches assisted the young women, sending representatives to meet them at the airport, helping them in setting up apartments, enrolling them for English as a Second Language (ESL) classes, and even offering driving lessons. Even those who did not attend church joined a religious lay group, the University Bible Fellowship, gathering each evening in one of the apartments 'to learn English and to keep and strengthen their faith.' Given their church activities, the young Koreans 'feel that they belong as members of the religious community in Canada.' So all-encompassing were their social ties that these women claimed to spend less time in the solitary activities of watching television and listening to the radio and more time visiting Winnipeg's museum, art gallery, and public library in the company of other Koreans.[50]

By the end of the century many immigrant women also were enlisting in ethnic feminist organizations. Ralston's 1995 study of East Indian women in Edmonton describes their participation in such organizations. The attraction was simple, contributing as they did to their 'social cohesion and empowerment by providing needed social, cultural, recreational and spiritual services.' In Edmonton the Indo-Canadian Women's Association, founded in 1984, became a proactive group, campaigning for women's rights in the media and addressing problems such as 'employment equity and sexual abuse.' This group also developed educational material, including collaborating with a local television station to produce two videos: *Crossing the Line*, dealing with 'girls abused by their parents because they want to be like every other Canadian-born girl'; and *The Bold Step*, telling a woman's 'own story of wife abuse and her "success story" of empowerment and enrollment in a social work program.' The Edmonton association even challenged fundamentalist religious ideas that kept 'women in a subservient and oppressed condition in family and society.'[51] Working women in egalitarian marriages and membership in women's organizations signalled significant changes in gender relations. That some of the households experienced conflict suggested the depth of the changes.

Primary Relations

Immigrant families were directly affected by the wider Canadian society. Deep intergenerational conflicts within the family could occur, resulting in rapid changes It often seemed that the concept of 'cultural maintenance' applied less directly to the primary world of the family than to secondary relations in social clubs, churches, and mutual aid societies where overt ethnic practices could be observed. Within the ethnic family, 'middle-class' behaviours such as the general usage of English were accepted in relatively short order. Here 'ethnicity' was often experienced as an imagined identity, rather than as a set of observable ethnic practices. As the East Indian immigrants of St James in Winnipeg formulated it, beef consumption in Canada could be tolerated without affecting their identity, for 'after all it's the Indian, not the Canadian cow, which is sacred to the Hindus.'[52] Their household eating customs could be Canadian because their religious identity was based in homeland culture.

Some family members clearly were more open to change than others. The most reticent, of course, were the elderly. And, of the urban elderly, victims of racism seemed the most resistant to change. Lordson Wai-Chung Luk's 1971 study of elderly Chinese residents in Saskatoon identified pre-Second World War discrimination as a cause for reclusive behaviour a generation later. Thus, many 'have stayed in this country for nearly all of their life without knowing the English language' and 'most ... identify themselves as Chinese instead of Canadian.'[53] Daniel Wing Leung Lai and J.R. McDonald's 1995 examination of elderly Chinese residents of Calgary Chinatown senior citizens' facilities also identified the elderly as relatively unintegrated into Canadian society. Staying primarily within their ethnic institution, they were integrated only in that they relied on the state-based social safety net: 76 percent received an old-age pension and 36 percent social welfare payments. Most of these immigrants had come to Canada from mainland China without the ability to speak English; in 1995 fully 83 percent of these migrants still 'did not know ... any English at all.' Within their tightly knit circle, the group experienced high levels of social support, personal control, self-esteem, and physical health. The males noted that 'life satisfaction' was linked to 'financial adequacy'; women said that it was linked to 'length of residency in Canada' and 'English capacity.' But the survey also indicated that neither the men nor the women were especially interested in relating to the non-Chinese world.[54] Their most important guarantor of personal satisfaction was their ethnic-based 'social support' systems.

Middle-aged family members followed a more complex pattern. Signs of an invented ethnicity could be observed within the ubiquitous suburban bungalow. A 1984 description of a Greek home in Calgary makes the point: 'Katherina's ... house from the outside is an ordinary bungalow, but inside is a little bit of Greece ... [The] house is ... dominated by plants ... which give an overall impression of a garden balcony in

Greece.' The study continues that 'treasures brought from Greece on the many trips are in evidence' and that both 'the living room and the entrance are dominated by a large picture of the Acropolis of Athens, hand stitched by Katherina and framed in Greece.'[55]

Other studies, however, suggest that such ethnic household practice was affected by generation and class. Work on Sansei Japanese Canadians in Edmonton by Yoko Nakahara notes that these third-generation Canadians experienced a home-based ethnicity in starkly different terms, depending on whether they were professionals or members of the working class.[56] A surprising irony existed. It was the 'less-educated' Japanese, showing weak public cultural relationships with Japanese, who had high degrees of 'lived ethnicity'; that is, they were able to speak Japanese, were married to a Japanese person, and were partial to Japanese foods. In contrast, professional families – those with post-secondary education and close primary relationships, including marriage to non-Japanese people – indicated significant interest in 'Japanese culture such as arts, language and sports.'[57]

Several studies, however, suggest that most family members learned English quickly and even began relying on it for daily conversation. Indeed, as Gordon Darroch has argued, 'rapid inter-generational assimilation to English-language usage' occurred among immigrants; it was the 'ethnic media, ethnic politics and ethnic cultural and academic activities' where one encountered the most 'striking visibility and apparent persistence' of ethnicity.[58] These findings correspond to specific examples of second- and third-generation urbanized ethnic groups, such as the Ukrainians. In 1980 a study by Jeffrey Reitz and Margaret Ashton concluded that among recently arrived Ukrainian Canadians, 'language learning occurred in the first five years of life for 95% of the second and third generation respondents.' The Ukrainian language was spoken chiefly not within the family, but within public ethnic sites such as the church. This study, based on the 1971 census, demonstrated that fluent speakers of Ukrainian spoke it only 32 percent of the time within family, but 39 percent of the time with friends and 61 percent of the time with clergy.[59]

Scholars have suggested that the youth and children especially impelled the immigrant family to change.[60] In a 1981 study of university students belonging to thirty different ethnic groups in a 'large western Canadian university,' University of Calgary scholars James Frideres and Sheldon Goldenberg argued that ethnic identity seemed of little importance to the general student body. Of these students, 83 percent indicated that they 'often or sometimes' thought 'about being Canadian,' but only 32 percent 'often or sometimes' identified with an ethnic group. The authors concluded that it 'could be the case that the flowering of ethnicity in Canada is over and only the lingering perfume remains now that we [academics] are turning our attention, however belatedly to it.'[61] This study may not be conclusive in its argument that immigrant youth eagerly embraced opportunities to assimilate. Life stories, however, do add weight to the argument. In such an account, a University of Calgary female student of East Indian descent spoke of deep familial conflict in 1999. Sona Khosla reported 'secretly' dating men in contravention to her parents' 'preference for arranged marriages' with someone from her cultural group. She found herself 'vehemently opposed to learning Hindi … thinking that learning a foreign language is absurd when every-one I know speaks English'; on trips back to India she made a point of 'proudly claim[ing] that I was Canadian and not Indian.' She concluded that 'rapid assimilation' and a 'proud identification' with 'the beautiful traditions' of her culture are not contradictory.[62]

Younger children especially contributed to changes in family practice. The most apt examples in prairie cities were children of late-century Chinese immigrants. The western Canadian–Chinese community had endured a significant change in the 1960s when Cantonese-speaking professional immigrants from large Chinese cities overwhelmed the rural language of Taishanese, the once-dominant language of prairie Chinese enclaves.[63] By the 1970s, however, these Cantonese speakers faced challenges of their own from their school-aged children. A Saskatoon Chinese woman recalled that in the 1970s, 'during my school years … I wanted to be just like the other kids, I didn't want to be differ-ent … I didn't want any Chinese part of me to show.' When her father told her to be proud of her heritage, she answered, 'but, Dad it's so easy for you to say that – you don't have to listen to kids call you names.'[64] It was a small step for children who bore the brunt of assimilation pressure in school to take home their newly learned behaviour. Thus, Winnipeg children from the tailor-shop family named Tang were observed to have difficulty speaking Cantonese in the 1970s and to experience 'difficul-ties in assuming the parents' ethnic identity.' The result was 'a great deal of talking … among the children themselves' but 'little conversation be-tween the children and the parents' and even a need for 'interpretation by bilingual members of the family … in complex matters.'[65] A survey of Calgary Chinese adults in 1981 discovered that fully 81 percent of these citizens read 'mostly English newspapers,' 67 percent spoke mostly English with their children, and 43 percent also spoke mostly English to their spouse. They insisted that one did 'not have to speak Chinese in order to be Chinese,' as culture was a matter of 'values, attitudes and conceptions towards life and towards treating other people.'[66] Finally, a 1998 study of Winnipeg Chinese children reported on their mothers who lived in unilingual Chinese worlds, visiting Chinese grocers, restaurateurs, doctors, and even hairdressers, and hence spent 81 percent of their time speaking Chinese. The study found that even in these ethnic households, young children spoke Chinese only 49 percent of the time, while older children spoke it 60 percent of the time.[67] If the family was a haven of psychological comfort for children, it was not one for cultural maintenance and the perpetuation of parental ways.

Conclusion

The family remained a crucial social organism for the prairie immigrant throughout the century. In each of the decades, family shaped the very migration, establishing its timing, its destination, and the economic well-being of the newcomer. Over time most immigrants seemed to value the nuclear family, seek marriage, and cultivate relations within an extended kinship group; refugees in the 1920s, 1940s, and 1990s alike seemed deeply concerned by the absence of family support.

If family was the site for the immigrants' most primary and intimate of relations throughout the century, it became less and less of a barrier against host-society influences over time. Especially in the late-century decades it underwent significant change. Increasingly, it seemed, immigrants amalgamated old and new perceptions of the masculine and the feminine, of generational difference, of household and kinship. Sometimes the changes occurred in the context of intense conflict, including domestic violence. They occurred at different rates for different immigrants, depending on class, education, gender, and generation. Some immigrant women spoke of isolation from the wider world and estrangement from publicly savvy husbands; others described companionship and mutuality with husbands, as well as heightened status and freedom. Men who faced underemployment and separation from old-world communal status faced a significant upheaval, while those who 'made good' in a liberal society claimed to possess status both within the ethnic community and the wider world. The elderly had the least incentive to change; both preteen and teenaged children had the most incentive and served as catalysts within the ethnic family.

By the end of the century family was central not only to the immigrants' ethnic consciousness, but also to their integration strategies. The

1971 story of a one-time-sojourner Chinese man in Saskatoon summed it up nicely: only since being 'reunited with his family and children had he begun to plan to settle down in Canada and think of Canada as his permanent home.'[68] The immigrant family seemed to have become the very heart of the adaptation process for immigrants and their children in a new world. The family established the path for the immigrants' entry into the wider world.

chapter seven

Racism, Anti-Racism, and Race in Winnipeg

By the late-century decades, prairie citizens had grown accustomed to the activities of ethnic cultural networks and to the steady arrival of strangers from other backgrounds. In a number of striking episodes, however, racist incidents broke the surface of urban life. These were isolated events, typically, though they seemed to feed on deeper sentiments. People's long experience with ethnicity, their mid-century burst of volunteer activism related to immigrant services, and their invention of city-wide multicultural festivals combined to combat such expressions of hate. Because citizens responded so calmly to the arrival of newcomers of different heritages and because some challenged even the concept of 'race' itself, the late-century story of race and racism in these cities is worthy of attention. Winnipeg, with its century-long history of cultural diversity, illustrates the broader theme.

Racism

Like other major Canadian cities, Winnipeg relied on new sources of population growth in the late-century decades: Aboriginal people from northern reserves; and migrants from economically less-developed regions of the globe, including parts of Asia, Latin America, the Caribbean, the Mediterranean, and Africa. Filipinos and Aboriginal Canadians constituted the largest groups, numbering over 40,000 each in a total population near 700,000 at the end of the century. Social strains developed not just because of the numbers of newcomers but because, in culture and history, these immigrants represented a noticeable change from the mid-century arrivals. Their presence underlined the continuing power of skin colour and cultural difference to provoke racist incidents and yet the prevailing social calm suggested that other factors might also be at work, ensuring a degree of civic harmony.

Aboriginal Manitobans were the original inhabitants of the land, descended from people who had lived on its resources for several hundred generations. They had been governed separately by race-based legislation since Canada annexed the West a century before. An expression of their perspective on racism was George Barker's autobiography, *Forty Years a Chief*, published in 1979. Raised by his Native grandparents, living almost all his life in the bush and on a reserve, Barker attended school from time to time as a child and acquired a competency in reading and writing. But he also lived a life close to his ancestors: in his memoir he described in matter-of-fact phrases what is known as foretelling in Aboriginal culture and devoted an entire chapter to Aboriginal dance and drum ceremonies. Barker consistently reported the racial identity of the people he met, from the premier in his big office to the workers on the boats. About the crews on the steamers, he wrote: 'I was very well treated by all those with whom I worked, both white and Indian. Most of the captains were of English or Icelandic descent, but one, by the name of Cook, was Cree.'[1]

Barker's clear perceptions of race difference were reflected in widespread Aboriginal recognition of white racism. Residential schools, the *Indian Act*, loss of resources: the catalogue was familiar to Winnipeg residents and the consequences dire. The Aboriginal reaction to the shooting of a community leader by a Winnipeg police officer in 1988 and the Manitoba Aboriginal frustration that was partly responsible for the death of the Meech Lake constitutional amendment in 1990 both had their roots in such tensions. Beneath these issues lay the fundamental matters of income and economic power: as one member of a crime-reliant Aboriginal gang explained, whites had taken his people's land and now he and his colleagues were taking back some of the wealth.[2] For reasons of history and cultural difference, Aboriginal people accepted race as a category, identified racism as a fact of life in the city, and responded in race-conscious ways.

A number of Caribbean immigrants, all of whom were black, saw the city in comparable terms. One explained to historian Esyllt Jones that, in a predominantly white community like Winnipeg, 'racism is a given.' Many, but not all, reported that they confronted racism in a variety of contexts, whether on the job, at their children's schools, in their search for housing, or in their quest for career advancement. A man who endured a period of mental illness arising from feelings of uncertainty was encouraged, paradoxically, when his wife responded to his worries by saying, '"okay, that's the way it is because you are scared"… She was here before me, so she had some experience. So that way, she would help me out, to cope. Guys in the community would help … I'd read black magazines that would help you to understand a little bit better … It took a lot of hard, hard work, many years, even up until now.' Negative feelings were one part of the Caribbean immigrants' response to their new home.[3]

Outbursts of intolerance in the city were documented on a number of occasions. Several scuffles 'with racial overtones' occurred in local high schools in the 1970s and 1980s, one involving Filipino and white students; another, three black and three white girls. These springtime 'pushy-shovy things' (a principal's phrase) sometimes escalated into violence in which bottles were thrown or knives were pulled. The arrival of refugees from Vietnam in 1979 provoked a letter to a newspaper saying, 'Hitler would have known what to do …' An Asian defence committee alleged that 'the state has supported racist attacks against immigrants and other groups in Canada.' A representative of the Caribbean–Canadian Association reported 'inter-racial clashes and complaints of "blatant racism in job markets and schools" … [also] verbal abuse and threats directed towards East Indians.'[4] These moments of confrontation were noted and deplored in newspapers and public discussion before the news cycle moved on and citizens resumed their activities.

The most unsettling dispute in the public sphere arose not from differences of skin colour but, rather, from the century-old contest between defenders of the French and English languages. Having won a court case on their constitutional right to employ French in their relations with government, Franco–Manitobans sought a legal arrangement to implement the ruling. A wide range of established Canadians resisted the government's proposed solution with angry outbursts that, in some instances, could be described only as bigoted denunciations of French-speaking citizens. The so-called French-language crisis of 1983–84, one of the most shocking moments in Manitoba public life in several generations, underlined how fragile was the cultural and political consensus upon which democratic society rested.[5]

Despite the ugliness of such outbursts, the tenor of public commentary on racist incidents was remarkably calm. Time and again, from the 1960s through the 1990s, people in leading positions in the city insisted that racial discrimination was not a major public concern. A high school principal whose institution was, he said, 'as close to being a United Nations as possible,' commented in the aftermath of one scuffle: 'today's student is probably less biased racially than we were in my generation. We're not living on the edge of a precipice.' A teacher who ran 'tutorial classes for black youths experiencing problems in Winnipeg schools, said he is not aware of serious racial problems.' The Caribbean association spokesman who had noted racist abuse added that 'discrimination in Winnipeg against West Indians who are black, East Indians and Chinese was at a very low level.'[6]

How can the individuals' experience of racism and civic leaders' calm reactions to racist incidents be reconciled? Local stories seemed to demonstrate that a change in atmosphere did occur around mid-century. In the early-century decades, when 'race' applied variously to nation, religion, language, and skin colour, many British Canadians believed that Scottishness was a race, that English–Protestant and French–Catholic peoples should not mix, and that eastern Europeans were lesser beings. This link between national heritage and biology died a slow death in mid-century. So, too, did restrictions that targeted specific religious groups such as Jews. In 1944 Manitoba legislators ensured that quotas on the admission of Jews to medical school would be abandoned and, some years later, that restrictive covenants in land sales ended.[7] During the medical school debate, Dr. Dwight L. Johnson, a member of the legislature, expressed a widespread sentiment: 'at this particular time in the history of our country citizens of both sexes, all religions and every ethnic group represented in our land are giving of their blood and their lives, to destroy an international system based on prejudice, intolerance and racial discrimination. Are they coming back to find that we have allowed intolerance, prejudice and discrimination to become recognized principles in our own national life?'[8]

Civic leaders frequently associated the changes with the Second World War, when individuals from every group and occupation trained together and learned to rely on each other. Business leader Arthur Mauro, a university student in the late 1940s, recalled: 'Many of the very best [veterans] ... were now students. To my mind one of the finest national policies ever devised was D.V.A. [Department of Veterans' Affairs] support ... for post-secondary education ... there was this tremendous release of latent talent ... Discussions as to national and international developments were frequently intense. The impact we had on Winnipeg was that we knew each other. Many of the prejudices and misconceptions of prior generations were no longer sustainable.'[9] Mauro's belief that civic leaders outgrew many aspects of the city's race-based history during these short years is sustained, to a degree, by historians. Franca Iacovetta suggests that 'an ideology of cultural pluralism' developed in Canada during the mid-century decades.[10] Carmela Patrias and others have explained that a number of anti-discrimination laws gave expression to this 'upsurge of egalitarian idealism,' including city bylaws, provincial employment and housing legislation, and a national Bill of Rights.[11] But was this the idealism of elites rather than the practice of the people?

Winnipeg journalist Val Werier, writing in 1960, outlined the effect of 'second-hand discrimination ... a Canadian specialty.' In three cases, he said, black persons were refused jobs or accommodation in the city but the individual who practised discrimination blamed the decision on someone else, perhaps a husband or a co-worker whose sentiments allegedly forbade the hiring or housing of the newcomer. Werier had changed his opinion by 1965, however, when he wrote a long article suggesting that 'Some of the old prejudices may be wearing away.'[12] In retrospect, it is possible to say that he was right on both occasions.

If racist outbursts and pluralist celebration coexisted, one must still question why the positive view, the view that prejudices were eroding, came to prevail in late-century Winnipeg and whether such a claim ignored serious rifts in local society. One important thread in recent historical interpretation suggests that, in the United States, one-time immigrants, or second-generation children of immigrants, had simply been co-opted by the old elites. A seemingly generous, if belated, inclusiveness on the part of established citizens, these scholars argue, came at the expense of newcomers whose skin colour and cultures differed from the British and European standard. Was the quiet, soothing Winnipeg response to racist outrages merely the voice of complacency on the part of one-time targets of racial discrimination? Did the new members of the established classes owe their recently elevated status to the arrival of non-whites from northern reserves and less-developed countries?[13] These questions can be answered only by considering the public conversation on anti-racism and popular perceptions of race itself.

Anti-Racist Activities

By the late-century era Winnipeg had lost much of the lustre imparted by the rapid economic growth of the early-century decades. Eclipsed by its Alberta counterparts, its residents retained just a few significant advantages, among which an atmosphere of cultural pluralism and a diversified economy were often trumpeted by boosters. While Calgary and Edmonton, driven by boom and bust and boom again, adjusted hastily to waves of immigrants, and while their immigrant newcomers retained dual identities, Winnipeg's residents adapted to slow growth and talked more about civic pluralism. Perhaps because the city grew so slowly, its anti-racist public education activities had important consequences.

Winnipeg's social services for immigrants became much more extensive in the 1970s and 1980s. The International Centre, for example, introduced a weekly Saturday morning coffee party in 1970. This social event commenced at the request of provincial immigration officials as part of 'a more systematic procedure for welcoming newcomers to Winnipeg.' The party was choreographed by volunteers and, in the first instance, was aimed at young Filipino women who had been brought to the city to work in garment factories. It began at 11:00 and often ran as long as three or four hours, serving not just to introduce the new International Centre and its facilities to newcomers but as a means of teaching the centre's volunteers about the needs of the women. It featured a candle-lighting ceremony borrowed, volunteers assumed, from a church group's ritual, in which the most recent immigrant in attendance lit a 'candle of hope' at the front of the room to symbolize his or her hope 'for a good life in this new country,' and a representative of the International Centre lit a 'candle of friendship' to declare that 'the people of Canada were stretching their hands out in friendship.' After the two candles at the front of the room were lit, guests lit candles from them and placed these candles in centrepieces on tables around the room. Centre staff thought the idea was 'a bit folksy or naive' at the beginning but it quickly grew into an expected part of the routine and was said to be meaningful for those who participated. In just over three years, 182 parties had been held and over ten thousand people, newcomers and established Canadians, had attended, an average of over fifty guests per week, every week.[14]

The International Centre grew into a model institution and received national attention for its programs. When Prime Minister Pierre Trudeau introduced his government's new multiculturalism policy in 1971, he noted: 'Existing multicultural centres, like that in Winnipeg, have proven their value in providing services to help new immigrants to adjust to Canadian life, and in promoting inter-ethnic activity on a continuous basis.' Both aspects of this observation – immigrant adjustment and intergroup relations – spoke to the strengths of the institution. Increasingly, the centre's staff recognized that the immigrants themselves should manage the programs. Together, the established and the newcomers tackled the seemingly eternal problem of accreditation for previously acquired learning and skills. They set up more classes to teach English as a second language and more daycare places for mothers who wanted to study. They also recognized that counselling about domestic violence must be a priority. The centre's newly founded Language Bank called on the volunteer translation skills of interpreters in dozens of languages when hospitals, police, and courts needed such help. By 1987, when it moved into its fourth and largest home, the centre could claim, literally, to be a million-dollar facility offering a million-dollar program, and to mobilize sixteen thousand volunteer hours per year on behalf of over a thousand new 'clients' each year. As one of its senior officers explained, 'Our whole job is to help people to become the best Canadians they can be. Whatever you can do to get them there.'[15]

As the centre grew more reliant on public money, it ran into new sources of tension. Was its role primarily to coordinate volunteer social convenors and citizenship educators or to act as a professional agency working on immigrants' behalf? The new director of the centre observed that the 'old guard [were] nice people, they served coffee and held Bavarian nights' but they were no longer relevant. Greater numbers of refugees, and the shift in immigrant recruitment to globe-wide sources, meant that newcomers were often quite different in appearance and cultural background from the Winnipeggers who met them. The centre's leaders, by this time, were full-time employees. They decided that racism was the pressing challenge and that the International Centre must be the voice of the newcomers in the wider community. Not just a mediator in disputes, it was actually taking the immigrants' side in their struggles with the federal department of immigration and in their confrontations with racist behaviour in the city. Discrimination in employment, housing, education, and in public places all pushed the centre into the roles of advocate and defender.

Governments intervened in many other ways during the post-1970 decades as issues of racism rose to prominence on the public agenda. Despite its location in state institutions, however, one of the most noteworthy anti-racist campaigns was not originally driven by government intervention. Rather, teachers in the classroom, administrators in the school system, and faculty members in the University of Manitoba's Faculty of Education decided to make cross-cultural or multicultural understanding a central message within teacher education and in the schools. Teacher-training classes began to focus on how to counter racism and how to introduce themes related to plural citizenry and an immigration-based society. This teachers' initiative was followed up by civil servants in the province's Department of Education who helped to introduce a pluralist perspective into all the schools.[16]

Given that race-related tensions were so evident, how might the community consolidate what Charles Taylor describes as 'a politics of equal dignity'? In his discussion of this theme, Taylor revives Jean-Jacques Rousseau's proposal that a true republic hold open-air public festivals expressing its social ideal. Rousseau had written: 'Plant a stake crowned with flowers in the middle of a square; gather the people together there, and you will have a festival. Do better yet; let the spectators become an entertainment to themselves; make them actors themselves; do it so that each sees and loves himself in the others so that all will be better united.'[17] Civic leaders in Winnipeg unwittingly stumbled upon Rousseau's ideal in 1970 and nurtured it for the next four decades.

The festival notion began to develop decades earlier when Winnipeg's elites first recognized that cultural diversity was one of the city's distinctive features and could be relied upon to produce exciting ceremonial events. The discovery may have dated from an annual competitive music festival, founded just after the First World War, which presented school choirs 'made up of children of over twenty races, singing with perfect English diction, and without a sheet of music in evidence, the fine songs that are prescribed ...'[18] It was in full flight by the time of the city's sixtieth celebration of Canada's confederation in 1927 and the Canadian Pacific Railway's huge handicraft exhibition in 1928. Public acknowledgment of pluralism was then extended to the promotion of citizenship. The Imperial Order Daughters of the Empire introduced 'official ceremonies of welcome to newly-naturalized citizens' in the 1930s. Out of their struggle to find ways of expressing the city's variety in positive terms came the discovery that a ceremonial celebration, multicultural in nature, actually struck a chord with both the newcomer and the established Canadian.[19]

Canada's preparations for its centennial in 1967 moved the expressions of community identity to a new plane. As early as 1964, Ottawa's Centennial Commission planners were encouraging ethnic groups to plan special events for the country's 100th birthday. They held out the prospect of federal grants for 'projects of a performing arts, educational, and archivistic nature ...' Their enthusiasm happened to coincide with a growing interest in 'folk arts,' particularly in Toronto, where Stephan

Davidovich and Leon Kossar, council member and chair, respectively, of the city's Community Folk Art Council, proposed the founding of a 'national cultural coordinating council' for the movement. Winnipeg civic and ethnic leaders received this message enthusiastically and, in 1965, created their own Folk Arts Council of Manitoba. Its mandate was to coordinate folk festivals and exhibitions of folk arts, and to develop what an organizer described as 'an energetic programme [that] is truly an expression of the people and an integral part of a new, very fresh and very active, coast to coast cultural movement, a true movement of *the people*.'[20]

The Manitoba council's first enterprise was a concert called Folkways '66. It was succeeded by annual concerts in late winter through the late 1960s and early 1970s. The event typically featured song and dance performances by as many as twenty-five national groups, on at least one occasion accompanied by the city's symphony orchestra. Museums, as discipline and medium, provided a second source of inspiration. In 1967, as part of the celebration of Canada's centennial year, Sonja Roeder, a leader of the Citizenship Council, developed *Treasures from Many Lands* at a major downtown exhibition venue, the display windows of Eaton's department store. With the members of her organizing committee, she 'borrowed paintings, ceramics, furniture, clothing, old photographs, jewellery and other artifacts for display, with the intention of creating a better understanding between individuals and ethnic groups in Winnipeg. Written descriptions accompanied each object, emphasizing the object's owner, and his or her effort to maintain a distinct identity in Canada. The description also highlighted the individual's willingness to share [his or her] most beloved possessions with the Winnipeg community.'[21] It was a successful show, a version of a people's museum or gallery, and it encouraged thoughts of a repeat performance.

The council's next adventure was a brilliant stroke that combined the strengths of *Treasures from Many Lands* and Folkways while maintaining the vitality of grassroots commitment. As the provincial government approached Manitoba's centennial in 1970, it urged communities to undertake appropriate means of celebration. Cecil Semchyshyn, chair of the Folk Arts Council, who was always 'interested in preserving Canadian folk art,' suggested to the city's centennial celebrations committee that 'Winnipeg's cosmopolitan population' should provide 'the theme in a unique centennial festival ...' The city responded with a grant of $1500 to the council, specifying that the 'ethnic festival' be called Folklorama, a name borrowed from a similar event held in Fort William in 1967 and

modelled in part on that event and on Toronto's Caravan festival. Twenty
ethnic groups responded to his appeal for 'a display of the costumes,
crafts, foods and customs of their particular country of origin.' Folklorama
was an instant hit. The 'pavilions,' set up by volunteers, received nearly
one hundred thousand visitors, an average of five hundred visitors each
per night.[22]

Folklorama has been held annually since 1970. Though it has been
described at times as belonging in the context of major international
tourist attractions, such a claim is inappropriate. It is fairer to locate it as
a local and amateur event, not an international and professional one.
The festival mobilizes local cultural leaders to teach children about a
national heritage through the media of song, dance, and public exhibition. It oils the wheels of local ethnic organizations by placing considerable demands on their members, giving them an opportunity to earn
significant sums of money, and to renew annually the social connections
that accompany such a commitment. It involves citizens as performers,
parents of performers, administrators, exhibit guides, cooks, waiters,
and ushers who, as a cultural group, teach thousands of visitors a little
about their heritage. In these activities, they offer the rest of the city an
opportunity to survey a few artifacts, dances, dishes, and beers in the
rather utilitarian settings of local halls. More importantly, they situate
each group as equal to the others and they situate all groups as components of the city itself. That is Folklorama's merit: if every group has a
wine, a beer, some songs, and handsome child performers, then each
group is more or less like the others. Folklorama is a lesson in civics dis-
guised as people's entertainment. A recent executive director described
the festival as an 'authentic experience,' that rare treasure desired above
all else by those who market tourist attractions. What makes it authentic
is amateur performance and its creative expression of important tensions within the city. And the music, dance, and cuisine, though easily
mocked, provide ideal vehicles for community cultural renewal and self-
expression.[23]

When Tekla Obach died in 2005, her grandchildren recorded in her
newspaper obituary that 'Baba truly enjoyed Folklorama. We remember
how she introduced us to this festival. We also remember how we, as
young kids, couldn't keep up with her as she ran from one pavilion to
another. [She] was also extremely proud of her Ukrainian heritage. She
meticulously made each granddaughter a full Ukrainian outfit, including fine and precise embroidery on every piece of the ensemble. She
also had her doll collection which she clothed in Ukrainian attire. Her

embroidery was a work of art ... The stitches were tiny and precise, each one perfect.' The relation between the material expressions of a national heritage and the festival is unmistakable. Ms Obach's grandchildren interpreted her life as one in which pride in heritage was expressed through folk art. The art, in turn, was linked in their minds to her enthusiastic participation in Folklorama. The obituary was a measure of how the festival pulled heritage, family, folk cultural production, and the city into a single tangible and comforting expression.[24]

A survey of one thousand Winnipeg adults in 2006 demonstrated that significant currents of racism and of pluralism coexisted in the city. On the surface, the survey seemed to say that Winnipeggers had 'learned to accept people of other races.' It reported that

> 13 per cent of respondents believe racism has decreased in the last five years, and another 57 per cent believe the situation remains about the same ... A definitive majority of Caucasians, people of dark skin, and aboriginals all agree Winnipeg provides a welcoming environment for immigrants, while admitting some racial groups still have trouble adapting to life here. A similar majority of respondents across racial lines believes that people of all races are welcome in Winnipeg stores or businesses and that Canada on the whole is a much more interesting place to live because of our ethnic diversity ... A total of 91 per cent of respondents said they would be comfortable if a person from a different race moved in next door, and 92 per cent said they wouldn't cross the street to avoid a person of a different race. In terms of the company we keep, 91 per cent of respondents said they count people of different races in their circle of friends. And 61 per cent of respondents said they challenged someone face to face for treating a visible minority with disrespect because of their race.

'But is it an accurate picture?' asked Dan Lett, the journalist who wrote the story on survey responses. Though 70 percent believed racism had decreased or remained the same over the past five years, 22 percent believed it was on the increase. And how many of the respondents had experienced actual racial incidents? 'Eighteen per cent. But when the question was asked of aboriginals or people with dark skin, a much different response is given. Nearly four in 10 respondents with dark skin and 35 per cent of aboriginal respondents said they had experienced racism.' As Lett concluded: 'Leaders of visible-minority communities, immigration advocates and sociologists believe the poll results show that although racism has been driven underground, it remains part of the fabric of Winnipeg society. "If you're talking about people in general, attitudes are changing," said University of Manitoba sociologist Lori Wilkinson. "There is less acceptance now of racial slurs. But we're still fighting some battles on the covert forms of racism."[25]

A half-century of anti-racist campaigns had made a difference. They did not eliminate racism but they did establish accommodation and restraint as dominant notes in Winnipeg's public sphere. The expansion of social services and anti-racist activities at the International Centre, the development of anti-racist education in the schools, and the city-wide success of the Folklorama phenomenon ensured that the mid-century elites' pluralist language and ideals now touched all levels of society. But, if the tone of public conversation had moderated, the expression of racist attitudes should have remained a concern. Given the arrival of immigrants from northern Manitoba and the Global South, American historians such as Roediger and Jacobson would argue, the racist challenge had simply moved to new spheres. Still, the relative calm of civic leaders' responses bears further reflection. Was there something distinctive about the Winnipeg, and prairie, pluralist outlook by the end of the twentieth century? The answer may lie in popular perceptions of race.

Race: Masako Kawata and Her Parents

The differences between mid-century and late-century perceptions of race may be encapsulated in the experience of one Winnipeg family. The changes embodied by two generations of the Kawata family illustrate how rigid boundaries between peoples diminished over time and how an increasingly hybrid prairie culture reinforced anti-racist rhetoric.

Masako Kawata was four years old in 1942 when government authorities ordered her Japanese–Canadian family to leave their farm south of Vancouver. In June of that year, they travelled by train to a Manitoba sugar beet farm where they were housed in a granary. Masako excelled in her studies, received a bursary to attend university, graduated with a Bachelor of Science in Home Economics degree, taught for a few years, and then switched to an administrative position where she flourished for three decades. Determined to recover her family's story, she collaborated in an oral history project and interviewed her parents when they were in their nineties.[26] She was surprised by the result:

My mother's story is amazing. She was born in 1915 in Vancouver. She was
the eldest of nine surviving children. At the age of six or seven, she travelled

on her own from Canada to Japan and lived there for six years. She complained a lot, she says. After all, she had been born in Canada and the village in which she lived in Japan with her grandparents was very poor. She returned when she was twelve, received a few years of schooling, and then worked as a domestic. She married when she was nineteen.

My father's story is also amazing. He was born in Honolulu, Hawaii, in 1905, the youngest of four children, and his family soon moved back to Japan. When he was very young, his father died. Father received some schooling in Japan and, at the age of twenty-four, in 1930, he came to Canada as an immigrant farm labourer sponsored by a Japanese family in Delta [British Columbia]. He had to work for them for three years. In 1934, he married my mother and they bought land near her parents. They cleared the land and raised chickens and sold eggs and strawberries. Four children followed in the next few years.

The Kawata family story illustrates how perceptions of 'race' changed over the course of the twentieth century. The elder Kawatas, like Saul Cherniack, were born early in the century. They were regarded by others as belonging to a distinct, racially defined group, they accepted such categories themselves, and they perceived this 'race'-based identity as biological and inescapable. They joined thousands of others in the government-ordered expulsion of the Japanese from coastal areas of British Columbia in the early months of 1942. Five years and three homes later, they moved to Winnipeg and adapted to life in the polyethnic North End. 'Dad found work with the help of a friend but the authorities would not approve. They said that workers were needed in the [Winnipeg] public abattoir so he took a job there, though he didn't like the job ... He also found a house and paid two months rent but, again, the authorities would not approve because there were too many Japanese families already living in the East Kildonan area ...' In short, government and military officials determined the Kawatas' migrations, place of work, and choice of home, in each case basing their decisions on 'racial' or 'national' factors.[27]

Informal racism also shaped the Kawatas' daily life in Winnipeg during the 1940s. Masako Kawata recalled: 'Racism existed but it was not a big issue ... I think that life in ... Winnipeg was marked by a subtle racism. Some people treat you differently. You sense it, feel their body language, so you walk away. You don't confront it. It's often not verbal because people don't want to voice such opinions. Children will say such things out loud, especially younger kids. We would chase them all the way home to their parents. They would think we were Chinese. The kids must have learned these views from someone in order to have voiced them. Most clerks in stores would serve you last, even Eaton's and the Bay. We would try to avoid the small stores that treated us in this way. We did hear racist remarks but we would always try to avoid confrontation.' This view of 'race' as an irreducible barrier was, seemingly, a fact of life in the elder Kawatas' generation.

Travel forward thirty or forty years, however, and 'race' was not an inevitable aspect of daily life. Masako Kawata's career illustrated the change. She was conscious of skin colour and other physical identifiers as factors shaping her family's experience when she was a child. But she did not see such categories as meaningful during her adult years. When asked directly about her race, Ms Kawata said:

I never think of myself as Japanese alone. I say Japanese-Canadian because I haven't retained a lot of Japanese ways and, basically, as I said, I lived a Canadian life. My 'race' is Japanese-Canadian. My features and everything – I can't say I'm a Canadian, I look different. People to this day ask me where I'm from. They don't really mean to say that, they're asking if I'm Chinese, Vietnamese. What they mean is 'what is your ancestry?' There are a few who think you're from another country. They ask how you learned to speak English so well. There are so many new immigrants ... Is it race? *Something* is shaping you differently. I don't know if it's biological, but it's ingrained from when you were born. Maybe the attitudes that you learn at an early age. You're taught certain things ... I'm not competent to talk about race at a genetic level but there aren't inner differences.

And that was her conclusion. She may have looked different from someone of European ancestry, may have had responses to the world that were learned from her parents and inherited from earlier generations, but 'there aren't inner differences.' Race was a thorny concept for her and not one to which she could attach unambiguous meanings.

One of the highlights of the Kawata family history was the 'redress' settlement of 1988, the Canadian government's official apology for the wartime evacuation. When she came to this point in her story, Masako Kawata said: 'I was never Japanese. I'm a Canadian in every way in my outlook. I had very little from my heritage. [What did I do with the redress settlement?] ... I thought it was a good idea to buy some Japanese cultural works – I thought it was better than just spending the money. We never had original prints or pottery in our family – so I bought some

– in Vancouver, in Hawaii, in Winnipeg – some beautiful prints and some pottery and this little lacquered tray that I got in a garage sale for a dollar – a beautiful work, an heirloom, and it was in this sale that I found by accident.'

Masako Kawata's feeling about alleged racial differences reflected changes in the wider community and in the scholarly world. Race mattered less when she made these comments than in earlier generations. Racism still existed in her world, and so did race-based judgments, but 'race' as a category distinguishing meaningfully between and among humans was now contested. Such a debate was new. It was being conducted by such scholars as the sociologist Paul Gilroy, who argued that race must be rejected as an organizing category in discussions of contemporary humankind.[28] Though she did not follow the academic literature, Ms Kawata travelled the same path. For her, racism was an important historical and contemporary issue but physical differences – skin colour, hair, facial and body characteristics – were not matters of relevance in the public sphere. In her view, the intellectual or social or cultural differences often associated with such characteristics had other explanations than the biological.

In the terms employed by political philosopher Charles Taylor, the Kawata family story offers valuable illustrations of individuals' perceptions of their 'identity.' Taylor defines identity as 'a person's understanding of who they are, of their fundamental defining characteristics as a human being.' In modern societies, he writes, discussions of identity are accompanied by analyses of 'recognition and misrecognition'; that is, estimates of how one's identity is shaped by the perceptions of others, 'so a person or group of people can suffer real damage, real distortion, if the people or society around them mirror back to them a confining or demeaning or contemptible picture of themselves ... imprisoning someone in a false, distorted, and reduced mode of being.' Taylor suggests that democratic societies such as modern Canada embrace 'a politics of equal recognition, which has taken various forms over the years, and has now returned in the form of demands for the equal status of cultures and of genders.'[29]

The Kawata family narrative offers two illustrations of that demand for the equal status of cultures. The first is represented by the senior Kawatas, who sustained significant reverses in the course of their lives, especially because of the decisions taken by government in wartime. They wanted the label of 'alien' removed. The second is associated with Masako Kawata, who believed that her own claim to citizenship had been accepted with little or no dissent during her adult life. She looked at redress from the perspective of a thoroughly integrated Canadian whose history contained one stain and whose commitment to the community required that the historic error be acknowledged.

Both generations supported the redress campaign, though for different reasons. The elder Kawatas were not bitter. They chose to 'look forward rather than back ...' They did not 'impose their Japanese views' on their children, says Masako, because they believed such inheritances 'had to be suppressed in order to get along in society.' But they did believe that an official government apology was necessary. Masako, in contrast, retained only a few of the conventional markers of ethnicity in her daily life, including food ('my mother always cooked half-Japanese and half-Canadian'), and a few – though strong – links to the local Japanese–Canadian community. She had fewer connections to such other markers of ethnicity as language, faith, and national memory. But she accepted both the history of the Japanese–Canadian group's forced resettlement and a family history that concentrated on integration rather than consciousness of ethnic cultural differences. The 'Japanese' aspect of her identity had two meanings: one that was based on her *social* attachments and another that had *civic* and *political* dimensions. She joined her parents and the local ethnic community in the redress campaign partly from a desire for vindication of her community and partly from a desire to educate Canadians about respect for the rights of all citizens. Thus, the two generations of the Kawata family looked at redress from different angles. The elders wanted an apology and then to forget and move on; the younger generation wanted to remember, to commemorate, and to teach. Both emphasized Japanese Canadians' equal place in Canadian society, as Charles Taylor emphasized.

The Winnipeg encountered by the two Kawata generations also differed. The elder Kawatas experienced the effects of racism in Winnipeg during the 1940s, recognized that public attitudes to 'race' shaped their lives in Canada, and accepted these categories. Masako Kawata's fulfilling career began in the 1960s and 1970s. Outside her workplace, she found spheres in which to make voluntary contributions, including the Japanese–Canadian cultural centre and a pavilion in Winnipeg's summer festival, Folklorama. In these institutions she was able to address racism and explore her ethnicity in practical, everyday ways. She felt a greater degree of individual authority – greater control over her own life and greater responsibility for the wider community – than her parents had known. She established a sense of belonging within civil society, a sense of 'ownership' of the whole, that was greater than had been possible in previous generations. In Charles Taylor's terms, her identity was more complete, less distorted by the views of those around her, than was possible for her parents. Moreover, in the terms originally set out by Fredrik Barth, the boundary zones in which Masako Kawata encountered the host society had become more benign, more genuinely plural in their acknowledgement of her group's equal status and of her worth as an individual.

Conclusion

Experience of racism and anti-racism takes place at the level of the city and region as well as on a national and global scale. In Winnipeg, expressions of racist hostility occurred through the half-century after 1945. They evoked concern but not panic, however, as civic leaders came to recognize that the outbursts were not likely to degenerate into broadly based confrontations between groups. The one exception was the battle over the status of the French language in 1983–4. In many arenas, including citizenship ceremonies, Folklorama pavilions, the International Centre, and the schools, public conversations about race and racism – and anti-racism – increasingly involved ordinary citizens.[30] The city's construction of cultural pluralism through public education provided a more inclusive context within which citizens could interpret and communicate their daily experience. And the Kawata family experience, which moved in two generations from a rigid construction of race to rejection of the concept, and from bleak experiences of racism to confidence in one's ability to transcend it, offered a ray of hope for all plural societies at the turn of the twenty-first century.

chapter eight

Prairie Links in
a Transnational Chain

The networks that defined the immigrant worlds in the prairie city grew more complex throughout the late-century decades.[1] During this time the various prairie centres became interwoven into a series of transnational lines connecting the immigrants to familiar and unfamiliar sites around the globe. A globalizing economy and neo-liberal policies overtook what Eric Hobsbawm has referred to as 'older units such as the "national economies" defined by the politics of territorial states.'[2] Added to technological innovation, these economic changes meant that newcomers increasingly charted their lives within social and cultural webs that had not just one centre, but two or even three. One point was located in their new prairie home – in urban households, ethnic centres, places of worship, sites of employment. But the others were situated in the old homeland across the seas or in a third country, perhaps an economically necessary place of sojourn. Simply put, the immigrants increasingly lived 'their lives across national borders'[3] and pursued their 'life projects in multiple contexts,' in settings Dirk Hoerder has suggested constituted a 'trans-regional' or a 'transcultural space.'[4]

Life in those spaces may have highlighted 'shifting identities,' as Adam McKeown has argued, but that did not erase 'pressing issues of local politics and acceptance.'[5] These links, for example, shaped the immigrants' social behaviour: they could dictate the migration pathways and the range of available economic choices; they could enable consumer habits, health strategies, manners of communication, childhood education, life-cycle rituals, and even leisure activities. Transnational webs could also shape the immigrants' very world views; certainly, they reflected what Robin Cohen dubs diasporic cultures with their ambivalent yearning and nostalgia for the 'homeland'[6]; and those networks were informed by a mental map, anchoring immigrant imaginings in old homelands, ironically providing cultural resources that enabled their adjustment to new settings.

Technological, economic, social, and political changes associated with the increased late-century momentum of economic globalization affected the prairie city in specific ways. Changes in technology radically shortened the very long distances between places of origin and city of immigrant destination. Neo-liberal trade policies made the Canadian metropolises and the country's capital seem less important, while competition for world recognition made an image of international, cosmopolitan, inclusive culture more important. The resulting economy linked the Prairies' resource-driven and agriculturally driven sectors even more indelibly in a global market economy. That economy rewarded cosmopolitan-minded professional and entrepreneurial classes of immigrants who came to work the oil patch, the increasingly scientific farm and farm-service industries, the transportation sectors, and the supporting social services. That economy itself benefited from the unseemly consequence of globalization; that is, from disrupted local economies overseas that created a mobile, internationalized labouring class willing to work in a regional economy with the hope of returning home with the 'golden fleece.'

Finally, a prairie-driven transnationalism was spurred on by provincial governments. Certainly national governments had long benefited from transnationalism: sending states for immigrant remittances and diplomatic ties; and receiving states for economic advantages brought by skilled immigrants and for the opportunity to hone national mythologies rooted in a generous, inclusive image as a home to the newcomer, especially the refugee.[7] Canada may have repositioned its international image from valuable partner in the British Empire to independent, socially conscious global neighbour, but the prairie capitals did their own reconfiguring. Not only did they support trade missions seeking to sell regionally derived commodities and wares, they produced cultural and educational exchanges that built on the rich cultural tapestry of the immigrants of former decades.

Both the economic and cultural analyses of transnational behaviour challenge notions of unilinear integration. In the older nation-centred view, the migrant travelled in one direction, into a nation-state that saw itself as an unshakeable, territorialized thing. But from the perspective of an increasing number of immigrants, travel was transnational rather than one way; migrants moved within a web of nations and citizenships with relative ease. Still, one might assert that transnationalism simply recognizes the effect of technology, politics, and cultural diversity on the lifeworlds of the migrants. For all urban newcomers, destination and points of origin became increasingly blurred, at least within their own views of self, locale, region, and state.

Precursors of Transnational Ties in Prairie Cities

In order to understand the late twentieth-century prairie migrants' transnational web, it is instructive to trace its development over the course of the century. Early mechanized travel relied on slow-moving ships and trains, and was informed by equally slow-moving overseas mail and immigrant newspapers. The trip into Canada's interior was itself arduous enough to spell separation from the homeland. In the early days, prairie-bound immigrants faced a lengthy transoceanic voyage and then the demands of a strenuous multi-day trip by train, and many seemed to wonder whether the extra leg of the journey was worth the effort. Laments such as Winnipeg-bound Jewish immigrant S.F. Rodin's in 1882 were not uncommon: only after travelling 'about a thousand Persian miles from the Atlantic Ocean' did his party reach Winnipeg, where he witnessed 'abhorrent tears ... stream from the cheeks of the people who came here with me' and he himself felt 'like an outcast ... looking towards the sky ... grief in an arid and sunken land.'[8] The very fatigue and exhaustion the immigrants experienced during the trip inland kept most from considering an equally arduous return migration. Compared to the personal links made possible by late-century communications technology, the migrants' ties to the homeland in 1900 were relatively more fragile.

Still, some transnational linkages existed in the first third of the century. The prime transnational agent during this time was, of course, the prairie sojourner. The foreign workers, the so-called navvies, who built the Canadian Pacific and Canadian Northern railways, worked the mines in the Rockies, and served in threshing gangs for farm families were restless men. They arrived in western Canada having traversed half a dozen countries along the route and fully expecting to travel back to the old homeland. And they might return to Canada several times. Marriage often put an abrupt stop to these transnational wanderings, leaving only memories and an openness to communication across cultural lines. Remarkable exceptions existed, of course, revealing just how strong the lure of the economy in the new world and the pull of the village in the old world could be.

Dirk Hoerder recounts the story of Giovanni Veltri, who lived in Winnipeg for most of the years from 1905 to 1931. Veltri had first travelled to the

United States from Italy via France and Belgium in 1885 as a single eighteen-year-old sojourner on the advice of an older brother. He returned home a few years later, served a stint in the Italian army, married Rosa Anselmo, and then, in 1895, with Rosa pregnant, he left again, alone, as a sojourner for North America. He renamed himself John Welch and came to western Canada, where he worked as a Canadian Pacific Railway supervisor until 1900, when he returned to Italy again, rejoined his wife, and began working the land of Calabria. In 1905 'after the grape harvest' he returned a third time to North America, now accompanied by his eldest son, but with his wife and daughters remaining in Italy. From a base in Winnipeg he ran railway-related businesses with fellow Italian–Canadian partners. He returned to Italy once between 1905 and 1924, during which time his wife and daughters finally joined him in Canada. But in 1931 they convinced him to return to Italy a final time. Mentally the aging Veltri lived 'suspended between Calabria and the prairies,' but knew that 'living in two cultures and many locations never hindered his efficient functioning.'[9]

Nationalist loyalties in the homeland also sent some early-century migrants home for times of visit and interaction. Immigrants could easily refashion themselves as warriors, willing to fight in old-world struggles. In 1912 Greek immigrants Athanassios Papadopoulos and Louis Georgopoulos left the Calgary homes they had established in 1903 and returned to Greece to battle the Bulgarians in the Balkan Wars. Papadopoulos died in the Battle of Tjourmayia, while Georgopoulos returned to Calgary a hero and successfully cajoled the Calgary Greek community to support war relief in Greece.[10] Just how many Ukrainian Canadians responded to Bishop Nicetas Budka's call is not known, but during the First World War this Winnipeg Ukrainian Catholic cleric publicly denounced 'Russian policy in the Ukraine,' and in 'a pastoral letter … spoke of Austria as the threatened fatherland' and urged all male Ukrainians to 'immediately report to the consulate and leave for the old country.'[11] Similar calls for political support in the old world also reached the Prairies' Chinese residents. Prasengit Duara has argued that the Chinese government had successfully used the sentiments of 'pan-Asianism to incorporate peripheral peoples … into the empire.'[12] With equal success, political activists travelling through western Canada brought Chinese politics to the periphery. Local chapters of the Empire Reform Association, the Bo Wung Wai, were founded in prairie cities in 1910 as a result of transnational visits. This interest in the homeland escalated in 1916 when military units were formed among the small Saskatoon and

Edmonton Chinese communities. Some two hundred men from Canada headed off to Shandong province to resist the resurgence of old imperial forces and to bolster constitutional armed forces.[13]

For most of the early-century migrants, however, transnational lines served less to direct behaviour than to shape a simple, lasting, imaginative construct. Those left behind daily recalled their adventurous kin, just as newcomers made frequent 'mental visits' to their old-world kin. Brian Ross's study of early-century Italians in Winnipeg notes that when sojourners came to Canada, a type of transnationalism ensued among those in the homeland, one in which 'the migrant was still counted within the social organization he had left behind' for 'he was still considered to be an active and viable [member] although [a] "temporarily" removed component.'[14] This imagined transnationalism was also true for the migrants themselves. Often it was bolstered by continued legal ties; Canada, for example, might not have granted the Chinese citizenship until 1947, but the Chinese practised *jus sanguinis*, the automatic conferring of Chinese citizenship on any son born outside China, even though there was little chance the son would return home.[15] Even for those both legally and physically removed from the homeland, a ceaseless transoceanic yearning was common. Russian Jews, for example, were barred from returning by threat of pogroms and yet, as Gerald Tulchinsky explains, 'connections with kinfolk still in *der alter Heim* ... continued.' They 'corresponded with their families in Europe, sending news, remittance and photographs of their spouse and children ... and in return received family and regional news, gossip and publications.' Moreover, an overpowering nostalgia accompanied the singing of 'songs like *Belz*, an enormously popular Yiddish theatre song that expressed longing for hometowns in Eastern Europe.'[16]

Such transnational yearnings were certainly expressed more often as sentiments within immigrant organizations in prairie Canada than as actual return migrations. Among the most vibrant of organizations with a transnational focus were women's groups. Frances Swyripa writes that Ukrainian women in particular were involved in seeking independence and status for their homelands. An early women's nationalist organization was the 1922 socialist Women's Section of the Ukrainian Labour-Farmer Temple Association, with some four hundred members in Winnipeg. A second organization, the Ukrainian Women's Association of Canada (UWAC), was a pan-Canadian association of Greek Orthodox Church women who espoused a 'nationalist cause' and an international perspective, from its base in the Saskatoon Ukrainian girls' residential school, the Mohlylianky. A third and even more important organization, the right-wing Ukrainian Women's Organization of Canada (UWOC), was founded in 1930 among the 'women's branches of the Ukrainian War Veteran's Association'; in Saskatoon these women raised monies for a variety of overseas causes, while in Winnipeg they protested 'anti-Ukrainian pogroms in Galicia.'[17] Krystyna Lukasiewicz describes similar behaviour among Polish women during the 1930s. In Calgary these women were encouraged by the Polish consulate to express their nationalism and especially to celebrate national Polish anniversaries. As one woman recorded, 'just before the Second World War ... I organized a concert for the 3rd of May. We invited the Polish consul from Ottawa, ... Bishop Carrol of Calgary and [representatives from] other institutions ... I put in a lot of work but it was worth it as everyone was congratulated and satisfied.' Another woman, who taught Polish dances and history at the Polish Society, or the Club, as it was known, noted that 'I enjoyed this kind of activity. And although it was very exhausting physically, it gave me a great inner satisfaction.'[18] Here was a virtual transnationalism, an imagined link in lieu of actual physical interaction.

This chasm between new and old worlds would widen before it narrowed. Indeed, during the mid-century decades the immigrants were cut off from their homelands by political fortunes. Many were displaced persons, refugees from war-ravaged countries. They had left behind the Eastern bloc European or Southeast Asian countries that were governed by communist regimes. Mid-century refugees from eastern Europe may have been dedicated 'to the liberation of their homelands,' but their lands were out of reach, firmly under Soviet control. The immediate goals of these immigrants were overwhelmingly domestic and even isolationist: 'to keep their homeland culture and language alive in Canada, uncontaminated by the influences of Soviet communism.'[19]

Canadian policy did not sanction political contact between its immigrants and liberation movements in former homelands. Immigrants with roots in the wartime Axis and post-war communist countries were the most affected. After 1938 when Adolf Hitler's Kristallnacht signalled the potential of his terror, and especially after the outbreak of war in 1939, German immigrants faced a stark choice: quietly cultivate the transnational Volkish ties or assimilate completely into Canadian society. Italian Canadians faced the same choice and they responded similarly: when Calgary Italian leader Consul Antonio Rebaudengo was arrested in 1940, his wife destroyed all his papers, not to exonerate Rebaudengo, but 'to prevent any other Italian from being interned.'[20] Similar breaks occurred for immigrants from socialist countries. Leftist and nationalist Ukrainian women's organizations declined as the Cold War set in. When, during the 1950s, the UWOC in Winnipeg and Edmonton sought renewal, it downplayed nationalistic goals and emphasized its 'liaison with the Canadian Red Cross and other mainstream women's organizations.'[21] Increasingly, the symbol of hope for second-generation urban Ukrainians was not revolution in Ukraine but the romanticized grandmother pioneer, the Baba of the Canadian Prairies. Indeed, the 'baba as an icon,' complete with coloured Easter eggs and ethnic crafts, helped Ukrainians lay claim to their place in nation building, as one of the founding peoples of western Canada.[22] By 1954, when Ukrainian novelist Vera Lysenko wrote *Yellow Boots*, the main protagonist, the 'strong-willed' Lili, gained ascendancy through 'a successful blending of the Old and New Worlds.' As Tamara Palmer suggests, Lili's 'death and recovery … [was] an important and unifying symbol of immigrant adaptation to the New World.'[23]

When mid-century immigrants created organizations to plan for transnational encounters, their impossible agenda was the liberation of their homelands from Soviet domination. All they could hope to do was to bring attention to the oppressiveness of Soviet-imposed communism. Polish veterans, argues Joanna Matejo, often 'became bitter and divorced themselves from Canadian realities, living in the past and remembering days of glory on the battlefields.'[24] Post-war Calgary Polish newcomers, writes Kathryn-Anne Rhea Watts, despaired over the prospect of Poland's liberation during the Cold War and turned their resources to the building of an 'imagined homeland' in Canada. In the end they could show their old-world nationalism only by associating 'with one another and emphasiz[ing] their Polishness' in a rich array of community institutions. But in doing so they maintained 'a Polish community outside of Poland' and used it 'as an asset' in the ideological battles of the Cold War.[25] The best way to liberate the homeland was to perpetuate it overseas.

Post-war immigrants able to cultivate transnational ties, such as Italians and Greeks, sometimes seemed uninterested in doing so. Antonella Fanella's study of Calgary Italians does reveal some active links, such as the Italian Canadian Club's contacts with the Italian government to 'assist Italians through the entire emigration-immigration process.' But these connections ensured that the migrants made a one-way voyage, not that they maintained close bonds with Italy. Aside from the ritual planting of grape vines in their backyards or perhaps a fig tree in a greenhouse, the Italians seemed content to celebrate memories of the old world within their new settings. Then, too, they venerated 'their value system, *la via vecchia*,' and sought to cultivate it in Calgary; after all, it provided a useful identity in Canada, a conservative moral code for child rearing, an explanation of the meaning of migration, and, indeed, a tool for upward mobility. This ethnic invention was especially practical as immigrants integrated into Calgary's booming middle-class culture. But it also reflected the antipathy they felt for Italy. Life in wartime and postwar Italy had been difficult, but more importantly, many immigrants fundamentally disagreed with Italian government policies. Hailing mostly from the more tradition-bound southern Italian states of Abruzzi and Calabria, the prairie Italians were skeptical of Rome's cultural liberalism and economic might. Specifically, they questioned Italy's post-war nationalism, asking how the new education laws of 1948 that required 'reading Dante or learning Latin was going to result in an improved standard of living.' Moreover, they questioned Rome's integrity, spoke of shattered dreams, said they were 'tired of broken promises' and that in economic terms they, the southerners, 'would never catch up to the north.' Modern Italy had failed them.[26]

Certainly transnational ties and yearnings existed in the first two-thirds of the century. But the great distances between the prairie city and the immigrants' points of origin, coupled with cumbersome and expensive transportation links, made such ties tenuous at best during the first third of the century. Wartime destruction and Cold War politics in the 1950s compromised even the ties that had existed. All this changed in the late-century decades.

The Ascendancy of Late-Century Transnational Ties

Transnational linkages increased dramatically in the last third of the century. A series of contradictory forces worked in concert to create a tighter and more emotionally charged entanglement with the homelands. A globalized economy linked both sending and receiving societies into a single economy, while locally oriented ethnicities and state-less nationalities solicited strong loyalties. Meanwhile the world became smaller as the ability to traverse great spaces with jet travel, long-distance telephone, cable television, and the World Wide Web grew exponentially. Moreover, some of Canada's immigration selection policies favoured educated or skilled immigrants, and most of these newcomers were able to move quickly into the middle class and acquire the means to cultivate personally and economically rewarding ties with homeland contacts. By the 1980s, too, the nature of Canada's own national identity had evolved, leading it to champion multiculturalism, plural citizenship, international peacekeeping, and a relatively liberal refugee policy. Finally, seemingly impenetrable barriers suddenly opened as Soviet communism collapsed and Chinese communism embraced a mixed economy and relationships with the West. Each of these phenomena helped turn the immigrant into a transmigrant, a transnational citizen, a traveller who could feel at home in several nations.

The most obvious causes of increased transnational activities were post-war technological changes. Jet travel had itself made migration seem less permanent. Families now were usually a day from home, and they returned regularly. Studies document the new-found ease of international travel. East Indians of Winnipeg flew home to maintain their transplanted caste-based cultures by seeking the right mates for their children: Pereira's 1971 study suggested that 'a high caste Hindu of marriageable age normally feels the pressure to select a mate from his region and his caste, even though he (or she) may have to spend several thousands of dollars to travel to India for this purpose.'[27] Filipinos in Winnipeg, according to Buduhan's 1972 study, flew home in large numbers at Christmas, using 'annual chartered vacation flights to the home country' to courier 'mail, gifts or information ... to and from each other's families.'[28] Chinese people of Calgary took flights back to China to nurture native languages: one family described in 1980 how they took their children to China for a period of 'three years so they could learn more about Chinese culture and language' and overcome a developing 'language barrier.'[29] For Greeks in Calgary, it was a matter of using 'modern communication techniques [and] air transportation' to maintain kinship ties. Minions's 1984 study asserted that all the migrants who had been interviewed for her study had 'visited Greece since migration, some regularly every two to four years,' and all migrants 'kept in touch regularly with close relatives in Greece,' if not by travel, then 'through a monthly phone call.'[30]

These transnational ties were also encouraged by a globalizing economy that relied on cross-border labour markets. The highest profile migrants in this economy were skilled workers and executives of multinational corporations who moved easily from one country to another. Donald Smith points out that 'thanks to the investment ... in the oil and gas industry by French and Belgian interests, a number of companies such as

Aquitaine, Elf and Total of France [became] … active in Alberta [and] … employed a number of French personnel in the province, particularly in Calgary.'[31] Similarly, Max Rubin documents two different groups of Jews in the Alberta cities: one group that 'settled in Calgary because of the city's position as the petroleum capital of Canada, many [of whom] associated with the petroleum industry in Israel'; and a second, being mostly 'from professional classes,' whose friends tended to be fellow Israelis.[32] Transnational business ties also included small business, often import enterprises, specializing in foods and gifts. According to Chow's 1981 study, one Winnipeg Chinese man used 'connections that his family in Hong Kong [had] established with the jewellers in Bangkok, and [was] selling precious stones, pearls and the like to local jewellers in Winnipeg.' Later, he also began 'acting as a middle-man for big distributors such as Eatons, Sears, K-Mart and Shell for such items as vacuum bottles, and toys from Hong Kong.'[33]

At the other end of the class spectrum were labourers guided to the Canadian Prairies as one district in a global labour market. Teal's study of Korean workers in Edmonton puts the phenomenon in starkly formulaic terms: 'the incorporation of Korea into the international division of labour as a source of cheap labour power' began with the 'subordination of Korean labouring classes as a reserve army of labour and a cheap labour force for foreign capital operating in Korea.'[34] Buduhan's work on Filipino garment workers in Winnipeg offers the same interpretation through the stories of young women. Having first left their families in northern Luzon province for American textile factories in the vicinity of Manila, these women were recruited by the hundreds by Winnipeg textile companies and Canadian Pacific Airlines. Their apprehensive families agreed to allow their daughters to leave for 'America' for a simple reason: the *mahirap* and *walang natapos* 'are better off for they have someone in America sending them dollars, [the great] *nagpapadala*.' A diary entry of a Winnipeg garment worker in about 1968 recorded the happy event of sending the first remittances: 'Oh my salary is big but the tax is also big … $7.35 is the income tax removed from $61.51! However, I am thankful to the Almighty God … for He gave me great things. I got the money order of $25.00 to send tomorrow. This will be used to buy benches for the … home barrio chapel.' A short time later came this entry: 'Now I have sent my very first money order to my parents. I sent only $16.00 to them for this is only a trial to see if it will really reach them without problem. I even wrapped it with carbon paper and then hid it inside a Christmas card. I should have sent more but this is only a trial.'

The response from home by letter completed this transnational act. His family replied: 'how fortunate the immigrant is to be rich and safe, and how the family is sharing in this fortune through the cheque.'[35]

Efficient transportation links made even the most desperate immigrants, the political refugees, consider Canada merely a 'way station' to a better life back in the homeland. Carmen Alicia Robles-Milan's study of Chilean refugees in Regina in 1981 indicates that despite experiences of torture in Chile, their affection for the homeland had not diminished. Indeed, the majority of the seventy-nine households that arrived in Regina between 1975 and 1978 hoped to return to the country of their birth. What made these transcultural expressions significant was that the Regina community was, by all reports, a well-adjusted one. Respondents indicated a speedy adjustment with assistance from federal government and non-profit agencies. Fully 86 percent of the men and 82 percent of the women were employed, and more than 60 percent participated in Spanish-language social clubs, 40 percent in the Regina Chilean Association. Members of the community had created a Saturday cultural school, La Escuela de Salvador Allende, for children of all ages and even organized a human rights conference for the people of Regina to 'spread awareness of the social and political issues that affect Chileans in exile.' Many participated in Regina's summer 'music, food and dance' multicultural festivity known as Mosaic. Two competing soccer clubs, El Club Deportivo-Colo-Colo and El Equipo Lautero, played other city teams. Fifty-four percent of the migrants even declared that 'they had adjusted to Saskatchewan winters' and the majority, 68 percent, declared that 'they were well received' in Regina. Yet they were ambivalent about integrating forever into Canadian society. Almost 70 percent stated that they 'would go home ... tomorrow' if they could, while only 7 percent described Canada as 'home.' Perhaps the fact that most of these one-time professionals were working at 'blue-collar' jobs in Regina accounted for this desire, but it did not explain why only a small percentage, 14 percent, 'stated a desire that their children become Canadian citizens.' Clearly, after three to five years in Canada, they remained strongly attached to Chile and its distinctive culture. In fact 64 percent stated they preferred that their children not 'become attached to Canadian culture' and about 80 percent declared that material possessions, the promise of North American culture, were not important in creating a 'best life' situation.[36]

The Regina story was not unique. Katherine MacRury's 1979 work on Vietnamese migrants in Edmonton discovered that 72 percent of its informants expressed 'either a desire to leave Canada or indecision about their plans,' with some speaking of Edmonton as 'a way-station between two cities.' Indeed, Edmonton was sometimes seen simply as a site that offered 'a chance to rest ... and figure out where ... to go next'; and for many, the future still lay in Vietnam where they could respond to the heartfelt duty 'to help rebuild their homeland.'[37] Ransford Danso's 1997 work on Africans in Calgary introduced yet another mindset. Here was a group of migrants who, although citing 'violence and want' as causing the migration in the first instance, 'always regarded themselves as transients or sojourners and never as permanent settlers.' To their mind, only a return to the homeland could truly legitimize their absence in the first place, for their only aim was 'to bring back the golden fleece' for the benefit of those left behind.' Any thoughts about permanent life in Canada were considered 'tantamount to cultural betrayal.'[38]

Transnational sentiments were also affected by the fact that many late-century immigrants had been sojourners in other countries, part of a shifting, evolving diasporic culture long before their arrival in Canada. In one way, this had been true for early-century immigrants, especially Volksdeutsche German migrants from eastern Europe.[39] But, during the late century, fleeting 'third country' experiences seemed much more prevalent, resulting in ties to two or more different homelands. It was a migration path that constituted a multi-sited transnational experience. Many immigrants thus were transnational in orientation even before coming to Canada. Chinese in Winnipeg and Calgary were usually transmigrants from Hong Kong, Malaysia, or Vietnam. For these migrants from mainland China, Canada represented a second major destination. Most Africans in Calgary had also lived in a country outside their continent before coming to Canada, including 'Britain, USA, Germany and Belgium, as well as the oil-rich states of the Middle East.'[40] Most members of the large Sikh population in Alberta did not come directly from Punjab, or indeed from India, but from east African countries, and many had lived for a time in Britain before arriving in western Canada.[41] In a unique pattern, Canadian-descendent Low German Mennonites whose ancestors had migrated to Mexico and Paraguay in the 1920s, protesting Manitoba and Saskatchewan's English-only school laws, now 'returned' to prairie towns, but also to Winnipeg and Saskatoon. And, adding complexity to their story, many came via Belize or Bolivia and came to 'work in factories owned by the children of early- or mid-century Mennonite refugees from the Soviet Union, all of whom had arrived via Germany, with some adding way stations in Paraguay or Mexico.[42]

The consequence of these 'third country' experiences was significant. Africans who spent time in Europe or the United States are said to have benefited by encountering the 'social, economic and cultural systems of western industrialized societies' before coming to the prairie cities.[43] Norman Buchignani points out that South Asians who arrived in Alberta in the 1960s with 'overseas experiences of one sort or another, such as university training, work in Britain or in Third World countries' are said to have 'pre-adapted' to life in Canada as virtually 'all men spoke English and had received their higher education in English.' Other groups had experienced the workings of transnational ethnicities, inventing ways of maintaining ties between ethnic enclaves in foreign lands and the original sending society. The small community of Gujarati Indians of Alberta, for example, spoke a language distinct from those of the Hindi and Punjabi peoples, and hailed not only from India, but also from Uganda, Kenya, Tanzania, and Malawi. This diversity ultimately did not undermine the unity of the immigrant community because such 'close communication between Gujaratis in East Africa and those in India' had existed prior to migration to Canada that in Alberta they formed 'essentially one community.'[44]

Immigrants also maintained transnational ties to enrich and sustain a life of cultural quality. These immigrants seemed put off by Canada's advanced economy and its atomizing culture, and spoke nostalgically of traditionalist societies, places where kinship and localistic ties were especially strong. Perhaps North America had a technological and economic advantage over the sending society, but it was the latter that possessed attractive traditional, spiritual, holistic cultures.

Bat-Ami Klejnei's 1994 study of Calgary's Latin Americans notes that they often spoke openly of the superiority of social relations and cultural values in the homeland. Typical was the testimony of an alienated young Guatemala woman, who noted that, given the 'different lifestyle' in Canada, 'one can never have those deep friendships' common in 'my country.' Representative, too, were denunciations of Western materialism by a young Argentine woman who asserted that 'I don't know what ... interests [Canadians] besides money.' In Argentina, she said, 'because of the economic problems ... you focus ... on other things such as family, your group of friends, getting together to have fun.' Other informants cited Canada's shallow culture. A middle-aged Chilean woman testified: 'if we (Latinos) go to the movies ... we talk about it, back and forth trying to find things that maybe were not there ... or a book ... you read it and we discuss it, its meaning, the message, the symbols ... I can't find that with the Canadians.'[45] The sentiment crossed gender lines. A thirty-eight-year-old Calgary male from El Salvador may have praised the more open Canadian class structure but he was quick to add that he also missed 'the warmth of our families, our language, our traditions. It would be so beautiful to be able to have that again.'[46]

Many Asian immigrants, too, believed that their homeland cultures were superior in some way. Jinjin Zhang's 1998 study of health cultures among Calgary Chinese cast doubt on the progressive, scientifically based Western medical culture, but spoke highly of traditional approaches in China. Chinese immigrants suffering from arthritis consulted regularly with Chinese doctors, even after moving to Canada. They believed that Chinese medicine cultivated 'a holistic approach towards health which teaches that good health is a state of spiritual and physical harmony with nature.' According to one immigrant patient, Wei, Chinese medicine was 'extremely enigmatic ... very abstract and ... perceived through the senses, that is, Yin and Yang' and enabled one to determine just when one was 'lacking in vital energy.' Wei further criticized Western medicine for focusing on 'the partial and the immediate,' and failing to 'pay much attention to how this part will influence your whole body.' Other immigrants criticized Canadian doctors for their formal manner, for prescribing 'toxic' drugs with side effects, for performing unnecessary surgeries, for lacking 'intuition and medical knowledge,' and for relying on the analysis of less educated laboratory technicians for their diagnosis of illness. The irony, according to immigrant Li, was that 'Canada has so many psychologists while physicians treat patients like inanimate objects' and forget their patient is 'an organic entity with thoughts and emotions.'[47]

A rigorous transnational consultation accompanied the Chinese immigrants' observations of Canada's health system. Sometimes they returned to their homeland for treatment. One informant in Zhang's study recalled that 'in December 1994 when I went back to Taiwan I consulted a Chinese healer [who] ... gave me Chinese medicine powder.' Others maintained links with Chinese health traditions by planning month-long trips back to Taiwan or China. Informant Ya, for example, noted that he would 'probably go back to mainland China for two months next year ... [and look for] an excellent, old Chinese doctor,' while Lu announced that 'next week, I will go back to China for a few months [and] see a former Chinese doctor first.'[48]

The transnational worlds described above had been facilitated by jet travel and long-distance telephones. With the introduction of cable television and the World Wide Web during the 1980s and 1990s, respectively, another phase of transnational culture commenced. As Lynn Hershman Leeson begins a 1996 anthology, *Clicking In*, the 'digital age exploded into existence not with a whimper but a bang. The globe still shakes from its entry. The journey was long, but the impact was immediate.'[49] One effect, as John Quaterman, editor of the newsletter *Matrix News*, noted in a 1995 publication, was that 'the appropriate metaphor for use of computer networks may not be communications with its familiar analogies of telephones, paper post, fax, radio and televison but travel, with its immediacy of experience and its tendency toward total immersion.'[50] The effect of the World Wide Web on immigrant cultures was varied: instant access to homeland media, free communication via e-mail or interactive forms via MSN, immediate information on any cultural aspect of the homeland, and updates on immigration laws and regulations in Canada all had an impact. Very little scholarly analysis has been completed on the effect of the Internet on immigrant cultures, ethnic identities, or even transnational behaviour. Unrestricted searches on databases such as America: History and Life yields almost one thousand pieces on the word 'internet,' but only three for 'internet and ethnicity,' and four for 'internet and immigration,' and most of these are for articles on how the Internet can be used to research 'ethnicity' and 'immigration,' not on how immigration culture has been changed by it.

A search in 2006 for immigrant group Web sites, however, yielded a very rich array of cultural sites. Each pointed to an explosive change in the transnational cultures of immigrant groups in prairie cities. One example was <http://www.manilawinnipeg.com>, a site committed to enriching the large Filipino community in Winnipeg. Its host, Rod Layco, noted that he had arrived in Winnipeg in 1984 and had become a Canadian citizen. He insisted that continued ties to the Philippines were crucial for the residents of Winnipeg. The site opened with the words: 'Mabuhay! Welcome to two of the friendliest cities in the entire universe, Manila and Winnipeg. Manila is home to more than 12 million Filipinos and an exciting metropolis of gourmet food, fashionable dresses, tropical weather and a vibrant nightlife. Winnipeg is home to 50,000 Filipino-Canadians, mild to extreme winter, and a mosaic of cultural diversity.' It went on to present a dizzying array of links, everything from one that reported the results of a Filipino bowling league in Winnipeg to a dozen

different Philippines government sites, and other sites providing information on overseas news, local business opportunities, travel tips, and
prepaid long-distance phone services. Like no other tool, the Internet
created an indelible link between the old homeland and the diasporic
community.

Hundreds of other Web sites offering media and community services
to newcomers were accessible. The Indo-Canada Web site for Calgary
provided addresses to almost a hundred and seventy other Indo-Canadian
organizations across the country and a link to the Ministry of Overseas
Indian Affairs, including its Diaspora Services Division at <http://moia.
gov.in>. The Calgary Ethiopian Community Association's site at <http://
ethio-calgary.ab.ca/cecahistory.html> similarly linked Canada and
Ethiopia. It described the historic Western Canada Ethiopian Soccer
Tournament held in Calgary in 1996, as well as a community drive in
1998 by the association to address famine and war in Ethiopia; the effort
reportedly 'raised a substantial amount of money' and saw it sent 'to the
needy through the World Food Program.' Some sites, such as the Korean
Edmonton Association's at <http://www.edkor.org>, were welcoming
and sophisticated, a shifting kaleidoscope of soft images and esoteric
characters that required reading ability in the Korean language. The
Regina Hungarian Club Web site, <http://www.reginahungarian club.
com/Main.html>, provided a link to the history of Hungary, to the story
of Magyar Ország dating to 900 AD, as well as to the Web site of Mosaic,
the Regina Multicultural Council. The Chinese Cultural Association of
Saskatchewan, Saskatoon branch, at <http://www.sfn.sas katoon.sk.ca/
arts/chinese> had further links to the Chinese Canadian National
Council, the Embassy of the People's Republic of China in Canada, and
Chinese Students and Scholars Association in the United States.[51] At the
beginning of the twenty-first century, then, amidst revolutionary communications links, an exponential growth in the sophistication and reach
of the transnational web seemed in the offing.

Conclusion

Despite the location of prairie cities in the continental interior, its immigrants cultivated an increasing variety of transnational links over the
course of the twentieth century. To understand the late-century immigrant mindset is to replay the process by which the newcomers negotiated the space between the sending village and the receiving suburb.

Strong emotional ties to kinship networks and familiar cultural sites, continuing national imaginings, and actual links with the homeland informed the process by which the immigrants integrated into the new. Such ties allowed newcomers to find full and satisfied lives in the face of an oftentimes strange, and even suspicious or racist, host society. Transnational ties could provide financial resources, social networks, and spiritual and mythological truths.

The transnational mindset was not static. Sojourner worlds and emerging nationalisms charted some transnational pathways in the early century, but great distances and costly travel technologies restricted the general movement of people. Some early transnational links did exist among both peripheral and powerful immigrant groups, among the rich and the working class, women and men, Christian and Buddhist, but most were emotional ties, yearnings, and affinities expressed by a diasporic people through local organization and occasional fund-drives for projects in the old world. The devastation of the Second World War, a rising suburban middle-class culture in Canada, and communist politics across the seas dampened this nascent historical force during the middle decades of the century. Immigrants may have spoken of their links to the homeland, but they did so in symbolic terms, creating vestiges of them within the prairie cities, or internalizing inherited mythologies and turning them into the cultural resources required for integration into suburbia.

Late-century technological innovations and a globalizing economy invigorated transnational cultures as an unprecedented historic force. Affordable jet travel and long-distance telephone calls connected the prairie communities to the sending societies in new ways in the 1970s, and during the 1990s the revolutionary tools of cable television and the World Wide Web transformed even these close links. Ironically, as Canada opened its doors to immigrants of races from southern continents, it found newcomers whose educational levels and cosmopolitan perspectives not only aided integration into Canada but provided the network for sustained transnational activity, including cultural and social ties to the homeland. The integration of immigrants to Canada was never the result of only governmental policy and market-driven economics; it was also a process that was shaped by localized and regionally specific cultural worlds of the immigrants, oftentimes outside the purview of the nation-state. And for the immigrants, the world never consisted of disconnected geographic points, but a dynamic web of coordinates that included points of both birthplace and diaspora, or origin and destiny.

Conclusion

Cultural diversity in Canada is much more than a government policy or a tourism advertisement; it is an historic reality that varies from community to community and region to region. One of the variations grew out of the experiences of migrants of foreign origin, and their children, in the cities of Canada's prairie interior. The histories of these communities constitute a noteworthy chapter in the Canadian story of immigration. The cities possessed a particular set of social characteristics: they were relatively small, were situated a considerable distance from ports or large metropolises, and were home to sequential waves of immigration. In these cities no single immigrant group could remain aloof from other ethnic groups or from the state. Nor could any group take advantage of a critical mass sufficient to establish an exclusive ethnic enclave of any duration. Simply to get to the prairie cities, most immigrants had to take one more leg in what was already an arduous journey, either a long train ride after a transoceanic voyage in the early years of the century, or an expensive connecting flight in later years. Because of the region's continued growth, first in the farm economy and then in resource-extraction industries, immigrants arrived in every decade with the exception of short hiatuses during the two world wars and the Depression. These structural characteristics set the limits for what could be achieved, but they also left spaces for creative exchanges within and amongst the ethnic groups, and between newcomers and established Canadians.

The pluralistic nature of prairie cities has been addressed in this book as the recreation of 'ethnic webs' and as social encounters in an imagined 'boundary zone.' Our first concern was the communities the newcomers constructed, including the ethnic identities that were crucial in establishing new homes. The focus here was on 'webs of significance,' the manner in which the immigrants made sense of their new worlds as they looked outward from their ethnic communities. In this approach social networks and cultural webs were intertwined: networks linked particular social units across city districts, between ethnic groups, or transnationally; webs consisted of shared symbols and understandings that translated into multi-layered ethnic identities.[1] The second image, the boundary zone, addressed how newcomers and Canadians encountered each other. They met in an interstitial space, a third space, one that was neither completely 'new Canadian' nor entirely 'old Canadian.' This zone changed in character over time, reflecting the hosts' increasing openness to strangers but also the influence of a wider range of newcomers and their greater opportunities for cross-boundary negotiation.

The two images, 'boundary zone' and 'ethnic web,' may appear contradictory. One focuses on interaction between newcomers and their Canadian hosts; the other on connections within ethnic communities, domestic and foreign. One celebrates an increased openness of the host society; the other, the ingenuity of the newcomer society. One suggests that a hybrid culture developed from the interaction; the other concentrates on the continued cultural creativity of each immigrant group. One may appear teleological or unilinear in nature, moving steadily in the direction of increased toleration; the other may seem stuck in a featureless ontological mist, lacking discernible outlines amid a welter of contradictions in the immigrant's world. Yet the images of boundary zone and social web establish fundamental aspects of the migrant experience. Both unite social and cultural features of the immigrant story, recognizing that behaviour and ideas existed in dialectical relationship with each other. What people did affected their thinking and what they thought affected their behaviour. Both perspectives recognize that human agency was bounded, as Edward Said has suggested, by cultural and linguistic processes in which groups defined themselves by stereotyping the 'other.' It was also shaped by accelerating global economic forces, as described by Eric Hobsbawm and others. Both boundary and networks also reflect the creative ways in which newcomers negotiated access to the fruits of the new land. And they are directly linked: what happened in the boundary zone shaped the very nature of the ethnic web and vice versa. A widening zone of interaction necessarily spread the ethnic web to include inter-ethnic, regional, and transnational links that were at once more extensive and more porous. While the ethnic web expanded over the decades to include suburbia and suburban organizations, and increasingly was embedded in transnational locations, it also encountered established Canadians more frequently. These webs, to employ Homi Bhabha's language, became spaces 'for elaborating strategies of self-hood,' 'spaces through which minorities translate ... gender, ethnicity, class ... into a solidarity.'[2]

Over the course of the twentieth century the webs and zones in which the immigrants played out their lives changed. In the first decades of the century, when the wider urban prairie society offered little opportunity for immigrants to participate in community-wide forums, immigrant groups organized their own institutional expressions of language, music, and reli gion. At the heart of immigrant communities was the private world of blood ties, one shared in a variety of ways, from that of nuclear Icelandic families to clans of Chinese men. The conversations within these kinship units were preoccupied with economic strategy, the well-being of children (in Canada or overseas), and appropriate masculine and feminine codes of behaviour. At the heart of the communities, too, was the compelling, subjective, and dynamic world of religion. Oftentimes it offered ordinary immigrants cosmological explanations for their stress, separation, and longing, and mythological grounding for an immigrant morality. It also defined ethnic boundaries and constituted the social networks of familiarity and trust. These ethnic worlds also relied on social clubs, some for purposes of entertainment, others for radical political critique, but all for mutual aid and the common benefit of the immigrant community.

A particular focus on an imagined boundary zone in early-century Winnipeg, the region's first major immigrant-receiving city, reveals sharply defined edges within a conflict-laden meeting place. Here new-comers and citizens of long standing groups, almost equal in size, jostled against each other as discrete and inherently divided communities. The host society was put on guard by what it saw as the immigrants' suspect loyalties, their nostalgia for home, religious peculiarity, sharp national memories, 'foreign' languages, and weak character. When the newcom-ers turned to observe the host society, they saw arrogance and intimida-tion. Even when the newcomer was from England and Scotland, division was etched into the cityscape, albeit a less pronounced difference than that which awaited such groups as the Ukrainian and Chinese, who were more likely to be labouring at poorly paid tasks and living in wretched conditions. It seemed in these first decades of the twentieth century as if the borders between groups were so impenetrable that no real zone of interaction existed.

Though sharp divisions marked people's understanding of the new prairie metropolis, a geography of negotiation was developing. In the market and the media, in schools and politics, the newcomers encountered long-standing residents. All immigrants, whether from Western capitalist or peasant cultures, quickly adapted to wages and monetary exchanges, just as the long-settled recognized the purchasing power of the newcomers in street markets and department stores. A similar exchange existed in the education system. Principals of public schools coaxed religiously informed Europeans to permit the enrolment of their children in British–Canadian education; the newcomers exerted pressure on politicians to provide multilingual instruction. Immigrants also encountered their hosts in politics. Oftentimes the newcomers opposed the parties of the elites, and favoured progressive, working-class politicians who were more conscious of the needs of the poor. These encounters in market, school, and politics illuminated a sharp class-based divide but they also generated awareness of common interests among the working people.

Ethnicity changed in character around mid-century. In the burgeoning cities of Alberta and Saskatchewan post-war migrations undermined British–Canadian hegemony and lent a new saliency to reconstructed ethnic networks. Of special importance to this study, two concurrent migration waves entered these cities: second- and third-generation Euro–Canadian farm families uprooted from their homesteads by economic forces, and first-generation foreign immigrants dislodged from their homelands by war and political repression. The two streams interacted, oftentimes conflicting on questions of politics, religion, and ethnic meaning. They flowed into the newly built suburbs where they mixed with people from other ethnic groups. Many of these new city dwellers moved from the labouring classes to the middle class, becoming entrepreneurs and professionals, all the while growing increasingly confident that the old model of British Canadianism must be replaced by a more open and ethnicized European Canadianism. Within this dynamic world, ethnicity acquired a symbolic meaning, expressed in household ornamentation, in linguistic colloquialism, folk art, distinctive holiday cuisine, shared history, and differing views on gender and religion. In its reinvention, ethnicity provided many types of cultural resource that enabled the mid-century immigrant to take advantage of opportunities in a more prosperous economy and more welcoming society.

Winnipeg at mid-century, too, evolved into a plural society in which new Canadians and old worked out a civic compromise in an atmosphere of mutual accommodation. Once-exclusive groups such as Jewish and

Japanese Canadians were keenly aware of ethnic differences but they also developed a strong sense of belonging within the wider community. Just as Saul Cherniack found in an amateur theatre company and the armed forces tolerant pathways into the heart of a new prairie Canada, so did many other second-generation Jews enter higher education and obtain professional certification without serious obstacles to advancement. Nisei Japanese Canadians established themselves in Winnipeg's post-war polyethnic neighbourhoods, entered integrated schools and universities, and became members of its churches. The younger Sansei generation now chose the life of acculturated Canadians. Other groups, too, including the post-war German immigrants who were assisted by earlier German Catholic and Lutheran arrivals, and anti-modern, Low German-speaking Mennonites returning from a one-generation sojourn in Latin America, found relative tolerance and institutional support. Winnipeg's Citizenship Council and International Centre illustrated how ordinary citizens welcomed newcomers, both post-war European immigrants and, later, Asian, African, and Latin American immigrants, and sought to ease their integration. Crucial in this story were second-generation Canadian women who focused on language training and counselling for newcomers, programs that eventually reached over a thousand immigrants per year. At the same time citizenship court ceremonies and other public receptions offered evidence of a mobilized host society that was intent on opening up the middle class to the newcomers, even intent on guiding them into it.

Immigrants from the Global South – the Southeast and South Asians, South and Central Americans, Africans, and Caribbean islanders – provoked yet another expression of ethnicity in the 1970s and 1980s. This phenomenon was especially apparent in the fastest growing of the interior cities, Calgary and Edmonton, where Asian newcomers far outnumbered those from Europe, and Latin Americans those from the United States. On the one hand ethnicity here was less visible than ever as many immigrants qualified under Canada's points system, meaning that they more often arrived with experience of modern cities, English language proficiency, and a readiness to settle into the suburbs. On the other hand these immigrants were also more confident. They capitalized on the Alberta cities' association of multiculturalism with cosmopolitanism and on most Albertans' openness to refugees. They invested their professional earnings in a rich array of ethnic institutions, often located in the suburbs, and offered extensive social welfare resources to the elderly as well as to youth. They also happily assumed the label 'ethnic' and in their contributions to public debates they oftentimes boldly decried systemic racism and underemployment. Ironically, these immigrants embraced the image of the 'other' to counter the hegemony of the 'centre.'

Despite Canada's individualizing points system immigration policy, the immigrant family in its late-century manifestation still provided the centre and the anchor for newcomers, whether they were suburban professionals or inner-city labourers. Where family life had been dramatically uprooted – as happened to many refugees and young, single immigrants – the longing for household activities and the wish to recreate family ties were very strong. Though these households remained crucial as places from which Canadian ways were viewed, they less often fit the early-century image of 'haven in a heartless world.' Indeed, they more often were the very locus of change. In the late-century prairie city, old ideas of gender, childhood, and extended family were tested by the cross-current of Canada's points system. Children acquired English rapidly in the public school system and English as a Second Language programs. Women took jobs outside the home or became the prime negotiators in the public world of social services. Meanwhile, many men encountered challenges to traditional male authority in the home. Middle-class families seemed to disperse seamlessly into the suburbs, while working-class parents seemed especially intent on attaining middle-class status for their children. The family still stood as the bastion of the immigrant world, but it had become the very site of fundamental social and cultural change.

A focus on an imagined boundary between newcomers and long-time Canadians in late-century Winnipeg suggests that many cultural barriers had vanished but that racism remained a deeply entrenched obstacle to full acceptance of the new immigrants. Revulsion at the international racial politics of the 1930s and 1940s had combined with Canada's post-war cultural changes to make a new start possible. The old racial assumptions faded in the 1950s, a shift given expression in the Bill of Rights passed by Saskatchewan Member of Parliament and Prime Minister John G. Diefenbaker. Multiculturalism became generally accepted and new policies permitted the development of public schools built upon other languages of instruction and on an anti-racism ethos. Most forms of religious discrimination receded from public view. Insistence on an unhyphenated Canadianism also became less urgent as governments accepted dual citizenship and binationalism.

As in every society, racism continued to be a blot on the public record. Numerous racist incidents took place in Winnipeg, for example, touching international migrants from the Global South just as they touched Aboriginal migrants from the province's North. Civic leaders responded calmly to such challenges and, through such anti-racist institutions as the International Centre and Folklorama, emphasized that ethnic diversity was central to city life. The most optimistic gauge of the atmosphere in Winnipeg's boundary zones was the history of the Kawata family. In the course of two generations, one rooted in the first half of the century, the other in the second, the capacity of racism to infect Masako Kawata's daily life was diminished and the power of race to override her own and others' perceptions of her qualities was undermined. A more accommodating view of newcomers may have been part of a longer term pattern in the city but, as immigrant support workers declared, the struggle against racism was not over. [3]

By the closing decades of the century prairie immigrants honed a social resource that oftentimes strengthened their hand in the new land. The convergence of new communication technologies and a more globalized economy propelled their family- and community-centred social networks outward with unprecedented energy. Transnational linkages shaped the newcomers' worlds. Such ties in themselves were not new on the Prairies, as was evident in the lives of early-century sojourner labourers, old-homeland nationalists, and migrants who followed circuitous routes to their new homes. Mid-century immigrants were less transnational only because wartorn economies and repressive political regimes in their former homelands forbade such activity. But late-century migrants took advantage of air travel, long-distance telephone connections, satellite television, and the Internet to increase their connections to old homelands. In an age reshaped by international production and trade, they were both the pawns of globalized labour markets and the beneficiaries of global trade routes. The worlds of these newcomers included encounters in the prairie cities' boundary zones as well as in international, more precisely translocal, webs that directly linked neighbourhoods in old and new lands.

Immigrants in prairie cities benefited from increasingly open boundary zones and creative webs of ethnicity. Though many rated their new homes highly, not all did so. And even the ratings offered by optimists were tempered by recognition of hardship and loss. The century ended, writes Eric Hobsbawm, in 'Crisis Decades [that] demonstrated the limitations of various Golden Age policies, but without – as yet – generating convincing alternatives.'[4] The promise of a modern 'social citizenship' in the Western world, once articulated by T.H. Marshall, had not come to pass for every newcomer in prairie Canada. Indeed, some critics in Canada charged that 'after several generations the "western" welfare state has made little systemic progress' in providing a sense of belonging. They argued that the discourse of citizenship had been used disingenuously, interlaced as it had been 'with the projects of a hierarchical social structure and exclusionary political order.'[5] These critics suggested that, at century's end, life for new immigrants was filled with difficulties.

In 1997, at the first national conference held by Canada's Metropolis Project, a federally funded program to facilitate research on immigration issues, Meyer Burstein observed that 'what underlies Metropolis is a judgment ... that the long term viability of our societies ... is contingent on our ability to address the challenges and to capitalize on the opportunities presented by international migration.'[6] He called for research and policy development 'to build productive, cohesive and egalitarian societies' in which immigration plays a 'positive, vital force.' In his address to the same conference, Baha Abu Laban, the director for the Metropolis Project's prairie centre based in Edmonton, recognized the craft of history as one discipline that could deliver such knowledge. Such a focus, according to Abu Laban, should assume 'that immigrants and host societies exert reciprocal influence, that integration is a process rather than a static end-state,' that integration would be affected 'by gender, by class and by immigrant group,' and would have 'visible effects.'[7]

A knowledge of history is crucial to the understanding of how immigrants integrate into new societies. Immigration initiates a complex, long-term process, one that is subtle in its parts and revolutionary in its overall impact. The Canadian prairie city illustrates this remarkable transition. In these small-scale, so-called second-tier communities, many new Canadians were able to establish a positive, productive, and cohesive presence, and long-time Canadians themselves became newcomers in a refashioned society. Certainly there were and still are shortcomings in these communities, obstacles to immigrants' full acceptance in the new land, but over time, a vital multicultural society came into being.[8]

In previous scholarly work, historians have rightly noted that minority groups appeared on the periphery of the dominant culture's canon and that class lines in these cities ensured the survival of ethnicity-linked economic inequality for at least one, if not two or more, generations. They have also insisted that forms of cultural and social colonialism were quite apparent in prairie cities. This book acknowledges these circumstances.

But it emphasizes that people, through what academics call 'human agency,' are able to construct institutions that address such injustices, and have been creative and courageous in addressing social ills. Throughout the twentieth century thoughtful Canadians in prairie cities sought ways in which to welcome newcomers and to assist their integration into their new homes. During these decades, too, immigrants reconstructed their own ethnic communities. These institutions and households supported an evolving collective expression that facilitated connections with later arrivals.

While acknowledging deep fissures in the world's cities, we share with such scholars as David Harvey a concern to oppose fragmentation, anomie, and disfranchisement. As Harvey writes in his *Spaces of Hope*, ordinary citizens can act as 'insurgent architects,' undertaking the 'construction of collective identities, of communities of action, of rules of belonging' that translate 'the personal and the political onto a broader terrain of human action.'[9] Our book has traced a century of 'human action' by newcomers and established Canadians who sought to build 'spaces of hope.' We have observed cultures, as Edward Said proposed, not in 'their essence or purity, but [in] their combinations and diversity, their countercurrents, the way that they have had of conducting a compelling dialogue' across boundaries and within networks.[10] The Canadian prairie city has long been, and still is, home to such a compelling multicultural dialogue.

Notes

Introduction

1 For some of the central historical case studies of immigrant groups in these
so-called Gateway Cities see Franca Iacovetta, *Gatekeepers: Reshaping Immigrant
Lives in Cold War Canada* (Toronto: Between the Lines, 2006); Wenona Giles,
Portuguese Women in Toronto: Gender, Immigration and Nationalism (Toronto:
University of Toronto Press, 2002); Rima Berns McGown, *Muslims in the
Diaspora: The Somali Communities of London and Toronto* (Toronto: University
of Toronto Press, 1999); Wing Chung Ng, *The Chinese in Vancouver, 1945–
80: The Pursuit of Identity and Power* (Vancouver: University of British
Columbia Press, 1999); Kay Anderson, *Vancouver's Chinatown: Racial
Discourse in Canada, 1875–1980* (Kingston: McGill-Queen's University Press,
1995); Ira Robinson and Mervin Butovsky, eds., *Renewing Our Days: Montreal
Jews in the Twentieth Century* (Montreal: Véhicule, 1995); Lillian Petroff,
Sojourners and Settlers: The Macedonian Community in Toronto to 1940
(Toronto: Multicultural History Society of Ontario, 1995); Ruth A. Frager,
*Sweatshop Strife: Class, Ethnicity, and Gender in the Jewish Labour Movement of
Toronto, 1900–1939* (Toronto: University of Toronto Press, 1992); Franca
Iacovetta, *Such Hardworking People: Italian Immigrants in Postwar Toronto*
(Montreal and Kingston: McGill-Queen's University Press, 1992); Bruno
Ramirez, *On the Move: French-Canadian and Italian Migrants in the North
Atlantic Economy, 1860–1914* (Toronto: McClelland and Stewart, 1991);
Franc Sturino, *Forging the Chain: A Case Study of Italian Migration to North
America, 1880–1930* (Toronto: Multicultural History Society of Ontario,
1990); John Zucchi, *Italians in Toronto: Development of a National Identity,
1875–1935* (Montreal and Kingston: McGill-Queen's University Press,
1988); Ruth Gumpp, *Ethnicity and Assimilation: German Postwar Immigrants*

in Vancouver, 1945–1970 (Vancouver: University of British Columbia Press, 1989); and Robert F. Harney, *Gathering Place: Peoples and Neighbourhoods of Toronto, 1834–1945* (Toronto: Multicultural History Society of Ontario, 1985). For an illustration of the Canadian self-perception see Marcus Gee, 'Born in 169 Other Countries,' *Globe and Mail,* 10 June 1998, A27.

2 Will Kymlicka, 'The Canadian Model of Diversity in a Comparative Perspective,' Eighth Standard Life Visiting Lecture, 29 April 2004, Canadian Studies, Edinburgh University. <http://www.cst.ed.ac.uk/_oldsite/ressources.html>.

3 This simple view has been critiqued by Richard Alba and Victor Nee as implying 'more or less autonomous cultural centers organized around discrete ethnic groups, with [little] interpenetration of cultural life.' Richard Alba and Victor Nee, *Remaking the American Mainstream: Assimilation and Contemporary Immigration* (Cambridge MA: Harvard University Press, 2003), 10.

4 Clifford Geertz, *The Interpretation of Cultures: Selected Essays* (New York: Basic Books, 1973), 14. For a similar aim see Matthew Frye Jacobson, *Special Sorrows: The Diasporic Imagination of Irish, Polish and Jewish Immigrants in the United States* (Berkeley: University of California Press, 2002), 6.

5 Edward Said, *Culture and Imperialism* (1993; reprint, New York: Vintage Books, 1994), 191 ff.

6 Fredrik Barth, *Balinese Worlds* (Chicago: University of Chicago Press, 1993), 8.

7 Ibid., 354.

8 Kathleen Neils Conzen, et al., 'The Invention of Ethnicity: A Perspective from the U.S.A,' *Journal of American Ethnic History* (Fall 1992): 3–41; Harold R. Isaacs, 'Basic Group Identity: The Idols of the Tribe,' *Ethnicity* 1 (1974): 15–41.

9 Iacovetta, *Gatekeepers*. On the question of immigrants and humanageny: Henry Yu, 'Refracting Pacific Canada: Seeing our Uncommon Past,' *BC Studies* 156–7 (2007–08): 6.

10 Homi K. Bhabha, *The Location of Culture* (London and New York: Routledge, 1994), 170. The authors thank Mary Ann Loewen for drawing their attention to this source.

11 Ibid, 3–5, 38; also Homi Bhabha, ed., *Narration and Nation* (London: Routledge, 1990).

12 The group titled the Winnipeg Immigration History Research Group was funded by the Prairie Centre of Excellence for Research on Immigration and Integration, an arm of the Canadian Metropolis project.

13 Ninette Kelley and Michael Trebilcock, *The Making of the Mosaic: A History of Canadian Immigration Policy* (Toronto: University of Toronto Press, 1998), 113, 142, 155, 184.

14 Ibid., 321.
15 Conzen, et al., 'The Invention of Ethnicity.'
16 Ibid. The original and decisive argument in this vein was Fredrik Barth, 'Ethnic Groups and Boundaries,' originally published as 'Introduction' to Fredrik Barth, ed., *Ethnic Groups and Boundaries: The Social Organization of Culture Difference* (Bergen: Waveland Press, 1969).
17 Will Kymlicka, *Finding Our Way: Rethinking Ethnocultural Relations in Canada* (London: Oxford University Press, 1998), 25, 31, 44; Howard Palmer, *Patterns of Prejudice: A History of Nativism in Alberta* (Toronto: McClelland and Stewart, 1982), 46, 47, 78; Robert Harney, '"So Great a Heritage as Ours": Immigration and the Survival of the Canadian Polity,' *Daedalus* 117 (1988; reprint, in C. Gaffield, ed., *Constructing Modern Canada: Readings in Post-Confederation History* [Toronto: Copp Clark Longman, 1994]), 529–66.
18 Paul Gilroy, *Nations, Cultures and the Allure of Race* (London: Penguin, 2000); on whiteness, a useful introductory survey is Valerie Melissa Babb, *Whiteness Visible: The Meaning of Whiteness in American Literature and Culture* (New York: New York University Press, 1998).
19 David Roediger, *The Wages of Whiteness: Race and the Making of the American Working Class* (London and New York: Verso, 1999). For a Canadian example see Vic Satzewich, 'Whiteness Limited: Racialization and the Social Construction of "Peripheral Europeans,"' *Histoire Sociale/Social History* 33 (2006).
20 Constance Backhouse, *Colour-Coded: A Legal History of Racism in Canada* (Toronto: University of Toronto Press, 1999) , 7, 8, 11, 13–14, 15. She argues, too, that the writing of the history of racism in Canada 'is still in its infancy.'
21 For another variation in Canada see Gerard Bouchard and Charles Taylor, *Building the Future: A Time for Reconciliation*. Abridged Report (Québec: Commission de consultation sur les pratiques d'accommodement reliées aux différences culturelles, 2008).
22 Leo Lucassen, *The Immigrant Threat: The Integration of Old and New Migrants in Western Europe since 1850* (Urbana: University of Illinois Press, 2005), 3, 4. An admirable vision that includes reference to the Canadian experience in presented by Bhikhu Parekh, *A New Politics of Identity: Political Principles for an Interdependent World* (Basingstoke: Palgrave Macmillan, 2008).

1. The Ethnic 'Centre'

1 Clifford Geertz, *The Interpretation of Cultures: Selected Essays* (New York: Basic Books, 1973), 5, 12.

2 Alan F.J. Artibise, 'Divided City: The Immigrants in Winnipeg Society, 1874–1921,' in G. Stelter and A. Artibise, eds., *The Canadian City: Essays in Urban History* (1966; reprint, Toronto: McClelland and Stewart, 1979), 300–36. In Winnipeg, Alan Artibise writes, the first concern of an immigrant descending from the CPR station in the years before 1914 was shelter, and immigrants could receive this at both the city immigration sheds and at the houses of 'relatives or old countrymen with whom he might board' (Artibise, 'Divided City,' 319).

3 A. Ross McCormack, 'Networks among British Immigrants and Accommodation to Canadian Society: Winnipeg, 1900–1914,' *Histoire Sociale/Social History* 17 (1984): 358.

4 Antonella Fanella, 'Family, Honour and Destiny: Southern Italian Immigrants in Calgary, 1910–1990,' MA thesis, University of Calgary, 1991. A similar arrangement was seen among the Italians in Winnipeg: 'The extended family units' brought kinsmen together who 'assumed the roles of coddlers, friends, protectors, patrons, babysitters and informal disseminators of cultural knowledge to their young cognates within the Italian family.' Brian Ross, 'In the Company of Other Italians: Voluntary Associations in Winnipeg's Italian Community,' MA thesis, University of Manitoba, 1983, p. 31.

5 Harry Con, *From China to Canada: A History of the Chinese in Canada* (Toronto: McClelland and Stewart, 1982), 92, 107.

6 Wing-sam Chow, 'A Chinese Community in a Prairie City: A Holistic Perspective of its Class and Ethnic Relations,' PhD diss., University of Michigan, 1981, pp. 103, 104. For a full discussion of the role of the family in Chinese communities in Canada see also David Chuenyan Lai, Jordan Paper, and Li Chuang Paper, 'The Chinese in Canada: Their Unrecognized Religion,' in P. Bramadat and D. Seljak, eds., *Religion and Ethnicity in Canada* (Toronto: Pearson, 2005), 89–110.

7 Tamara K. Hareven, 'The History of the Family and the Complexity of Social Change,' *American Historical Review* 96 (1991): 96.

8 Arthur Grenke, 'The German Community of Winnipeg and the English-Canadian Responses to World War I,' *Canadian Ethnic Studies* 20 (1988): 31.

9 Laura Salverson, *Confessions of an Immigrant's Daughter* (Toronto: University of Toronto Press, 1981), 474, 480, 499, 509, 517.

10 Quoted in Jean R. Burnet, with Howard Palmer, *'Coming Canadians': An Introduction to a History of Canada's Peoples* (Toronto: McClelland and Stewart, 1988), 67.

11 Ibid., 68.

12 Salverson, *Confessions of an Immigrant's Daughter*, 213.

13 Quoted in Howard Palmer and Tamara Palmer, 'The Romanian Community in Alberta,' in H. Palmer and T. Palmer, eds., *Peoples of Alberta: Portraits of Cultural Diversity* (Saskatoon: Western Producer Prairie Books, 1985), 259.

14 James S. Woodsworth, *Strangers Within Our Gates or Coming Canadians* (Toronto: F.C. Stephenson, Missionary Society of the Methodist Church, Canada), 261. In a more impoverished family, 'Pieter, the oldest boy, eight years old, has to go out along the streets and lanes ... find[ing] sticks of wood, empty barrels, etc., for which he gets a few cents to help to keep the family,' 261, and another household where poverty forces 'from 15 to 20 boarders [to] live in four rooms' and 'two of the older girls are "working out,"' 263.

15 Ibid., 65.

16 Dirk Hoerder, *Creating Societies: Immigrant Lives in Canada* (Montreal: McGill-Queen's University Press, 1999), 147.

17 Ibid., 148.

18 Ibid., 175.

19 John Marlyn, *Under the Ribs of Death* (1957; reprint, Toronto: McClelland and Stewart, 1971), 26.

20 Quoted in Tamara Palmer, 'Ethnic Responses to the Canadian Prairies, 1900–1950: A Literary Perspective of the Physical and Social Environment,' *Prairie Forum* 12 (1987): 67.

21 Kirsten Wolf, ed., *Writings by Western Icelandic Women* (Winnipeg: University of Manitoba Press, 1997), 90.

22 Ibid.

23 Brian Ross, 'In the Company of Other Italians: Voluntary Associations in Winnipeg's Italian Community,' MA thesis, University of Winnipeg/University of Manitoba, 2000, p. 75.

24 Edward John Hart, 'The History of the French-speaking Community of Edmonton, 1795–1935,' MA thesis, University of Alberta, 1971, p. 70.

25 These included the following: le Theatre Francais (1933); the Quebec-based l'Association Catholique de la Jeunesse Canadienne-francais subsidiary le Cercle Grandin (1931); the young women's group le Cercle des Bonnes Amies (1925) and its male counterpart, Les Jeunes Canadiens. Hart, 'The History of the French-speaking,' 150, 153.

26 Krystyna Lukasiewicz, 'Family and Work: Polish Interwar Immigrant Women in Alberta, 1920–1950,' MA thesis, University of Alberta, 1993, p. 102.

27 Frances Swyripa, *Wedded to the Cause: Ukrainian-Canadian Women and Ethnic Identity, 1891–1991* (Toronto: University of Toronto Press, 1993), 14, 50.

28 K.W. Sololyck, 'The Role of Ukrainian Sports Teams, Clubs and Leagues, 1924–1952,' *Journal of Ukrainian Studies* 16 (1991): 136, 140.

29 Donna Gabaccia and Franca Iacovetta, 'Work, Women and Protest in the Italian Diaspora: An International Research Agenda,' *Labour/le travail* 42 (1998): 179.

30 Steven Maynard, 'Rough Work and Rugged Men: The Social Construction of Masculinity in Working Class History,' *Labour/le travail* 23 (1989): 161.

31 Joy Parr, *The Gender of Breadwinners: Women, Men and Change in Two Industrial Towns, 1880–1950* (Toronto: University of Toronto Press, 1990), 141.

32 Salverson, *Confessions of an Immigrant's Daughter*, 462.

33 Constance Backhouse, 'White Chinese Help and Chinese-Canadian Employers: Race, Class, Gender and Law in the Case of Lee Clun [Regina], 1924,' *Canadian Ethnic Studies* 26 (1994): 41–43.

34 Ibid., 35.

35 Woodsworth, *Strangers Within Our Gates*, 166.

36 Burnet, '*Coming Canadians*', 66.

37 Ibid., 28.

38 Salverson, *Confessions of an Immigrant's Daughter*, 214.

39 Adele Wiseman, *The Sacrifice* (Toronto: Macmillan 1956), 61.

40 Marlyn, *Under the Ribs of Death*, 115, 179.

41 McCormack, 'Networks among British Immigrants,' 359.

42 Palmer, 'Ethnic Responses to the Canadian Prairies,' 67, 70.

43 Wiseman, *The Sacrifice*, 32, 109, 110, 25.

44 Marlyn, *Under the Ribs of Death*, 40, 97, 188, 18.

45 Arthur Grenke, *The German Community in Winnipeg, 1872–1919* (New York: AMS Press, 1991).

46 Lukasiewicz, 'Family and Work,' 100.

47 Myrna Kostash, *All of Baba's Children* (Edmonton: Hurtig, 1977), 213.

48 Woodsworth, *Strangers Within Our Gates*, 262.

49 Wsevolod W. Isajiw, ed., *Ukrainians in the Canadian City* (Calgary: Research Centre for Canadian Ethnic Studies, 1980), 69.

50 Swyripa, *Wedded to the Cause*, 71.

51 Lukasiewicz, 'Family and Work,' 89.

52 Frieda Esau-Klippenstein, 'Doing What We Could: Mennonite Domestic Servants in Winnipeg, 1920s–1950s,' *Journal of Mennonite Studies* 7 (1989): 165; see also Marlene Epp, 'The Mennonite Girls' Homes of Winnipeg: A Home Away from Home,' *Journal of Mennonite Studies* 6 (1988): 100–14.

53 Lukasiewicz, 'Family and Work,' 107.

54 Timothy L. Smith, 'Religion and Ethnicity in America,' *American Historical Review* 83 (1978): 1155–85.

55 Paul Bramadat, 'Beyond Christian Canada: Religion and Ethnicity in a Multicultural Society,' in P. Bramadat and D. Seljack, eds., *Religion and Ethnicity in Canada* (Toronto: Pearson Longman, 2005), 1–29.

56 Robert Orsi, 'The Center Out There, in Here, and Everywhere Else: The Nature of Pilgrimage to the Shrine of Saint Jude, 1929–1965,' *Journal of Social History* 25 (1991): 213–32; Enrico Carlson Cumbo, '"Your Old Men Will Dream Dreams": The Italian Pentecostal Experience in Canada, 1912–1945,' *Journal of American Ethnic History* 19 (2000): 35–81.

57 Anthony Rasporich, 'Utopian Ideals and Community Settlements in Western Canada, 1880–1914,' in H. Klassen, ed., *The Canadian West: Social Change and Economic Development* (Calgary: Comprint, 1977), 37–62.

58 Harry Con, *From China to Canada: A History of the Chinese in Canada* (Toronto: McClelland and Stewart, 1982), 79.

59 Chuenyan Lai et al., 'The Chinese in Canada: Their Unrecognized Religion,' 91; Alison R. Marshall, 'Chinese Immigration to Western Manitoban since 1884: Wah Hep, George Chong, the KMT and the United Church,' *Journal of Canadian Studies* 42 (2008): 28–54.

60 Lai, 'The Chinese in Canada,' 93.

61 Quoted in Woodsworth, *Strangers Within Our Gates*, 184, 179, 180.

62 Con, *From China to Canada*, 94.

63 Orest T. Martynowych, *Ukrainians in Canada: The Formative Period, 1891–1924* (Edmonton: Canadian Institute of Ukrainians Press, 1991), 267.

64 Charles Tilly, 'Contentious Repertoires in Great Britain, 1758–1834,' *Social Science History* 17 (1993): 264.

65 Kostash, *All of Baba's Children*, 122.

66 Paul Yuzyk, *The Ukrainians of Manitoba: A Social History* (Toronto: University of Toronto Press, 1953), 148. Also see June Dutka, *St. Nicholas Ukrainian Catholic Church: Celebrating 100 years: Together for Tomorrow* (Winnipeg: St Nicholas Ukrainian Catholic Church, 2006).

67 Gerald J. Tulchinsky, *Taking Root: The Origins of the Canadian Jewish Community* (Toronto: Lester, 1992), 164. For a similar link between clergy and ethnic identity see Hart, 'The History of the French-speaking,' 147.

68 Arthur Chiel, *The Jews in Manitoba: A Social History* (Toronto: University of Toronto Press, 1961), 69, 80, 87, 90.

69 John Cobb, 'German Lutherns in the Prairie Provinces Before the First World War: Their Church Background, Emigration and New Beginning in Canada,' PhD diss., University of Manitoba, 1991, p. 104.

70 Grenke, *The German Community*, 177, 213.

71 Hart, 'The History of the French-speaking,' 66, 138.

72 Ross, 'In the Company of Other Italians,' 51, 55, 58.

73 Rosaline Usiskin, 'Toward a Theoretical Reformulation of the Relationship Between Political Ideology, Social Class, and Ethnicity: A Case Study of the Winnipeg Jewish Radical Community, 1905–1920,' MA thesis, University of Manitoba, 1978, pp. 126, 128, 170.

74 Jack Switzer, 'Whoa Emma!! An Anarchist Visits Calgary, 1907,' *Alberta History* 55 (2007): 6-12. See also <http://www.lycos.com/info/emma-goldman–women.html>, accessed 30 January 2009.
75 Martynowych, *Ukrainians in Canada*, 268, 297, 288.
76 Grenke, *The German Community*, 3, 66.

2. Patterns of Conflict and Adjustment in Winnipeg

1   This is the point emphasized by Kenneth Lunn, 'Immigration and Reaction in Britain, 1880–1950: Rethinking the "Legacy of Empire,"' in J. Lucassen and L. Lucassen, eds., *Migration, Migration History, History: Old Paradigms and New Perspectives* (Bern: Peter Lang, 1997), 336–8.
2   Fredrik Barth, 'Ethnic Groups and Boundaries,' originally published as 'Introduction' to Fredrik Barth, ed., *Ethnic Groups and Boundaries: The Social Organization of Culture Difference* (Bergen: Universitetsforlaget; London: Allen & Unwin, 1969).
3   Jan Lucassen and Leo Lucassen, 'Migration, Migration History, History: Old Paradigms and New Perspectives,' in J. Lucassen and L. Lucassen, eds., *Migration, Migration History, History* (Bern: Peter Lang, 1997), especially pp 21–6; Russell A. Kazal, 'Revisiting Assimilation: The Rise, Fall, and Reappraisal of a Concept in American Ethnic History,' *American Historical Review* 100 (1995): 437–71.
4   Marvin McInnis, 'Canada's Population in the Twentieth Century,' in M.R. Haines and R.H. Steckel, eds., *A Population History of North America* (Cambridge: Cambridge University Press, 2000), 529–99. Throughout our book, Winnipeg's population is calculated as the sum of the city itself and the twelve adjacent municipalities that are now part of the Census Metropolitan Area and that were integrated into the single 'unicity' of Winnipeg in 1971. The population numbers will therefore differ substantially from those reported in earlier works, such as those by Alan Artibise and Ruben Bellan.
5   Census of Canada, quinquennial and decennial, 1891–1941. We would like to thank Jennifer Rogalsky for her work on these records. The populations of ethnic groups are based on the then roughly accurate index of the respondent's father's place or group of origin.
6   John E. Tooth, 'Sixty years in Canada: By an immigrant of 1910,' copy of handwritten manuscript in possession of Gerald Friesen. Mr Tooth wrote the manuscript in 1972–3. We would like to thank his grandson, also John Tooth, who provided information on the manuscript and its author.
7   Ibid., 159.

8 These chapters of the autobiography reveal much about the exceptional life course – one might even say the fallibility as historical witness – of this great artist of francophone Manitoba. Gabrielle Roy, *La Détresse et l'enchantement* (1984), translated by P. Claxton as *Enchantment and Sorrow: The Autobiography of Gabrielle Roy* (Toronto: Lester & Orpen Dennys, 1987).

9 Ibid., 3–5.

10 Adele Wiseman, 'Old Markets, New World,' in *Memoirs of a Book Molesting Childhood and Other Essays* (Toronto: Oxford University Press, 1987), 31, 35.

11 Ibid., 36.

12 Charles W. Gordon, *Postscript to Adventure: The Autobiography of Ralph Connor* (New York: Farrar & Rinehart, 1938), 75.

13 Ibid., 79.

14 Joseph Wilder, *Read All about It: Reminiscences of an Immigrant Newsboy*, ed. F.C. Dawkins and M.C. Brodeur (Winnipeg: Peguis, 1978), 23–4; 'Larry Zolf' interviewed by Danny Finkleman in John Parr, ed., *Speaking of Winnipeg* (Winnipeg: Queenston House, 1974), 137; Sybil Shack, 'The Education of Immigrant Children During the First Two Decades of This Century,' *Historical and Scientific Society of Manitoba Transactions*, Series III, 30 (1973–4), <http://www.mhs.mb.ca/docs/transactions/3/immigranteducation.shtml>.

15 Wiseman, *Memoirs of a Book Molesting Childhood*, 16.

16 James Gray, *The Boy from Winnipeg* (Toronto: Macmillan, 1970), 11–12. See also Jerry Szach, 'Playing in the Shadow of the Ukrainian Labour Temple,' ed. N. Reilly, *Manitoba History* 60 (Spring 2009): 28–46.

17 Shack, 'Education of Immigrant Children,' 26.

18 W.J. Sisler, 'Notebooks 1916–1921,' entry on 30 September 1917 in Sisler Papers, Archives of Manitoba. We would like to thank Jennifer Simons for this reference.

19 Ibid., entry on 8 September 1920.

20 W.J. Sisler, *Peaceful Invasion* (Winnipeg: Ketchen Printing Company, 1944), 39–40.

21 Ibid., 40; and Shack, 'Education of Immigrant Children,' 29.

22 If Catholic children attended the publicly funded or 'national schools,' they could apply for religious instruction after the regular school hours. This was one small victory for the Catholic population.

23 Statutes of Manitoba 1897, 60 Vic. Chapter 26, Section 10.

24 Manitoba, 'Return to an order of the House Shewing Statistics re Polish and Ruthenian School Districts,' 1915, cited in Robert Fletcher, 'The Language Problem in Manitoba's Schools,' *Manitoba Historical Society Transactions*, Series 3, Number 6, 1949–50 season; <http://www.mhs.mb.ca/docs/

transactions/3/languageproblem.shtml>. Typically each district operated a one-room school. No fewer than ninety-eight employed a teacher who spoke mainly Ukrainian or Polish, two employed a teacher who was bilingual (one in English and Polish and the other in English and Ukrainian), and fourteen employed teachers who were 'English speaking.' In other words, most of these rural schools were, in fact, unilingual and conducted little instruction in English. It was said that at least ten or twelve different languages were being taught under the bilingual rubric in rural districts.

25 *Manitoba Free Press*, 6 January 1902; see also G.R. Cook, 'Church, Schools and Politics in Manitoba, 1902–1912,' *Canadian Historical Review* 39, 1 (March 1958): 1–23; J.S. Woodsworth, 'The Strangers Within Our Gates,' *Methodist Magazine* (July 1905): 36.

26 J.T.M. Anderson, *The Education of the New Canadian: A Treatise on Canada's Greatest Educational Problem* (Toronto: J.M. Dent, 1918), 117–18.

27 Murray Donnelly, *Dafoe of the Free Press* (Toronto: Macmillan of Canada, 1968), 70–6.

28 Interestingly, though the law specified English-only instruction, Franco–Manitobans continued to teach in French. They even ran what appeared to be an independent, voluntary, province-wide examination system in French as well as English. The English-language hierarchy in the Department of Education seemed to be fully aware of the ruse. Robert Fletcher, one of the key figures in the language bill of 1916, reviewed the debate thirty years later and, in his last words, defended the use of French as a language of instruction: 'In closing I wish to pay tribute to our good friends in the City of St. Boniface who directed the schools there through these difficult years. They developed real bilingual schools which are a credit to the Province and demonstrated the feasibility of bilingual teaching when it is supported by the good-will of the community.' See Fletcher, 'Language Problem'; and Jean-Marie Taillefer, 'Les Franco-Manitobains et l'éducation 1870–1970 : une étude quantitative,' PhD diss., University of Manitoba, 1988.

29 Orest T. Martynowych and Nadia Kazymyra, 'Political Activity in Western Canada, 1896–1923,' in M.R. Lupul, ed., *A Heritage in Transition: Essays in the History of Ukrainians in Canada* (Toronto: McClelland and Stewart, 1982), 90.

30 Statutes of Manitoba 1901, c.22, s.17e, cited in Murray S. Donnelly, *The Government of Manitoba* (Toronto: University of Toronto Press, 1963), 72.

31 *Winnipeg Free Press*, 31 March 1901, cited in Donnelly, *Government of Manitoba*, 72–3.

32 Jean R. Burnet with Howard Palmer, *'Coming Canadians': An Introduction to a History of Canada's Peoples* (Toronto: McClelland and Stewart, 1988), 158.

33 Daniel Hiebert, 'Class, Ethnicity and Residential Structure: The Social
    Geography of Winnipeg, 1901–1921,' *Journal of Historical Geography* 17, 1
    (1991): 74. An alternative perspective is David Bright, *The Limits of Labour:
    Class Formation and the Labour Movement in Calgary 1883–1929* (Vancouver:
    University of British Columbia Press, 1998).
34 Tooth, 'Sixty years in Canada.'
35 Esyllt W. Jones, *Influenza 1918: Disease, Death, and Struggle in Winnipeg*
    (Toronto: University of Toronto Press, 2007).
36 The Hare proportional system was adopted by the legislature just for
    Greater Winnipeg in 1924. It created a single riding with ten members. The
    results are analysed effectively, and juxtaposed with census data on popula-
    tion, by Nelson Wiseman and K.W. Taylor in 'Ethnic vs Class Voting: The
    Case of Winnipeg, 1945,' *Canadian Journal of Political Science* 7, 2 (1974):
    314–28; K.W. Taylor and Nelson Wiseman, 'Class and Ethnic Voting in
    Winnipeg: The Case of 1941,' *Canadian Review of Sociology and Anthropology*
    14, 2 (1977): 174–87; Nelson Wiseman and K. Wayne Taylor, 'Class and
    Ethnic Voting in Winnipeg during the Cold War,' *Canadian Review of
    Sociology and Anthropology* 16, 1 (1979): 60–76; Nelson Wiseman and K.W.
    Taylor, 'Voting in Winnipeg during the Depression,' *Canadian Review of
    Sociology and Anthropology* 19, 2 (1982): 215–36.
37 Wiseman and Taylor, 'Ethnic vs Class Voting,' 319–20.
38 Several counts offered choices where the transfer could not be calculated
    and, in another, a candidate who evaded classification on such a scale
    presented a conundrum; Wiseman and Taylor, 'Ethnic vs Class Voting.'
39 Wiseman and Taylor, 'Ethnic vs Class Voting,' 322–5, 326.

3. Ethnic Cross-Currents in Mid-Century Alberta and Saskatchewan

1 Max Rubin, 'Alberta's Jews: The Long Journey,' in H. Palmer and T. Palmer,
   eds., *Peoples of Alberta: Portraits of Cultural Diversity* (Saskatoon: Western
   Producer Prairie Books, 1985), 383.
2 Henry C. Klassen, *A Business History of Alberta* (Calgary: University of Calgary
   Press, 1999), 131.
3 Gerald Friesen, *The Canadian Prairies: A History* (Toronto: University of
   Toronto Press, 1985), 422, 427.
4 Ibid., 424.
5 *Census of Canada*, 1961.
6 According to T.R. Balakrishnan, Calgary's rate of segregation was a low .263
   in 1951, compared to Toronto's high of .408. Thirty years later Winnipeg
   was the fourth most segregated in the country, compared to Edmonton and

Calgary, which were twelfth and fourteenth, respectively. T.R. Balakrishnan, 'Ethnic Residential Segregation in the Metropolitan Areas of Canada,' *Canadian Journal of Sociology* 4 (1995): 1–20.

7 Sheila McDonough and Homa Hoodfar, 'Muslims in Canada: From Ethnic Groups to Religious Community,' in P. Bramadat and D. Seljack, eds., *Religion and Ethnicity in Canada* (Toronto: Pearson, 2005), 142.

8 *Census of Canada,* 1941, 1951, 1961.

9 Ibid.

10 John Herd Thompson and Ian MacPherson, 'The Business of Agriculture: Prairie Farmers and the Adoption of "Business Methods," 1880–1950,' *Canadian Papers in Business History* 1 (1989): 258. John L. Shover makes a similar argument for farmers in the United States in his *First Majority, Last Minority: The Transforming of Rural Life in America* (Dekalb, IL: Northern Illinois University Press, 1976), 6.

11 For one study of this phenomenon, see Royden Loewen, *Diaspora in the Countryside: Two Mennonite Communities and Mid-Twentieth-Century North America* (Toronto: University of Toronto Press, 2006).

12 Between 1950 and 1970 the total number of Canadians who were recorded as 'rural' inhabitants dropped only slightly from 5.19 million to 5.16 million, but because of high post-war urban-bound migrations, with the number of Canadians designated 'urban' doubling in Canada from 8.8 to 16.4 million, the percentage of folks designated as 'rural' dropped from 37 percent to 24 percent of the population in Canada. *Census of Canada*; <www.usda.gov/agency/nass/pubs/trends/farmpop/-labor.csv,> accessed 17 April 2005. For a discussion on rural depopulation during these years see also John Porter, *The Vertical Mosaic: An Analysis of Social Class and Power* (Toronto: University of Toronto Press, 1965), 142, 146, 164.

13 Dirk Hoerder, *Creating Societies: Immigrant Lives in Canada* (Montreal: McGill-Queen's University Press, 1999), 150, 156.

14 Howard Palmer and Tamara Palmer, 'The Icelandic Experience in Alberta,' in H. Palmer and T. Palmer, eds., *Peoples of Alberta: Portraits of Cultural Diversity* (Saskatoon: Western Producer Prairie Books, 1985), 192.

15 Krystyna Lukasiewisz, 'Family and Work: Polish Interwar Immigrant Women in Alberta, 1920–1950,' MA thesis, University of Alberta, 1993, pp. 105, 124, 106, 108.

16 Gerald Tulchinsky, *Branching Out: The Transformation of the Canadian Jewish Community* (Toronto: Stoddart, 1998), 179–80.

17 Rubin, 'Alberta's Jews,' 331, 340.

18 The number of Jews of Calgary and Edmonton increased by 5 percent and 30 percent, respectively, and those in Regina and Saskatoon experienced a net loss. *Census of Canada,* 1941, 1951, 1961.

19 Tulchinsky, *Branching Out,* 124.

20 Eliane Leslau Silverman, 'Lena Hanen and the Conflicts of Leadership in the Twentieth Century,' in S. Carter, et al., eds., *Unsettled Pasts: Reconceiving the West through Women's History* (Calgary: University of Calgary Press, 2005), 363–70.

21 Rubin, 'Alberta's Jews,' 344.

22 Aya Fujiwara, 'From Anglo-Conformity to Multiculturalism: The Role of Scottish, Ukrainian and Japanese Ethnicity in the Transformation of Canadian Identity, 1919–1971,' PhD diss., University of Alberta, 2007, pp. 126, 234–6.

23 Elizabeth Macdonald, 'Japanese Canadians in Edmonton, 1969: An Exploratory Search for Patterns of Assimilation,' MA thesis, University of Alberta, 1970, p. 55.

24 Ibid., 48, 51, 55, 56, 62.

25 All acknowledged their minority status, but few dwelt on past discrimina-tions; 'one man said there was discrimination in 1949 from the veterans with respect to jobs at Imperial Oil,' but added quickly that discrimination had 'disappeared' in Edmonton. Ibid., 47. Also, note that these achieve-ment were based on inherited values: 'such a deep value orientation' did 'not disappear from *Issei* to *Nisei* images, even with their difficult experi-ences.' Ibid., 86.

26 Ibid., 80.

27 Zenon S. Pohorecky and Alexander Royick, 'Anglicization of Ukrainian in Canada between 1895 and 1970: A Case Study of Linguistic Crystallization,' *Canadian Ethnic Studies* 1 (1969): 158.

28 Frances Swyripa, *Wedded to the Cause: Ukrainian-Canadian Women and Ethnic Identity, 1891–1991* (Toronto: University of Toronto Press, 1993), 193.

29 In Saskatoon, the projects included the Sheptytsky Institute and a Ukrainian school. Ibid., 169.

30 Pohorecky and Royick, 'Anglicization of Ukrainian,' 149, 156, 157.

31 Howard Palmer, 'Patterns of Immigration and Ethnic Settlements in Alberta,' in H. Palmer and T. Palmer, eds., *Peoples of Alberta: Portraits of Cultural Diversity* (Saskatoon: Western Producer Prairie Books, 1985), 36; Howard Palmer and Tamara Palmer, 'The Romanian Community in Alberta,' in H. Palmer and T. Palmer, eds., *Peoples of Alberta,* 262; Howard Palmer and Tamara Palmer, 'The Estonians in Alberta,' in H. Palmer and T. Palmer, eds., *Peoples of Alberta,* 210, 212.

32 Bohdan Harasymiw, 'Political Participation of Ukrainian Canadians Since 1945,' in M.R. Lupul, ed., *A Heritage in Transition: Essays in the History of Ukrainians in Canada* (Toronto: McClelland and Stewart, 1982), 126; Howard Palmer and Tamara Palmer, 'The Religious Ethic,' in H. Palmer

and T. Palmer, eds., *Peoples of Alberta: Portraits of Cultural Diversity* (Saskatoon: Western Producer Prairie Books, 1985), 157; Gerhard Bassler, *The German Canadian Mosaic Today and Yesterday: Identities, Roots and Heritage* (Ottawa: German-Canadian Congress, 1991), 16, 17.

33 Palmer and Palmer, 'The Religious Ethic,' 159.

34 David Aliaga, 'Italian Immigrants in Calgary: Dimensions of Cultural Identity,' *Canadian Ethnic Studies* 26 (1994): 143.

35 Ninety-one percent of the farmers claimed this level of poverty. Ibid., 143.

36 Forty-nine percent reported working in general construction, and 34 percent as general labourers, two-thirds of whom reported working either for the city or for the CP rail yards; only 3.5 percent reported owning their own businesses, and these were usually 'subcontractors to companies they had previously worked for.' Ibid., 146.

37 Antonella Fanella, 'Family, Honour and Destiny: Southern Italian Immigrants in Calgary, 1910–1990,' MA thesis, University of Calgary, 1991, p. 71.

38 Howard M. Snider, 'Variables Affecting Immigrant Adjustment: A Study of Italians in Edmonton,' MA thesis, University of Alberta, 1966, pp. 85, 87.

39 Alan Thomas Rees-Powell, 'Differentials in the Integration Process of Dutch and Italian Immigrants in Edmonton,' MSW thesis, University of Alberta, 1964, pp. 3, 7.

40 For further analysis on the history of Dutch immigrants in Alberta see Palmer and Palmer, 'The Religious Ethic.'

41 Rees-Powell, 'Differentials in the Integration Process,' 130, vi.

42 Donna Mavis Minions, 'Three Worlds of Greek-Canadian Women: A Study of Migrant Greek Women in Calgary, Alberta,' MA thesis, University of Calgary, 1984, pp. 86, 67, 69, 70.

43 Ibid., 136, 74, 80, 88.

44 Kathryn-Anne Rhea Watts, 'Calgary's Polish Community: Social Factors Contributing to its Formation and Persistence,' MA thesis, University of Calgary, 1976, pp. 19, 53, 54, 56, 59, 60, 67.

45 Fanella, 'Family, Honour and Destiny,' 18, 73, 74.

46 T.D. Regehr, *Mennonites in Canada: A People Transformed* (Toronto: University of Toronto Press, 1996), 47.

47 Marlene Epp, *Women Without Men: Mennonite Refugees of the Second World War* (Toronto: University of Toronto Press, 2000).

48 Thomas R. Poetschke, 'Reasons for Immigration and Ethnic Identity: An Exploratory Study of German Immigrants in Edmonton,' MA thesis, University of Alberta, 1978, p. 35.

49 Minions, 'Three Worlds of Greek-Canadian Women,' 84, 85.

50 Steve Tötösy de Zepetnek, 'A History of the Hungarian Cultural Society of Edmonton, 1946–1986,' *Canadian Ethnic Studies* 25 (1993): 100–17.
51 Ibid., 106.
52 David Millet, 'Defining the "Dominant Group,"' *Canadian Ethnic Studies* 13 (1981): 73.

4. Accommodation in Winnipeg

1 This chapter relies on interviews with immigrants and their children. Researchers at the University of Manitoba and University of Winnipeg, guided by the co-authors of this book, were funded by the Prairie Centre for Excellence in Research in Immigration and Integration, part of Canada's Metropolis Project, to undertake investigations of prairie immigrant adaptation. The Winnipeg research included studies of the local Japanese community by Peter Nunoda; Germans, by Hans Werner; Mennonites, by Janis Thiessen; French Canadians, by Ken Sylvester; people of Caribbean origin, by Esyllt Jones; and of Winnipeg's International Centre, by Jennifer Rogalsky. Gerald Friesen interviewed Saul Cherniack, Toni Chiapetta, Masako Kawata, Sam Loschiavo, Arthur Mauro, Arthur Miki, and Keith Sandiford.
2 The interviews with Saul Cherniack were conducted by Gerald Friesen at Mr Cherniack's house, 333 St John's Avenue, Winnipeg, on 10 December 2002 and 7 January 2003, and corrected by Mr Cherniack during several later conversations.
3 Saul M. Cherniack, 'Canada and the Japanese Canadians,' lecture presented to the Jewish Historical Society of Western Canada, 1 December 1998.
4 J.A. Cherniack, 'Reminiscences of 40 Years of Jewish Community Life,' typed manuscript originally presented in Yiddish, translated by H.H. Herstein, ms. in Jewish Heritage Centre of Western Canada, Inc., Winnipeg.
5 W.L. Morton, 'Manitoba Schools and Canadian Nationality,' *Canadian Historical Association Annual Report,* 1951. <http://www.erudit.org/revuc/ram/1951/v30/n1/290034ar.pdf,> 58; also G.R. Cook, 'Church, Schools and Politics in Manitoba, 1902–1912,' *Canadian Historical Review* 39, 1 (1958).
6 John S. Matthiasson, 'Icelandic Canadians in Central Canada: One Experiment in Multiculturalism,' *Western Canadian Journal of Anthropology* 4, 2 (1974): 49–61.
7 Hans Werner, *Imagined Homes: Soviet German Immigrants in Two Cities* (Winnipeg: University of Manitoba Press, 2007); also his 'Integration in Two Cities: A Comparative History of Protestant Ethnic German Immigrants

in Winnipeg, Canada and Bielefeld, Germany, 1947–1989,' PhD diss., University of Manitoba, 2002, pp. 63–84, 96–9.

8 Werner, 'Integration in Two Cities,' 100–1, 121, 238.

9 Peter Nunoda, 'Harold Hirose on Integration and Citizenship for Japanese Manitobans, 1942–52,' *Prairie Forum* 27, 2 (2002): 209–20. The Manitoba government made a more generous gesture in December 1945 in its statement of policy on the issues raised by the presence of Japanese Canadians in the province: 'But with regard to the general body of Canadian citizens of Japanese origin whose loyalty is unquestioned, in our opinion their Canadian citizenship should be the same as that of all other Canadian citizens which carries with it unrestricted freedom of movement within Canada.' This document, entitled 'Press Release,' 20 December 1945, is filed in the Premiers' Papers, Advisory Committee on Post-War Reconstruction, Correspondence of Premier Garson, Box 4, Q 025303 (Archives of Manitoba). Speaking of these events in 1998, Saul Cherniack said: 'Many first generation immigrants of other ethnic groups have proved that they could survive hardships ... So it has been with the Japanese; but the Japanese had to overcome more than most other immigrants, including racism, rejection, humiliation, and uprooting.' Cherniack, 'Canada and the Japanese Canadians.' Other details in this paragraph come from the Kawata family interview and from Arthur Miki.

10 Janis Thiessen, 'Faith and Factory: Russian Mennonite Workers in Twentieth-Century Manitoba,' PhD diss., University of New Brunswick, 2005.

11 Ibid., 98.

12 Ibid., 196.

13 The organizing group was called the Welfare Council of Greater Winnipeg; Margot Morrish, 'The Origins of the Citizenship Council of Manitoba / International Centre,' in D.H. Poonwassie and A. Poonwassie, eds., *Adult Education in Manitoba: Historical Aspects* (Mississauga: Canadian Educators' Press, 1997), 57–94.

14 The Refugees Committee (1946) was later called the New Canadians Committee (1949), and then renamed the Citizenship Committee (1951). Its program is discussed in Citizenship Council document P649, 1948, cited in Jennifer Rogalsky, 'The Citizenship Council of Manitoba: Fifty Years of Service, 1948–1998,' unpublished manuscript prepared for the Citizenship Council on the occasion of its fiftieth anniversary. Also central in the following discussion is Jennifer Rogalsky, '"Good Canadians in Every Sense": The Citizenship Council of Manitoba 1948–1975,' MA thesis, University of Winnipeg/University of Manitoba, 2000. Both manuscripts relied on an oral history project carried out by Glen Smith in 1989, on

interviews with International Centre and Citizenship Council workers, and
on the papers of the two organizations housed in the Archives of Manitoba.

15 The active leaders included the director of the university's adult education
program (A.S.R. Tweedie), a representative of the Welfare Council (Mrs
McQueen), the principal of a high school (E. Morgan of Daniel McIntyre
Collegiate), a judge (W.J. Lindal), and a federal civil servant whose assign-
ment was to link the government to community groups (Jean Lagassé of the
Citizenship Branch). Rogalsky, 'The Citizenship Council'; and Rogalsky,
'"Good Canadians in Every Sense."'

16 Rogalsky, 'The Citizenship Council,' 18–19; discovering that other prairie
cities had developed independent constitutions for agencies like theirs, the
Winnipeggers left the Welfare Council and reorganized as the independent
Citizenship Council of Manitoba in 1957.

17 The individuals were Sonja Roeder, a German immigrant; Mary Panaro,
who came to Canada from Poland as a child before the First World War;
and Genevieve Brownell. The provincial government grant of $5000 was
approved by Sidney Spivak, Minister of Industry and Commerce in the
Conservative government in 1966. It was to provide immigrants with
language training and counselling. Rogalsky, 'The Citizenship Council';
and Rogalsky, '"Good Canadians in Every Sense."'

18 Rogalsky, 'The Citizenship Council,' 24–30.

19 The Winnipeg branch of Imperial Order Daughters of the Empire introduced 'official ceremonies of welcome to newly-naturalized citizens' in the
1930s. The ceremony was revived after the Second World War, beginning
with an event on 10 January 1947 following the passage of Canada's new
Citizenship Act. Kurt Korneski, ed., 'Citizenship Ceremony, 10 January 1947,'
Manitoba History 51 (February 2006); 'some grasp' in Citizenship Council
Annual Report 1952, 649 1a, cited in Rogalsky, 'The Citizenship Council,'
15; 'equal footing' cited in Morrish, 'Citizenship Council,' 85. We would
like to thank Mallory Richard for her research on these activities.

20 'That was it,' interview with Genevieve Brownell, C2061, Archives of
Manitoba, cited by Rogalsky, 'The Citizenship Council,' 23; 'little old lady'
in Edith Courtney interview, AM, C2050, and Myrtle Lawson interview,
C2049, cited in Rogalsky, 'The Citizenship Council,' 23–4; Rogalsky, '"Good
Canadians in Every Sense."' Toni Chiapetta, interview with Gerald Friesen.

21 Royal Commission on Adult Education, 'Minutes of Meeting, 17–24 April
1946,' Royal Commission Papers, Archives of Manitoba GR76/A0063;
Gerald Friesen, 'Stuart Garson, Harold Innis, and Adult Education in
Manitoba,' in P.J. Giffen, *Rural Life: Portraits of the Prairie Town, 1946*
(Winnipeg: University of Manitoba Press, 2004), 228–9.

22 Franca Iacovetta, *Gatekeepers: Reshaping Immigrant Lives in Cold War Canada*
    (Toronto: Between the Lines, 2006), 11.

5. The Global South in Calgary and Edmonton

 1 Henry C. Klassen, *A Business History of Alberta* (Calgary: University of Calgary
    Press, 1999), 276, 285, 290, 313.
 2 Doreen Indra, 'Khmer, Lao, Vietnamese and Vietnamese Chinese in
    Alberta,' in H. Palmer and T. Palmer, eds., *Peoples of Alberta: Portraits of
    Cultural Diversity* (Saskatoon: Western Producer Prairie Books, 1985), 437.
 3 Paul Y.M. Lin, 'Accessibility of Services to New Immigrants in Calgary,' MSW
    thesis, University of Calgary, 1977, p. 35.
 4 *Calgary Herald,* 25 November 1996.
 5 Ibid., 5 November 1997.
 6 Ibid., 24 June 1998.
 7 Lin, 'Accessibility of Services,' 36, 41.
 8 Howard Palmer, 'Patterns of Immigration and Ethnic Settlements in
    Alberta,' in H. Palmer and T. Palmer, eds., *Peoples of Alberta: Portraits of
    Cultural Diversity* (Saskatoon: Western Producer Prairie Books, 1985), 43.
 9 In 2006, 28,325 Albertans declared they had been born in the United
    States, compared to 41,525 who had been born in Central and South
    America and the Caribbean; 187,675 were born in Europe compared to
    233,980 who had been born in Asia and Oceana. <http://www40.statcan
    .ca/l01/cst01/demo34c.htm>, accessed 22 January 2008.
10 For a fuller discussion of the points system, see Ninette Kelley and Michael
    Trebilcock, *The Making of the Mosaic: A History of Canadian Immigration Policy*
    (Toronto: University of Toronto Press, 1998).
11 True, the single largest source-country for Alberta in 1989 was a European
    country, Poland, providing 11 percent of the province's immigrants. David
    H. Bai, 'Canadian Immigration Policy and the Voluntary Sector: The Case
    of the Edmonton Immigrant Services Association,' *Human Organization* 51
    (1992): 25.
12 David Harvey, *The Condition of Postmodernity: An Enquiry into the Origins of
    Cultural Change* (Oxford: Blackwell, 1989).
13 Raymond Breton, 'Institutional Completeness of Ethnic Communities and
    the Personal Relations of Immigrants,' *American Journal of Sociology* 70
    (1964): 193–205.
14 Bat-Ami Klejner, 'Latin American Immigrants in Calgary: An
    Ethnopsychological Study,' MSc thesis, University of Calgary, 1994, p. 90.

15 Ransford Kwabena Danso, 'Access to Housing and its Impact on the Adaptation Process: The Case of African Immigrants in Calgary,' MA (Geography) thesis, University of Calgary, 1997, p. 129.
16 Indra, 'Khmer, Lao, Vietnamese,' 459.
17 Norman Buchignani, *Continuous Journey: A Social History of South Asians in Canada* (Toronto: McClelland and Stewart, 1985), 434.
18 Lin, 'Accessibility of Services,' 130.
19 Patricia Marie Hackney, 'An Investigation of Problems Related to Recent Immigration andAccessibility of Services for Immigrants,' MSW thesis, University of Calgary, 1979, p. 75.
20 Ibid., 76.
21 *Calgary Herald*, 13 December 1988.
22 Lin, 'Accessibility of Services,' 132.
23 The ACAC, founded in about 1995, organized 'picnics, national day celebrations and cultural festivals ... forging a sense of ... solidarity and cooperation among its members.' Danso, 'Access to Housing,' 131.
24 Norman Buchignani, 'South Asians in Alberta,' in H. Palmer and T. Palmer, eds., *Peoples of Alberta: Portraits of Cultural Diversity* (Saskatoon: Western Producer Prairie Books, 1985), 423.
25 Ibid., 428.
26 Jinjin Zhang, 'Illness Management Strategies among Chinese Immigrants Living with Arthritis,' MSc thesis, University of Calgary, 1998, p. 74.
27 Buchignani, 'South Asians in Alberta,' 433.
28 This came after a series of stories by the *Calgary Herald* and after Forest Lawn's MLA Barry Pashak 'lashed out at the province for ignoring the needs of immigrant workers.' *Calgary Herald*, 5 July 1988.
29 *Calgary Herald*, 9 September 1982.
30 *Edmonton Journal*, 16 August 1976.
31 Ibid., 4 January 1984.
32 Lin, 'Accessibility of Services,' 47.
33 The group that Lin studied had 558 children aged up to four years old, 558 aged five to nine, 420 aged ten to fourteen, and 430 aged fifteen to nineteen.
34 Palmer, 'Patterns of Immigration,' 45.
35 Ibid. See also Lin, 'Accessibility of Services,' 48.
36 Hackney, 'An Investigation of Problems,' 40, 41. Indicating their healthy integration was the fact that '80.6% of the respondents had contacted Canada Manpower and Immigration ... however, Calgary Immigration Aid Society, Calgary Catholic Family Service Bureau and Alberta Social Services

and Community Health had not been contacted at all.' Hackney, 'An Investigation of Problems,' 42.

37 Howard Palmer and Tamara Palmer, 'The Romanian Community in Alberta,' in H. Palmer and T. Palmer, eds., *Peoples of Alberta: Portraits of Cultural Diversity* (Saskatoon: Western Producer Prairie Books, 1985), 269.

38 Indra, 'Khmer, Lao, Vietnamese,' 457.

39 R. Montgomery, 'The Economic Adaptation of Vietnamese Refugees in Alberta, 1979–84,' *International Migration* 24 (1986): 749.

40 Ibid., 755, 758.

41 Katherine A. MacRury, 'The Occupational Adjustment of Vietnamese Refugees in Edmonton, Canada,' MEd thesis, University of Alberta, 1979, pp. 4, 54.

42 Quoted in Danso, 'Access to Housing,' 135.

43 Danso, 'Access to Housing,' 149. They were among 'the least residentially segregated among the so-called "visible minorities" in the city the Chinese at .502 on the ID.'

44 Ibid., 142, 162, 163, 165, 168.

45 Kit Man Kitty Mok, 'Community Services for Immigrant Women in Forest Lawn,' MEnv Design, University of Calgary, 1991, p. 1.

46 Ibid., 32–4.

47 This contrasts to 15 percent of Calgarians who spoke a language other than English or French and 2 percent who spoke neither of the official languages. Ibid., 36, 37.

48 Kenneth J. Fairbairn and Hafzia Khatun, 'Residential Segregation and the Intra-Urban Migration of South Asians in Edmonton,' *Canadian Ethnic Studies* 21 (1989): 60.

49 Of this number 68 percent of the adult men from 152 households 'reported professional and managerial professions.' Fairbairn and Khatun, 'Residential Segregation,' 57, 50.

50 Ibid., 51. '78% rented before the move, 29% following it.' Ibid., 57.

51 See Li Wei, 'Building Ethnoburbia: The Emergence and Manifestation of the Chinese Ethnoburbia in Los Angeles's San Gabriel Valley,' *Journal of Asian American Studies* 2 (1999): 1–28.

52 Fairbairn and Khatun, 'Residential Segregation,' 60, 55.

53 Danso, 'Access to Housing,' 147.

54 Nancy Foner, *From Ellis Island to JFK: New York's Two Great Waves of Immigration* (New Haven: Yale University Press, 2000), 55.

55 Palmer, 'Patterns of Immigration,' 48.

56 Palmer, 'Immigration and Ethnic Settlement,' 46; Lin, 'Accessibility of Services,' 70.

57 Yvette Y.L. Knott, 'A Case Study on the Canadian Policy and Calgary Community Response to the Southeast Asian Refugees, 1979–1980,' MA thesis, University of Calgary, 1981, p. 88.

58 Cecille DePass, 'Centering on Changing Communities: The Colours of the South in the Canadian Vertical Mosaic,' *Canadian Ethnic Studies* 24 (1992): 99, 101.

59 Ibid., 101.

60 Hackney, 'An Investigation of Problems,' 11.

61 DePass, 'Centering on Changing Communities,' 104, 106.

62 Hackney, 'An Investigation of Problems,' 12.

63 Ibid., 90.

64 Klejner, 'Latin American Immigrants in Calgary,' 66, 70, 72, 96, 147.

65 Knott, 'A Case Study on the Canadian Policy,' i, 90.

66 Ibid., 71, 72.

67 Ibid., 74, 84, 85.

68 Ibid., 86.

69 'The admission of 60,000 SEA refugees in 1979 and 1980 is the largest refugee program undertaken since World War II.' Ibid., 96.

70 Ibid., 97, 99.

71 Lin, 'Accessibility of Services,' 81, 90, 93, 99, 101.

72 Ibid., 127.

73 Its 1976 incorporation came just 'one month after the Immigration Act of 1976 was tabled in the House of Commons.' Bai, 'Canadian Immigration Policy,' 23. A voluntary organization, the EISA consisted of 'persons of either sex, who are aged 25–44, well-educated, employed and married.' Bai, 'Canadian Immigration Policy,' 24.

74 Ibid., 27, 28, 29, 32.

75 Gerald Friesen and Royden Loewen, 'Romantics, Pluralists and Post-Modernists,' in Gerald Friesen, *River Road: Essays on Manitoba and Prairie History* (Winnipeg: University of Manitoba Press, 1996), 183–96. See Royal Commission on Bilingualism and Biculturalism, *Report Book IV: The Cultural Contribution of the Other Ethnic Groups* (Ottawa: The Author, 1969), Recommendation #14, 230.

76 Bai, 'Canadian Immigration Policy,' 25, 26.

77 *Calgary Herald*, 10 November 1978.

78 Ibid., 10 March 1979.

79 Ibid., 24 December 1982.

80 Ibid., 24 July 1982.

81 Quoted in Victor J. Ramraj, 'West Indian Canadian Writing in English,' *International Journal of Canadian Studies* 13 (1996): 164.

6. Gender and Family in Hybrid Households

1 <http://www.calgarymandir.com/History.htm>; <islamiccenter.sk.ca/community_1.htm>, accessed 24 January 2008.

2 Paul Bramadat and David Seljack, eds., *Ethnicity and Christianity in Canada* (Toronto: University of Toronto Press, 2008).

3 David H. Bai, 'Canadian Immigration Policy and the Voluntary Sector: The Case of the Edmonton Immigrant Services Association,' *Human Organization* 51 (1992): 26.

4 Charles M. Campbell, *Betrayal and Deceit: The Politics of Canadian Immigration* (West Vancouver: Jasmine Books, 2000), 28.

5 See Greg Teal, 'Urban Anthropology and the Problems of the Formation of Social Classes: With Reference to Korean Immigrants in Edmonton,' MA (Anthropology) thesis, University of Alberta, 1979.

6 See Cecil P. Pereira, 'East Indians in Winnipeg: A Study of the Consequences of Immigration for an Ethnic Group in Canada,' MA thesis, University of Manitoba, 1971.

7 Milton Gordon argued in his classic 1964 study that immigrants in the United States were able to impede assimilative forces within the network of family, church, and ethnic institution, but that they assimilated more easily within the realm of 'secondary relations,' in the arenas of work, education, and state-run social service. See Milton Gordon, 'Assimilation in America: Theory and Reality,' in R. Abrams and L. Levine, eds., *The Shaping of Twentieth Century America* (Boston: Little, Brown and Company, 1965), 70–89. John Bodnar seemed to agree in 1985: within 'the face of a sprawling and complex urban, industrial structure,' wrote Bodnar, the 'traditional' family 'forged a relatively simple device for maintaining order and purpose in [the immigrants'] lives.' John E. Bodnar, *The Transplanted: A History of Immigrants in Urban America* (Bloomington: Indiana University Press, 1985), 84. A similar notion was echoed in a more recent publication. Its preface notes that the assimilating forces in postmodern society of 'hybridisation and de-differentiation' have been checked by 'the multicultural world' in which 'minority cultures ... maintain their differences through the socialization of children and adults into family cultural traditions that are unique.' Biko Agozino, Introduction, in C.D.H. Harvey, ed., *Maintaining our Differences: Minority Families in Multicultural Societies* (Hampshire, England: Ashgate, 2001), xiii. See also Charles H. Mindel, Robert W. Habenstein, and Roosevelt Wright Jr., eds., *Ethnic Families in America: Patterns and Variations* (New Jersey: Prentice Hall, 1998), 8.

8   Christopher Lasch, *Haven in a Heartless World: The Family Besieged* (New York: Basic Books, 1979), xxiii.

9   R.W. Sandwell, 'The Limits of Liberalism: The Liberal Renaissance and the History of the Family in Canada,' *Canadian Historical Review* 84 (2003): 426.

10 See, for example, Yen Le Espirtu, '"We Don't Sleep Around like White Girls Do": Family, Culture and Gender in Filipina American Lives,' in D.R. Gabaccia and V.L. Ruiz, eds., *American Dreaming, Global Realities: Rethinking U.S. Immigration History* (Urbana: University of Illinois Press, 2006) 484–503; Paula S. Fass, 'Children and Globalization,' *Journal of Social History* 38 (2005): 937–53; Simone Cinotto, 'Leonard Covello, the Covello Papers, and the History of Eating Habits Among Italian Immigrants in New York,' *Journal of American History* 91 (2004): 497–521; Allison Varzally, 'Romantic Crossings, Making Love, Family and Non-Whiteness in California, 1925–1950,' *Journal of American Ethnic History* 23 (2003): 3–54; Fatima Husain and Margaret O'Brien, 'South Asian Muslims in Britain: Faith, Family and Community,' in C.D.H. Harvey, ed., *Maintaining our Differences: Minority Families in Multicultural Societies* (Hampshire, England: Ashgate, 2001), 15–28.

11 J.E. Smith, 'Our Own Kind: Family and Community Networks in Providence,' *Radical History Review* 17 (1978): 99–108. Smith writes that in Providence there was neither 'a sharp uprooting nor a simple continuity,' 395, and that 'immigration was itself a family response to changing conditions,' 398.

12 Norman Buchignani, 'South Asian Canadians and the Ethnic Mosaic: An Overview,' *Canadian Ethnic Studies* 11 (1979): 56.

13 Pereira, 'East Indians in Winnipeg,' ii, 165, 168.

14 Teal, 'Urban Anthropology,' 68, 96, 117, 173, 170.

15 Howard Palmer, 'Patterns of Immigration and Ethnic Settlements in Alberta,' in H. Palmer and T. Palmer, eds., *Peoples of Alberta: Portraits of Cultural Diversity* (Saskatoon: Western Producer Prairie Books, 1985), 46.

16 Linda L. Fuchs, 'Social Support, Life Events, Self Concepts and Happiness Among Southeast Asian Refugee Women in Saskatoon,' MA thesis, University of Saskatchewan, 1987, pp. 75, 162.

17 Stuart D. Johnson and Cornelia B. Johnson, 'Institutional Origins in the Chilean Refugee Community in Winnipeg,' *Prairie Forum* 2 (1982): 232, 230, 231.

18 Bernard Thraves, 'An Analysis of Ethnic Intra-Urban Migration: The Case of Winnipeg,' PhD diss., University of Manitoba, 1986, pp. 98, 99.

19 The number of single people never entering marriage in Britain rose from 12 percent in 1960 to 22 percent in 1980; the percentage of households in

the United States consisting of two parents with children fell from 44 percent in 1960 to 29 percent in 1980. For a full discussion of these late-century developments see Eric Hobsbawm, *The Age of Extremes: A History of the World, 1914–1991* (New York: Pantheon, 1994).

20 Cleto M. Buduhan, 'An Urban Village: The Effects of Migration on the Filipino Garment Workers in a Canadian City,' MA (Anthropology) thesis, University of Manitoba, 1972, pp. 117–20.

21 Bok-Nam Yoon, 'The Adjustment Problems and Education Needs of Korean Immigrant Women in the Winnipeg Garment Industry,' MEd thesis, University of Manitoba, 1983, pp. 34, 36, 88.

22 Amory Yuk Mui Ong, 'An Exploratory Study of the Life of Single Asian Immigrant Women in Winnipeg: Implications for Social Work Practice,' MSW thesis, University of Manitoba, 1987, pp. ii, 120.

23 Nancy Foner, *From Ellis Island to JFK: New York's Two Great Waves of Immigration* (New Haven: Yale University Press, 2000), 119.

24 Ibid., 129. See also Donna Gabaccia, *From the Other Side: Women, Gender and Immigrant Life in the U.S, 1820–1990* (Bloomington: Indiana University Press, 1994), 102–3. She argues that the 'foreign-born ... now seem more strongly committed to ... professional careers than their ... native-born ... counterparts,' finding, thus, no need to build 'careers as feminists or women's rights activists.'

25 E. Anthony Rotundo, *American Manhood: Transformation in Masculinity from the Revolution to the Modern Era* (New York: Basic Books, 1993), 282. For a description of masculinity among men in manual labour, see Steven Maynard, 'Rough Work and Rugged Men: The Social Construction of Masculinity in Working Class History,' *Labour/le travail* 23 (1989): 159–69.

26 E. Tatsoglou and G. Stubos, 'The Greek Immigrant Family in the United States and Canada: The Transition from an "Institutional" to a "Relational" Form, 1945–1970,' *International Migration* 30 (1992): 161.

27 Daniel Coleman, *Masculine Migrations: Reading the Postcolonial Male in the New Canadian Narratives* (Toronto: University of Toronto Press, 1998), xii.

28 David Aliaga, 'Italian Immigrants in Calgary: Dimensions of Cultural Identity,' *Canadian Ethnic Studies* 26 (1994): 145.

29 Paul Yee, *Struggle and Hope: The Story of the Chinese in Canada* (Toronto: Umbrella, 1996), 183.

30 Angela Djao, Lily Tingley, and Roxana Ng, *Doubly Disadvantaged: The Women Who Immigrate to Canada* (Saskatoon: Immigrant Women of Saskatchewan, 1985), 54.

31 Ibid., 48.

32 Kit Man Kitty Mok, 'Community Services for Immigrant Women in Forest Lawn,' MEnv Design thesis, University of Calgary, 1991, pp. 107, 110, 114, 116.

33 Paul Y.M. Lin, 'Accessibility of Services to New Immigrants in Calgary,' MSW thesis, University of Calgary, 1977, p. 106.

34 A third of the sixty-two married women who agreed that immigration had introduced changes to their marriages cited the changes as negative; only sixty-two of the ninety-five agreed that immigration had changed their marriages. Djao, Tingley, and Ng, *Doubly Disadvantaged*, 48.

35 Helen Ralston, 'Organizational Empowerment among South Asian Immigrant Women in Canada,' *International Journal of Canadian Studies* 11 (1995): 143.

36 Ibid., 142.

37 Tomoko Makabe, *The Canadian Sansei* (Toronto: University of Toronto Press, 1998), 84.

38 Ransford Kwabena Danso, 'Access to Housing and its Impact on the Adaptation Process: The Case of African Immigrants in Calgary,' MA (Geography) thesis, University of Calgary, 1997, p. 111.

39 Bat-Ami Klejner, 'Latin American Immigrants in Calgary: An Ethnopsychological Study,' MSc (Psychology) thesis, University of Calgary, 1994, pp. 76, 79.

40 Muhammad Siddique, 'Changing Family Patterns: A Comparative Analysis of Immigrant Indian and Pakistani Families of Saskatoon, Canada,' *Journal of Comparative Family Studies* 8 (1977): 180, 181, 193, 199. Only a third of the women worked, but they nevertheless reported significant joint decision making, 90 percent reporting joint decisions as to where to locate, 82 percent on when to purchase a house, and 86 percent on how to take vacations.

41 Helen Chan, 'Family Organization and Change Among the Chinese in Calgary,' MA (Sociology) thesis, University of Calgary, 1980, p. 66.

42 Franca Iacovetta, 'Making New Canadians: Social Workers, Women and the Reshaping of Immigrant Families,' in F. Iacovetta, P. Draper, and R. Ventresca, eds., *A Nation of Immigrants: Women, Workers and Communities in Canada, 1840s–1960s* (Toronto: University of Toronto Press, 2002), 482–513; Joan Sangster, 'Creating Social and Moral Citizens: Defining and Treating Delinquent Boys and Girls in English Canada, 1920–65,' in R. Adamoski, D.E. Chunn, and R. Menzies, eds., *Contesting Canadian Citizenship: Historical Readings* (Peterborough: Broadview, 2002), 337–58.

43 Alison Louise Dobbie, 'Health Beliefs and Behaviours of Arab Immigrants: A Canadian Perspective,' MN thesis, University of Saskatchewan, 1999, pp. 62, 63, 103.

44 Doreen Indra, 'Khmer, Lao, Vietnamese and Vietnamese Chinese in Alberta,' in H. Palmer and T. Palmer, eds., *Peoples of Alberta: Portraits of Cultural Diversity* (Saskatoon: Western Producer Prairie Books, 1985), 448.

45 Djao, Tingley, and Ng, *Doubly Disadvantaged*, 57.

46 Klejner, 'Latin American Immigrants in Calgary,' 86.

47 Chan, 'Family Organization,' 6, 18, 23, 59.

48 Ibid., 7.

49 Wing-Sam Chow, 'A Chinese Community in a Prairie City: A Holistic Perspective of its Class and Ethnic Relations,' PhD diss., University of Michigan, 1981, pp. 89, 91, 141.

50 Yoon, 'The Adjustment Problems,' ii, 33, 39, 52, 62, 65, 68, 71. By comparison to their membership in churches, only 10 percent belonged to the Korean Association and only 5 percent were members of unions. Yoon, 'The Adjustment Problems,' 50.

51 Ralston, 'Organizational Empowerment,' 140, 141.

52 Pereira, 'East Indians in Winnipeg,' 166.

53 Lordson Wai-Chung Luk, 'The Assimilation of Chinese in Saskatoon,' MA thesis, University of Saskatchewan, 1971, p. 103.

54 Daniel Wing Leung Lai and J.R. McDonald, 'Life Satisfaction of Chinese Elderly Immigrants in Calgary,' *Canadian Journal of Aging* 14 (1995): 544, 548.

55 Donna Mavis Minions, 'Three Worlds of Greek-Canadian Women: A Study of Migrant Greek Women in Calgary, Alberta,' MA thesis, University of Calgary, 1984, p. 151.

56 Yoko Urata Nakahara, 'Ethnic Identity Among Japanese Canadians in Edmonton: The Case of Pre-World War II Immigrants and Their Descendants,' PhD (Education) diss., University of Alberta, 1991, p. i.

57 About 30 percent indicated that they were 'very much interested' in Japanese culture, and 27 percent actually took lessons in the Japanese language. Ibid., 94.

58 Gordon Darroch, 'Urban Ethnicity in Canada: Personal Assimilation and Political Communities,' *Canadian Review of Sociology and Anthropology* 18 (1981): 93, 96.

59 Jeffrey Reitz and Margaret Ashton, 'Ukrainian Language and Identity Retention in Urban Canada,' *Canadian Ethnic Studies* 12 (1980): 39, 44.

60 True, some studies have shown high degrees of endogamy among young immigrants. Sociologist Leo Driedger, for example, found in 1982 that immigrant students at the University of Manitoba in Winnipeg expressed eagerness to marry within their cultural group, reflecting 'healthy' ethnic bonding among young immigrant adults, and a 'need for in group ethnic

identification.' Leo Driedger, 'Attitudes of Winnipeg University Students towards Immigrants of European and Non-European Origin,' *Prairie Forum* 7 (1982): 219.

61 Jim Frideres and Sheldon Goldenberg, 'Hyphenated Canadians: Comparative Analysis of Ethnic, Regional and National Identification of Western Canadian University Students,' *Journal of Ethnic Studies* 5 (1981): 98, 99.

62 Sona Khosla, 'Generational Conflict: The Impact of Cultural Baggage and Culture Clash on the Relationship Between East Indian Immigrant Parents and Their Canadian-Born Children,' undergraduate essay, University of Calgary, 1999, pp. 3, 7, 8.

63 Hong Xiao, 'Chinese Language Maintenance in Winnipeg,' *Canadian Ethnic Studies* 30 (1998): 87.

64 Yee, *Struggle and Hope*, 177.

65 Chow, 'A Chinese Community,' 114, 142.

66 Chan, 'Family Organization,' 55.

67 Xiao, 'Chinese Language Maintenance in Winnipeg,' 91. The experience of Chinese children in Saskatoon, Calgary, and Winnipeg was echoed by children of all ethnic groups during the last decades. Parents of many groups voiced a range of concerns about the pressures their children faced in the public arena. Some were concerned with 'ethnopaulism': African parents in Winnipeg in the 1980s observed that the vast majority of their children had experienced name-calling – 'blackie,' 'fudge bar,' 'black ass,' 'slit eyes,' or 'flat nose' – with signs that the children were 'hurt, upset or humiliated by the ethnic derogation.' Bohdanna Pankiw and Rita M. Bienvenue, 'Parental Responses to Ethnic Name-Calling: A Sociological Inquiry,' *Canadian Ethnic Studies* 22 (1990): 85.

68 Luk, 'The Assimilation of Chinese in Saskatoon,' 103.

7. Racism, Anti-Racism, and Race in Winnipeg

1 George Barker, *Forty Years a Chief* (Winnipeg: Peguis Publishers, 1979), 33; the legal context is discussed in Constance Backhouse, *Colour-Coded: A Legal History of Racism in Canada* (Toronto: University of Toronto Press, 1999).

2 Joe Friesen and Katherine O'Neill, 'Armed Posses Spreading Violence across Prairie Communities,' *Globe and Mail*, 9 May 2008.

3 Esyllt Jones, 'Health and the Immigrant Experience: Caribbean Migrants in Winnipeg,' manuscript, Winnipeg Immigration History Research Group, 2000, pp. 40–1, 61. Gerald Friesen conducted one interview with a Caribbean-origin professional, Keith Sandiford, who recognized the

existence of these racist sentiments but whose experience differed completely from those reported in this paragraph.

4 The *Winnipeg Tribune* clipping file on 'Racial Discrimination' contains dozens of stories dating from the 1940s to 1980s, including details on these matters on 23 March 1978; 31 July 1978; 19 February 1979; 3 August 1979; 28 September 1979; 10 and 11 October 1979; 1 March 1980.

5 The French language story is told in Raymond M. Hébert, *Manitoba's French-Language Crisis: A Cautionary Tale* (Montreal: McGill-Queen's University Press, 2004), and in Frances Russell, *The Canadian Crucible: Manitoba's Role in Canada's Great Divide* (Winnipeg: Heartland Associates, 2003).

6 *Winnipeg Tribune*, 'Racial Discrimination' file, 19 February 1979; 10 and 11 October 1979; 1 March 1980.

7 Frances Russell, *Mistehay Sakehegan: The Great Lake: The Beauty and Treachery of Lake Winnipeg* (Winnipeg: Heartland Publications, 2000), 128–34.

8 James H. Gray tells the story of his hometown, including its racism, in three volumes of memoir-histories: *The Boy from Winnipeg* (Toronto: Macmillan, 1970), 11, 20, 35–44; *The Roar of the Twenties* (Toronto: Macmillan, 1975), 142, 225–65; and *The Winter Years: The Depression on the Prairies* (Toronto: Macmillan, 1966) 126–40. The volume on the 1920s contains the medical school story, p. 240. Another view is contained in W.J. Waines, 'University of Manitoba Presidents I Have Known: Recollections and Impressions,' University of Manitoba Archives, MSS SC 58, Folder 1. We would like to thank Mel Myers for the gift of a remarkable file on these issues that contained Percy Barsky, 'How "Numerus Clausus" was Ended in the Manitoba Medical School,' a paper presented in March 1975 and later published in Jewish Historical Society of Western Canada, *Jewish Life and Times: A Collection of Essays*, vol. 3 (1983), 123–7; also Hyman Sokolov's speech to the Select Committee (no date), Chancellor A.K. Dysart's letter to the Select Committee (17 November 1944), the Select Committee's final report (ca. January 1945), and Dr. Dwight L. Johnson's letter as MLA to the Select Committee (5 January 1945). A transformation in the way scholars talked about race commenced in the early twentieth century with the entry into the social sciences of the concepts labelled 'culture,' 'pluralism,' and 'cultural relativism.' These terms emphasized that culture was not something carried in corpuscles but, rather, was malleable, subject to historical change, and likely to evolve in two-way relations among 'ethnic groups.' The academic pioneers in this way of thinking in Canada included T.F. McIlwraith, Watson Kirkconnell, and A.G. Bailey, though American models such as the so-called second Chicago school also played an important part; Susan Bellay, 'Pluralism and Race/Ethnic Relations in Canadian Social

Science, 1880–1939,' PhD diss., University of Manitoba, 2001; A.R.M. Lower, *Canadians in the Making: A Social History of Canada* (Toronto: Longmans, Green, 1958); Mark Mazower, *Dark Continent: Europe's Twentieth Century* (New York: A.A. Knopf, 1999); Allan Smith, *Canada – An American Nation?: Essays on Continentalism, Identity, and the Canadian Frame of Mind* (Montreal: McGill-Queen's University Press, 1994).

9   Arthur Mauro was interviewed by Gerald Friesen on 11 December 2001. The transcript was reviewed and approved, Mauro to Friesen, 10 January 2002; also Lorne Reznowski and Arthur Mauro sections in 'Memories of St. Paul's College,' Wendy MacDonald, ed., in G. Friesen and R. Lebrun, eds., *St. Paul's College, University of Manitoba: Memories and Histories* (Winnipeg: St Paul's College, 1999), 10–23.

10 Franca Iacovetta, *Gatekeepers: Reshaping Immigrant Lives in Cold War Canada* (Toronto: Between the Lines, 2006), 79.

11 On the 'rights' story: Carmela Patrias, 'Socialists, Jews, and the 1947 Saskatchewan Bill of Rights,' *Canadian Historical Review* 87, 2 (June 2006): 265–92; Carmela Patrias and Ruth A. Frager, '"This Is Our Country, These Are Our Rights": Minorities and the Origins of Ontario's Human Rights Campaigns,' *Canadian Historical Review* 82, 1 (March 2001): 1–35; they take the 'upsurge' quotation from R. Brian Howe, 'The Evolution of Human Rights Policy in Ontario,' *Canadian Journal of Political Science* 24, 4 (1991): 783–802. On the Jewish community's role: Irving Abella, 'Jews, Human Rights, and the Making of a New Canada,' *Journal of the Canadian Historical Association/Revue de la Société historique du Canada* (2000). On the political context: Robert Harney, '"So Great a Heritage as Ours": Immigration and the Survival of the Canadian Polity,' *Daedalus* 117, 4 (Fall 1988). The racism is discussed in Irving Abella and Harold Troper, *None Is Too Many: Canada and the Jews of Europe, 1933–1948* (Toronto: Lester & Orpen Dennys, 1982); Denis Smith, *Rogue Tory: The Life and Legend of John G. Diefenbaker* (Toronto: Macfarlane Walter & Ross, 1995), 346. Diefenbaker's introduction of new immigration regulations, according to Reg Whitaker, 'began the process of ending overt racial discrimination.' Reg Whitaker, 'Canadian Immigration Policy Since Confederation,' booklet (Ottawa: Canadian Historical Association, 1991), 18.

12 Val Werier, 'Our Second Hand Discrimination,' *Winnipeg Tribune*, 'Racial Discrimination' file, 12 March 1960; Werier, 'Some of the Old Prejudices May Be Wearing Away,' *Winnipeg Tribune*, 'Racial Discrimination' file, 26 January 1965. The province of Manitoba and the city of Winnipeg enacted laws and bylaws that forbade discrimination in hiring and accommodation practices during the 1950s: *Winnipeg Tribune*, 'Racial Discrimination' file,

3 and 17 October 1950; 2, 3, 5, 7, 13, 15, 17, 24 May 1952; 3, 12, 17
   February 1953; 6, 8, 12, 20 February 1960; 12, 15 March 1960.

13 These questions are posed for American audiences in Matthew Frye
   Jacobson, *Whiteness of a Different Color: European Immigrants and the Alchemy of
   Race* (Cambridge MA: Harvard University Press, 1998), 6, 8–9, 12. David
   Roediger presents a similar view: 'The extent to which U.S. history has
   turned on race and oppression, not voluntary belonging, for huge numbers
   of residents who were not black can disappear in a search for optimism.
   The ways in which race broadly and deliberately structured competition for
   jobs and shaped ideas regarding who was a fit citizen or neighbor can get
   lost in a story that uplifts ethnics and premises the uplift not on addressing
   injustice but on Americanization.' Roediger, *Working Toward Whiteness: How
   America's Immigrants Became White: The Strange Journey from Ellis Island to the
   Suburbs* (New York: Basic Books, 2005), 23, 33. Russell A. Kazal, 'Revisiting
   Assimilation: The Rise, Fall, and Reappraisal of a Concept in American
   Ethnic History,' *American Historical Review* 100 (1995): 437–71.

14 Lynne Panterics interview, C2060, and Alvina Giesbrecht interview, C2067;
   International Centre Annual Report 1972 AM, all cited in Jennifer
   Rogalsky, 'The Citizenship Council of Manitoba: Fifty Years of Service,
   1948–1998' (manuscript, Citizenship Council of Winnipeg, ca. 1998),
   pp. 35–7. Also central in the following discussion is Jennifer Rogalsky,
   '"Good Canadians in Every Sense": The Citizenship Council of Manitoba
   1948–1975,' MA thesis, University of Winnipeg/University of Manitoba,
   2000. Both manuscripts relied on an oral history project carried out by
   Glen Smith in 1989, on interviews with International Centre and
   Citizenship Council workers, and on the papers of the two organizations
   housed in the Archives of Manitoba.

15 The Trudeau statement is reported in the Citizenship Council, 'Annual
   Report 1971'; see Rogalsky, 'Fifty Years,' 38; for the rest of the paragraph,
   Rogalsky, 'Fifty Years,' 46–89; the quotation comes from Rogalsky's 1997
   interview with Mary Anne Gribben, quoted in 'Fifty Years,' 89. As immigrants
   took over the International Centre, so Aboriginal leaders took over the
   Indian and Metis Friendship Centre and ran it as they saw fit; Leslie Hall,
   'The Creation of the Winnipeg Indian and Metis Friendship Centre 1954–
   1964,' MA thesis, University of Manitoba/University of Winnipeg, 2004.

16 Interviews with professors Jon Young and Kenneth Osborne, Faculty of
   Education, University of Manitoba, conducted by Gerald Friesen, 2004 and
   2005; Jon Young and Robert J. Graham, 'School and Curriculum Reform:
   Manitoba Frameworks & Multicultural Teacher Education,' *Canadian Ethnic
   Studies/Études ethniques au Canada* 32, 1 (2000): 142–55; Kogila A. Moodley,

'Multicultural Education in Canada: Historical Development and Current Status,' in J.A. Banks, ed., *Handbook of Research on Multicultural Education* (New York: Simon & Schuster Macmillan, 1905), 801–19.

17 Rousseau, *Lettre B D'Alembert,* quoted in Charles Taylor, *Multiculturalism: Examining the Politics of Recognition* (Princeton: Princeton University Press, 1994), 48, 44–9.

18 Edith Paterson, 'Winnipeggers Enjoy First "Folklorama" – 1928.' This story, taken from a Winnipeg newspaper ca. 1972–4, was part of a clipping file in the papers of the Folk Arts Council of Winnipeg Inc. [henceforth FACWI]. Papers related to the Folk Arts Council of Winnipeg Inc., including planning documents dating from 1965 to 1967, are part of the FACWI collection now housed in the Archives of Manitoba. Friesen conducted his research in the Folk Arts offices before the papers were transferred and before file numbers were assigned.

19 John Murray Gibbon, *Canadian Mosaic: The Making of a Modern Nation* (1938; reprint, New York: Dodd, Mead, 1939), 413–25; Dora Dueck, 'A "Grand Patriotic Pageant of Progress": The Diamond Jubilee of Canada's Confederation, 1927,' manuscript, Winnipeg, 1999–2000; Paterson, 'Winnipeggers Enjoy First "Folklorama" – 1928'; Stuart Henderson, '"While There Is Still Time …": J. Murray Gibbon and the Spectacle of Difference in Three CPR Folk Festivals, 1928–1931,' *Journal of Canadian Studies* 39, 1 (2005): 139–74. As noted in Chapter 4, volunteers who worked with immigrants in the post-war decades developed this citizenship ceremony into an event that has since become part of national and even international discussion. Doug Saunders, 'I'd Rather Pledge Allegiance to a Notion, Not a Nation,' *Globe and Mail,* 18 February 2006, F9; Joe Friesen, 'Blame Canada (for Multiculturalism),' *Globe and Mail,* 20 August 2005, F8. We would like to thank Mallory Richard for research assistance on the history of the citizenship ceremony.

20 Details of the Folk Arts Council founding were reported in a 'Memorandum re 12 August 1964 Exploratory Meeting of Winnipeg and Toronto Folk Art Representatives,' 18 August 1964, in FACWI papers. The quotation about *the people* appears in a letter from Cecil Semchyshyn (Folk Arts Council) to Mary Elizabeth Bayer (Centennial Corporation of Manitoba), 1 January 1967. Charles Dojack, local entrepreneur and leader of ethnic heritage-based movements, noted at the 1965 meeting the existence of an important local festival, 'the Manitoba Mosaic show … the first comprehensive stage effort to put together an international festival in Winnipeg. He also mentioned the Red River Exhibition and the groups that were asked to participate there,' suggesting presumably that these concerts

provided a foundation upon which such a folklore group could be built. As early as 1967, Winnipeggers were treating this multicultural type of event as representative of their city. When seventy Quebec journalists visited Winnipeg in that year, the council arranged 'one hours entertainment for them – various ethnic dance groups will entertain.' Recorded in FACWI, 'Minutes,' 9 February 1967.

21 Roeder Archives, press release, Citizenship Council of Manitoba Centennial Project, 'Treasures From Many Lands,' 1967, cited in Rogalsky, 'Fifty Years,' 27.

22 FACWI papers, 'Minutes,' 1967–76; 'Press Clippings,' 1967–76; and Dr. Sam Loschiavo, 'Early History of Folklorama.' Also Dr. Sam Loschiavo interview with Gerald Friesen, 20 December 2001.

23 In 2000 the pavilions received over four hundred thousand visitors in two weeks and coordinated the efforts of twenty thousand volunteers. The central organization generated $1.5 million in revenue and the pavilions another $1.2 million. Some observers might place Winnipeg's Folklorama in the category of 'folklorization' but we do not believe such a judgment does justice to the agency of the performing groups. Judy Murphy, Executive Director, Folk Arts Council of Winnipeg, Inc., interview with Gerald Friesen, 13 December 2001. Franca Iacovetta, in her analysis of the post-war reception of immigrants, provides an important complementary argument: she notes, for example, that a Canadian government official possessed a 'hazy form of liberalism [that] also included a strong element of the folklorization of immigrants ... quaint traditions that can be put on display for Canadian consumption.' Iacovetta, *Gatekeepers*, 61.

24 'Tekla Obach (Tutkaluk, nee Hawryliuk),' obituary in *Winnipeg Free Press*, 19 November 2005, C13.

25 Dan Lett, 'The Colour of Our Skin: How Accepting Are We? Poll Shows Racism Still a Part of City's Fabric,' *Winnipeg Free Press*, 13 March 2006. The poll surveyed one thousand adults in mid-February 2006.

26 Masako Kawata collaborated with Gerald Friesen and interviewed her parents between 2003 and 2008.

27 Peter Nunoda mentions a discriminatory city bylaw on minimum wages in 'Harold Hirose on Integration and Citizenship for Japanese Manitobans, 1942–52,' *Prairie Forum* 27, 2 (Fall 2002): 209–20; Saul Cherniack, 'Canada and the Japanese Canadians,' lecture presented to the Jewish Historical Society of Western Canada, December 1998.

28 Paul Gilroy, *Between Camps: Nations, Cultures, and the Allure of Race* (London: Allen Lane Penguin Press, 2000, 2001). Similar views were expressed by J. Craig Venter, the American biologist who released the decoded sequencing

of his own genome, all forty-six of his chromosomes, in 2007. Venter's pioneering feat demonstrated the complexity of each individual's genetic composition and the narrow range of differences within the human family. As Venter commented, he did not discover the existence of 'racial differences in DNA: "Race is a social composition, not a scientific one" … We are all originally related, and all of us genetically mixed, he said, so that no "bright lines" can be drawn to cleanly divide populations at the level of DNA.' Venter's feat was announced in the on-line journal *PloS (Public Library of Science) Biology*. This quotation appeared in Carolyn Abraham, "This Human's Life, Decoded,' *Globe and Mail*, 4 September 2007, A1, p. 8.

29 Charles Taylor, *Multiculturalism: Examining the Politics of Recognition* (Princeton: Princeton University Press, 1994), 25, 27; Stuart Hall and Paul du Gay, eds., *Questions of Cultural Identity* (London: Sage, 1996); Bhikhu Parekh, *A New Politics of Identity: Political Principles for an Interdependent World* (Basingstoke: Palgrave Macmillan, 2008).

30 An example of the anti-racist movements that have developed in the city is the Maples Collegiate Unity Group's annual march against racism. *Winnipeg Free Press*, 29 May 2003, 20 May 2004, 31 May 2005, 31 May 2006, 5 May 2007.

8. Prairie Links in a Transnational Chain

1 This chapter was first published as 'Transnational Webs and the Late-Century Interior Canadian City,' in N. Besner and M. Conceicao Monteiro, eds., *(A)Symmetries in the Americas – Brazil/Canada: Cultures and Literature* (Rio de Janeiro: Editora Caetés, 2007).

2 Eric Hobsbawm, *The Age of Extremes: A History of the World, 1914–1991* (New York: Pantheon, 1994), 15.

3 Nina Glick Schiller and Linda Bash, 'From Immigrant to Transmigrant: Theorizing Transnational Migration,' *Anthropological Quarterly* 68 (1995): 55. See also Donna R. Gabaccia, 'Is Everywhere Nowhere? Nomads, Nations and the Immigrant Paradigm of United States History,' *Journal of American History* 86 (1999): 1115–34.

4 Dirk Hoerder, 'Historians and Their Data: The Complex Shift from Nation-State Approaches to the Study of People's Transcultural Lives,' *Journal of American Ethnic Studies* (Summer 2006): 91.

5 Adam McKeown, *Chinese Migrant Networks and Cultural Change: Peru, Chicago and Hawaii, 1900–1936* (Chicago: University of Chicago Press, 2001), 10.

6 Robin Cohen, *Global Diasporas: An Introduction* (Seattle: University of Washington Press, 1997).

7 Prasenjit Duara, 'Transnationalism and the Predicament of Sovereignty: China 1900–1945,' *American Historical Review* 102 (1997): 1033.

8 Gerald Tulchinsky, *Taking Root: The Origins of the Canadian Jewish Community* (Toronto: Lester, 1992), 115.

9 Dirk Hoerder, *Creating Societies: Immigrant Lives in Canada* (Montreal: McGill-Queen's University Press, 1999), 144.

10 Donna Mavis Minions, 'Three Worlds of Greek-Canadian Women: A Study of Migrant Greek Women in Calgary, Alberta,' MA thesis, University of Calgary, 1984, p. 86.

11 John Herd Thompson, *Forging the West* (Toronto: Oxford University Press, 1998), 78.

12 Prasenjit Duara, 'Transnationalism and the Predicament of Sovereignty: China 1900–1945,' *American Historical Review* 102 (1997): 1049.

13 Harry Con, *From China to Canada: A History of the Chinese in Canada* (Toronto: McClelland and Stewart, 1982), 75, 105, 188, 191, 193.

14 Brian Ross, 'In the Company of Other Italians: Voluntary Associations in Winnipeg's Italian Community,' MA thesis, University of Manitoba, 1983, p. 27.

15 Con, *From China to Canada*, 75, 105, 188, 191, 193.

16 Gerald Tulchinsky, *Branching Out: The Transformation of the Canadian Jewish Community* (Toronto: Stoddart, 1998), 26.

17 Frances Swyripa, *Wedded to the Cause: Ukrainian-Canadian Women and Ethnic Identity, 1891–1991* (Toronto: University of Toronto Press, 1993), 14–17, 170.

18 Krystyna Lukasiewicz, 'Family and Work: Polish Interwar Immigrant Women in Alberta, 1920–1950,' MA thesis, University of Alberta, 1993, p. 103.

19 Howard Palmer, 'Patterns of Immigration and Ethnic Settlements in Alberta,' in H. Palmer and T. Palmer, eds., *Peoples of Alberta: Portraits of Cultural Diversity* (Saskatoon: Western Producer Prairie Books, 1985), 39.

20 Antonella Fanella, 'Family, Honour and Destiny: Southern Italian Immigrants in Calgary, 1910–1990,' MA thesis, University of Calgary, 1991, p. 62.

21 Swyripa, *Wedded to the Cause*, 189, 190, 198.

22 Indeed, the simple memory of the homeland now became a tool for upward mobility and full participation in Canadian society. In the words of Wsevolod Isajiw, the third generation's lasting symbols of Ukrainianess were no longer found in political agendas, but in the 'turn back to the primary experience of food, embroidery and the teaching of a few words in Ukrainian.' Wsevolod W. Isajiw, ed., *Ukrainians in the Canadian City* (Calgary: Research Centre for Canadian Ethnic Studies, 1980), 128.

23 Tamara Palmer, 'Ethnic Responses to the Canadian Prairies, 1900–1950: A Literary Perspective of the Physical and Social Environment,' *Prairie Forum* 12 (1987): 55.

24 Joanna Matejo, 'The Polish Experience in Alberta,' in H. Palmer and T. Palmer, eds., *Peoples of Alberta: Portraits of Cultural Diversity* (Saskatoon: Western Producer Prairie Books, 1985), 291.

25 In 1948, for example, the Canadian Polish Ex-Combatants Association set up shop in Calgary and established a credit union, a library, a program of youth activities, and an array of social events that included 'plays, concerts, dances and picnics.' Kathryn-Anne Rhea Watts, 'Calgary's Polish Community: Social Factors Contributing to its Formation and Persistence,' MA thesis, University of Calgary, 1976, pp. 32, 41, 59.

26 Fanella, 'Family, Honour and Destiny,' 36, 40, 73, 90.

27 Cecil P. Pereira, 'East Indians in Winnipeg: A Study of the Consequences of Immigration for an Ethnic Group in Canada,' MA thesis, University of Manitoba, 1971, p. 170.

28 Cleto M. Buduhan, 'An Urban Village: The Effects of Migration on the Filipino Garment Workers in a Canadian City,' MA (Anthropology) thesis, University of Manitoba, 1972, p. 113.

29 The trip actually convinced the couple that their English-speaking children did not have to 'speak Chinese in order to be Chinese.' Helen Chan, 'Family Organization and Change Among the Chinese in Calgary,' MA (Sociology) thesis, University of Calgary, 1980, p. 55.

30 Minions, 'Three Worlds of Greek-Canadian Women,' 97.

31 Donald B. Smith, 'A History of French-Speaking Alberta,' in H. Palmer and T. Palmer, eds., *Peoples of Alberta: Portraits of Cultural Diversity* (Saskatoon: Western Producer Prairie Books, 1985), 105.

32 Max Rubin, 'Alberta's Jews: The Long Journey,' in H. Palmer and T. Palmer, eds., *Peoples of Alberta: Portraits of Cultural Diversity* (Saskatoon: Western Producer Prairie Books, 1985), 346.

33 Wing-Sam Chow, 'A Chinese Community in a Prairie City: A Holistic Perspective of its Class and Ethnic Relations,' PhD diss., University of Michigan, 1981, p. 78.

34 Greg Teal, 'Urban Anthropology and the Problems of the Formation of Social Classes: With Reference to Korean Immigrants in Edmonton,' MA (Anthropology) thesis, University of Alberta, 1979, p. 92.

35 Buduhan, 'An Urban Village,' 54, 127, 129.

36 Carmen Alicia Robles-Milan, 'The Personal Adjustment and Acculturation of the Chilean Émigré in the City of Regina,' MSW thesis, University of Regina, 1981, pp. 63, 65, 66, 84, 105, 113, 115, 117.

37 Katherine A. MacRury, 'The Occupational Adjustment of Vietnamese Refugees in Edmonton, Canada,' MEd thesis, University of Alberta, 1979, p. 79.
38 Ransford Kwabena Danso, 'Access to Housing and its Impact on the Adaptation Process: The Case of African Immigrants in Calgary,' MA (Geography) thesis, University of Calgary, 1997, p. 13. 'Paradoxically ... when asked if, given the overall situation that they face in Calgary they would want to go back home to their countries, respondents frequently answered that over the long term, yes, but for now there were not such plans,' leading Danso to conclude that 'the tendency is to distance one's self in which case the new society becomes even more inaccessible ...' Danso, 126.
39 Hoerder, *Creating Societies*, 127.
40 Danso, 'Access to Housing,' 105.
41 Norman Buchignani, 'South Asians in Alberta,' in H. Palmer and T. Palmer, eds., *Peoples of Alberta: Portraits of Cultural Diversity* (Saskatoon: Western Producer Prairie Books, 1985), 422.
42 See various articles in the special 'Return of the Kanadier' section of the 2004 issue of the *Journal of Mennonite Studies*. See also Marlene Epp, *Women Without Men: Mennonite Refugees of the Second World War* (Toronto: University of Toronto Press, 2000); Janis Thiessen, 'Faith and Factory: Russian Mennonite Workers in Twentieth-Century Manitoba,' PhD diss., University of New Brunswick, 2005.
43 Danso, 'Access to Housing,' 105.
44 Buchignani, 'South Asians in Alberta,' 420, 427.
45 Bat-Ami Klejner, 'Latin American Immigrants in Calgary: An Ethnopsychological Study,' MSc (Psychology) thesis, University of Calgary, 1944, pp. 91, 92, 93.
46 Ibid., 89.
47 Jinjin Zhang, 'Illness Management Strategies among Chinese Immigrants Living with Arthritis,' MSc thesis, University of Calgary, 1998, pp. iii, 58, 83–86, 90, 103.
48 Ibid., 102.
49 Lynn Hershman Leeson, 'Introduction,' in L. Leeson, ed., *Clicking In: Hot Links to a Digital Culture* (Seattle: Bay Press, 1996), vii.
50 John S. Quaterman, 'Telecomputing in the New Global Networks,' in D. Crowly and P. Heyer, eds., *Communication in History: Technology, Culture, Society* (White Plains, NY: Longman, 1995), 343.
51 The sites listed in the paragraph were accessed 24 December 2006.

Conclusion

1   They could even reflect Edward Said's ideas 'for a possibly counterhegem-
    onic stance.' See Hans Bertons, *The Basics: Literary Theory* (New York:
    Routledge, 2001), 206.
2   Homi K. Bhabha, 'Frontlines/Borderposts,' in A. Bammer, ed., *Displacements:
    Cultural Identities in Question* (Bloomington: Indiana University Press, 1994):
    269–72.
3   Elizabeth Comack, 'Racialized Policing' (Winnipeg: Canadian Centre for
    Policy Alternatives, <www.policyalternatives.ca>). Accessed 20 January 2009.
4   Eric Hobsbawm, *The Age of Extremes: A History of the World, 1914–1991* (New
    York: Pantheon, 1994), 565.
5   Robert Adamoski, Dorothy E. Chunn, and Robert Menzies, eds., Introduction,
    Contesting Canadian Citizenship: Historical Readings (Peterborough: Broadview,
    2002), 19, 20. For similar conclusions regarding the mid-century decades
    see also Franca Iacovetta, *Gatekeepers: Reshaping Immigrant Lives in Cold War
    Canada* (Toronto: Between the Lines, 2006).
6   Baha Abu-Laban and Tracey M. Derwing, eds., *Responding to Diversity in the
    Metropolis: Building an Inclusive Research Agenda: Proceedings of the First
    Metropolis National Conference on Immigration* (Edmonton: Prairie Centre of
    Excellence for Research on Immigration and Integration, 1997), 18.
7   Ibid., 63.
8   An illustration is Lori Wilkinson, 'Visualizing Canada, Identity and
    Belonging among Second Generation Youth in Winnipeg,' *Canadian
    Diversity/Diversité Canadienne* 6, 2 (Spring 2008): 84–6.
9   David Harvey, *Spaces of Hope* (Edinburgh: Edinburgh University Press,
    2000), 244, 240–1.
10 Edward W. Said, *Humanism and Democratic Criticism* (New York: Columbia
    University Press, 2004), 10.

Bibliography

Primary

Calgary: The Glenbow Museum

The Calgary Herald

Winnipeg: Jewish Heritage Centre of Western Canada, Inc.

Cherniack, J.A. 'Reminiscences of 40 Years of Jewish Community Life,' typed manuscript originally presented in Yiddish, translated by H.H. Herstein, 1969.

Winnipeg: Archives of Manitoba

Folk Arts Council of Winnipeg Inc. Papers
W.J. Sisler Papers
Premiers' Papers, Advisory Committee on Post-War Reconstruction, Correspondence of Premier Garson, Box 4, Q 025303
Papers of Manitoba Royal Commission on Adult Education, GR76/A0063

Winnipeg: Mel Myers (Private Collection)

File on University of Manitoba Medical School quota controversy

Winnipeg: University of Manitoba Archives

Waines, W.J. 'University of Manitoba Presidents I Have Known: Recollections and Impressions,' President's Office Papers, MSS SC 58

Winnipeg Free Press
Winnipeg Tribune

Interviews

Conducted by Gerald Friesen

Saul Cherniack
Masako Kawata
Sam Loschiavo
Arthur Mauro
Judy Murphy
Kenneth W. Osborne
Keith Sandiford
Jon Young

Unpublished Documents

Dissertations, Theses, and Unpublished Manuscripts

Beaujot, Roderic Paul. 'Ethnic Fertility Differentials in Edmonton.' PhD diss.,
    University of Alberta, 1975.
Beimcik, Jacek. 'Immigration and its Effect on Marital Satisfaction and Violence
    Against Wives in Polish Families in Winnipeg.' MA thesis, University of
    Manitoba, 1996.
Bellay, Susan. 'Pluralism and Race/Ethnic Relations in Canadian Social
    Science, 1880–1939.' PhD diss., University of Manitoba, 2001.
Blackburn, Magdalena. 'Creating Identities: A Case Study of Polish Immigrants
    in Manitoba after the Second World War.' MA thesis, University of
    Manitoba/University of Winnipeg, 2009.
Buduhan, Cleto M. 'An Urban Village: The Effects of Migration on the Filipino
    Garment Workers in a Canadian City.' MA (Anthropology) thesis, University
    of Manitoba, 1972.
Chan, Helen. 'Family Organization and Change Among the Chinese in
    Calgary.' MA (Sociology) thesis, University of Calgary, 1980.
Cherniack, Saul M. 'Canada and the Japanese Canadians.' Lecture presented to
    the Jewish Historical Society of Western Canada, 1 December 1998.
Chow, Wing-sam. 'A Chinese Community in a Prairie City: A Holistic Perspective
    of its Class and Ethnic Relations.' PhD diss., University of Michigan, 1981.

Cobb, John. 'German Lutherans in the Prairie Provinces Before the First World
    War: Their Church Background, Emigration and New Beginning in Canada.'
    PhD diss., University of Manitoba, 1991.
Comack, Elizabeth. 'Racialized Policing.' Winnipeg: Canadian Centre for Policy
    Alternatives. <www.policyalternatives.ca>. Accessed 20 January 2009.
Danso, Ransford Kwabena. 'Access to Housing and its Impact on the
    Adaptation Process: The Case of African Immigrants in Calgary.' MA
    (Geography) thesis, University of Calgary, 1997.
Dickens, Thomas W. 'Winnipeg, Imperialism, and the Queen Victoria Diamond
    Jubilee Celebration, 1897.' MA thesis, University of Manitoba, 1982.
Dobbie, Alison Louise. 'Health Beliefs and Behaviours of Arab Immigrants: A
    Canadian Perspective.' MN thesis, University of Saskatchewan, 1999.
Dueck, Dora. 'A "Grand Patriotic Pageant of Progress": The Diamond Jubilee
    of Canada's Confederation, 1927.' Undergraduate essay, Winnipeg, 1999–
    2000. Copy in possession of Gerald Friesen.
Fanella, Antonella. 'Family, Honour and Destiny: Southern Italian Immigrants
    in Calgary, 1910–1990.' MA thesis, University of Calgary, 1991.
Fuchs, Linda L. 'Social Support, Life Events, Self Concepts and Happiness
    Among Southeast Asian Refugee Women in Saskatoon.' MA thesis,
    University of Saskatchewan, 1987.
Fujiwara, Aya. 'From Anglo-Conformity to Multiculturalism: The Role of
    Scottish, Ukrainian and Japanese Ethnicity in the Transformation of
    Canadian Identity, 1919–1971.' PhD diss., University of Alberta, 2007.
Hackney, Patricia Marie. 'An Investigation of Problems Related to Recent
    Immigration and Accessibility of Services for Immigrants,' MSW thesis,
    University of Calgary, 1979.
Hall, Leslie. 'The Creation of the Winnipeg Indian and Metis Friendship Centre
    1954–1964.' MA thesis, University of Manitoba/University of Winnipeg, 2004.
Hart, Edward John. 'The History of the French-speaking Community of
    Edmonton, 1795–1935.' MA thesis, University of Alberta, 1971.
Herstein, Harvey H. 'The Growth of the Winnipeg Jewish Community and the
    Evolution of its Educational Institutions.' MA thesis, University of Manitoba,
    1964.
Jones, Esyllt. 'Health and the Immigrant Experience: Caribbean Migrants in
    Winnipeg.' Manuscript. Winnipeg Immigration History Research Group,
    2000.
_____. 'Searching for the Springs of Health: Women and Working Families in
    Winnipeg's 1918–1919 Influenza Epidemic.' PhD diss., University of
    Manitoba, 2003.

Khosla, Sona. 'Generational Conflict: The Impact of Cultural Baggage and Culture Clash on the Relationship Between East Indian Immigrant Parents and Their Canadian-Born Children.' Undergraduate essay, University of Calgary, 1999.

King, Mona. 'Some Aspects of Post-War Migration to Edmonton, Alberta.' MA (Geography) thesis, University of Alberta, 1971.

Klejner, Bat-Ami. 'Latin American Immigrants in Calgary: An Ethnopsychological Study.' MSc (Psychology) thesis, University of Calgary, 1994.

Knott, Yvette Y.L. 'A Case Study on the Canadian Policy and Calgary Community Response to the Southeast Asian Refugees, 1979–1980.' MA thesis, University of Calgary, 1981.

Lin, Paul Y.M. 'Accessibility of Services to New Immigrants in Calgary.' MSW thesis, University of Calgary, 1977.

Luk, Lordson Wai-Chung. 'The Assimilation of Chinese in Saskatoon.' MA thesis, University of Saskatchewan, 1971.

Lukasiewicz, Krystyna. 'Family and Work: Polish Interwar Immigrant Women in Alberta, 1920–1950.' MA thesis, University of Alberta, 1993.

Luscombe, Barry Wayne. 'Social Distance and Spatial Distance: Segregation and Dispersion of Social Classes in Regina, Saskatchewan.' MA thesis, University of Regina, 1977.

Macdonald, Elizabeth. 'Japanese Canadians in Edmonton, 1969: An Exploratory Search for Patterns of Assimilation.' MA thesis, University of Alberta, 1970.

MacRury, Katherine A. 'The Occupational Adjustment of Vietnamese Refugees in Edmonton, Canada.' MEd thesis, University of Alberta, 1979.

Marshall, Alison R. 'Chinese Immigration to Western Manitoba since 1884: Wah Hep, Geore Chong, the KMT and the United Church.' *Journal of Canadian Studies* (forthcoming).

Minions, Donna Mavis. 'Three Worlds of Greek-Canadian Women: A Study of Migrant Greek Women in Calgary, Alberta.' MA thesis, University of Calgary, 1984.

Mok, Kit Man Kitty. 'Community Services for Immigrant Women in Forest Lawn.' MEnv. Design thesis, University of Calgary, 1991.

Nakahara, Yoko Urata. 'Ethnic Identity Among Japanese Canadians in Edmonton: The Case of Pre-World War II Immigrants and Their Descendants.' PhD (Education) diss., University of Alberta, 1991.

Nunoda, Peter Takaji. 'A Community in Transition and Conflict: The Japanese Canadians, 1935–1951.' PhD diss., University of Manitoba, 1991.

Ong, Amory Yuk Mui. 'An Exploratory Study of the Life of Single Asian Immigrant Women in Winnipeg: Implications for Social Work Practice.' MSW thesis, University of Manitoba, 1987.

Pereira, Cecil P. 'East Indians in Winnipeg: A Study of the Consequences of Immigration for an Ethnic Group in Canada.' MA thesis, University of Manitoba, 1971.

———. 'A Study of the Effects of the Ethnic and Non-ethnic Factors on the Resettlement of the Ugandan Asian Refugees in Canada.' PhD diss., University of Wisconsin–Madison, 1981.

Poetschke, Thomas R. 'Reasons for Immigration and Ethnic Identity: An Exploratory Study of German Immigrants in Edmonton.' MA thesis, University of Alberta, 1978.

Rees-Powell, Alan Thomas. 'Differentials in the Integration Process of Dutch and Italian Immigrants in Edmonton.' MSW thesis, University of Alberta, 1964.

Robles-Milan, Carmen Alicia. 'The Personal Adjustment and Acculturation of the Chilean Emigré in the City of Regina.' MSW thesis, University of Regina, 1981.

Rogalsky, Jennifer. 'The Citizenship Council of Manitoba: Fifty Years of Service, 1948–1998.' Manuscript, prepared for the Citizenship Council on the occasion of its fiftieth anniversary. Winnipeg, 1999.

———. '"Good Canadians in Every Sense": The Citizenship Council of Manitoba 1948–1975.' MA thesis, University of Winnipeg/University of Manitoba, 2000.

Ross, Brian. 'In the Company of Other Italians: Voluntary Associations in Winnipeg's Italian Community.' MA thesis, University of Manitoba, 1983.

Siddique, Muhammad. 'Patterns of Familial Decision-Making and Division of Labour: A Study of the Immigrant Indian-Pakistani Community of Saskatoon, Canada.' MA thesis, University of Saskatchewan, 1974.

Snider, Howard M. 'Variables Affecting Immigrant Adjustment: A Study of Italians in Edmonton.' MA thesis, University of Alberta, 1966.

Spina, Giovanni (John). 'Winnipeg's Little Italy: A Developmental Model.' MA thesis, University of Manitoba, 1998.

Swyripa, Frances. 'Storied Landscapes: Aspects of Ethno-Religious Identity on the Canadian Prairies.' Winnipeg: University of Manitoba Press, forthcoming.

Taillefer, Jean-Marie. 'Les Franco-Manitobains et l'éducation 1870–1970: une étude quantitative.' PhD diss., University of Manitoba, 1988.

Teal, Greg. 'Urban Anthropology and the Problems of the Formation of Social Classes: With Reference to Korean Immigrants in Edmonton.' MA (Anthropology) thesis, University of Alberta, 1979.

Thiessen, Janis. 'Faith and Factory: Russian Mennonite Workers in Twentieth-Century Manitoba.' PhD diss., University of New Brunswick, 2005.

Thischler, Kurt. 'The German Canadians in Saskatchewan with Particular Reference to the Language Problem, 1900–1930.' MA thesis, University of Saskatchewan, 1978.

Thraves, Bernard. 'An Analysis of Ethnic Intra-Urban Migration: The Case of Winnipeg.' PhD diss., University of Manitoba, 1986.

Tooth, John E. 'Sixty Years in Canada: by an immigrant of 1910.' Handwritten Manuscript, ca. 1972–73. Copy in possession of Gerald Friesen.

Usiskin, Rosaline. 'Toward a Theoretical Reformulation of the Relationship Between Political Ideology, Social Class, and Ethnicity: A Case Study of the Winnipeg Jewish Radical Community, 1905–1920.' MA thesis, University of Manitoba, 1978.

Watts, Kathryn-Anne Rhea. 'Calgary's Polish Community: Social Factors Contributing to its Formation and Persistence.' MA thesis, University of Calgary, 1976.

Werner, Hans. 'Integration in Two Cities: A Comparative History of Protestant Ethnic German Immigrants in Winnipeg, Canada and Bielefeld, Germany, 1947–1989.' PhD diss., University of Manitoba, 2002.

Yoon, Bok-Nam. 'The Adjustment Problems and Education Needs of Korean Immigrant Women in the Winnipeg Garment Industry.' MEd thesis, University of Manitoba, 1983.

Zhang, Jinjin. 'Illness Management Strategies among Chinese Immigrants Living with Arthritis.' MSc thesis, University of Calgary, 1998.

Books

Abella, Irving, and Harold Troper. *None Is Too Many: Canada and the Jews of Europe, 1933–1948*. Toronto: Lester and Orpen Dennys, 1982.

Abu-Laban, Baha, and Tracey M. Derwing, eds. *Responding to Diversity in the Metropolis: Building an Inclusive Research Agenda: Proceedings of the First Metropolis National Conference on Immigration*. Edmonton: Prairie Centre of Excellence for Research on Immigration and Integration, 1997.

Adamoski, Robert, Dorothy E. Chunn, and Robert Menzies, eds. *Contesting Canadian Citizenship: Historical Readings*. Peterborough: Broadview, 2002.

Alba, Richard, and Victor Nee. *Remaking the American Mainstream: Assimilation and Contemporary Immigration*. Cambridge: Harvard University Press, 2003.

Anderson, J.T.M. *The Education of the New Canadian: A Treatise on Canada's Greatest Educational Problem*. Toronto: J.M. Dent, 1918.

Anderson, Kay. *Vancouver's Chinatown. Racial Discourse in Canada, 1875–1980*. Kingston: McGill-Queen's University Press, 1995.

Avery, Donald H. *Reluctant Host: Canada's Response to Immigrant Workers, 1896–1994*. Toronto: McClelland and Stewart, 1995.

Babb, Valerie Melissa. *Whiteness Visible: The Meaning of Whiteness in American Literature and Culture.* New York: New York University Press, 1998.

Backhouse, Constance. *Colour-Coded: A Legal History of Racism in Canada.* Toronto: University of Toronto Press, 1999.

Bailey, A.G. *Culture and Nationality: Essays by A.G. Bailey.* Toronto: McClelland and Stewart, 1972.

Barker, George. *Forty Years a Chief.* Winnipeg: Peguis Publishers, 1979.

Barth, Fredrik. *Balinese Worlds.* Chicago: University of Chicago Press, 1993.

_____, ed. *Ethnic Groups and Boundaries: The Social Organization of Culture Difference.* Bergen: Waveland Press, 1969.

Bassler, Gerhard. *The German Canadian Mosaic Today and Yesterday: Identity, Roots and Heritage.* Ottawa: German-Canadian Congress, 1991.

Bertons, Hans. *The Basics: Literary Theory.* New York: Routledge, 2001.

Bhabha, Homi K. *The Location of Culture.* London and New York: Routledge, 1994.

_____, ed., *Narration and Nation.* London: Routledge, 1990.

Bodnar, John E. *Remaking America: Public Memory, Commemoration, and Patriotism in the Twentieth Century.* Princeton: Princeton University Press, 1992.

_____. *The Transplanted: A History of Immigrants in Urban America.* Bloomington: Indiana University Press, 1985.

Bouchard, Gerard, and Charles Taylor. *Building the Future: A Time for Reconciliation.* Abridged Report. Québec: Commission de consultation sur les pratiques d'accommodement reliées aux différences culturelles, 2008.

Bramadat, Paul, and David Seljak, eds. *Ethnicity and Christianity in Canada.* Toronto: University of Toronto Press, 2008.

_____. *Religion and Ethnicity in Canada,* Toronto: Pearson, 2005.

Bright, David. *The Limits of Labour: Class Formation and the Labour Movement in Calgary, 1883–1929.* Vancouver: University of British Columbia Press, 1998.

Buchignani, Norman. *Continuous Journey: A Social History of South Asians in Canada.* Toronto: McClelland and Stewart, 1985.

Burley, David. *Living on Furby: Narratives of Home. Winnipeg, Manitoba, 1880–2005.* Winnipeg: Winnipeg Inner-City Research Alliance, Institute of Urban Studies, University of Winnipeg, Westminster Housing Society, 2008.

Burnet, Jean R., with Howard Palmer. *'Coming Canadians': An Introduction to a History of Canada's Peoples.* Toronto: McClelland and Stewart, 1988.

Buruma, Ian. *Murder in Amsterdam: The Death of Theo Van Gogh and the Limits of Tolerance.* New York: Penguin Press, 2006.

Calder, Alison, and Robert Wardhaugh, eds. *History, Literature, and the Writing of the Canadian Prairies.* Winnipeg: University of Manitoba Press, 2005.

Campbell, Charles M. *Betrayal and Deceit: The Politics of Canadian Immigration.* West Vancouver: Jasmine Books, 2000.

Chan, Kwok B., and Doreen Marie Indra, eds. *In Uprooting, Loss and Adaptation: The Resettlement of Indochinese Refugees in Canada.* Ottawa: Canadian Public Health Association, 1987.

Chiel, Arthur. *The Jews in Manitoba: A Social History.* Toronto: University of Toronto Press, 1961.

Cohen, Robin. *Global Diasporas: An Introduction.* Seattle: University of Washington Press, 1997.

Coleman, Daniel. *Masculine Migrations: Reading the Postcolonial Male in the New Canadian Narratives.* Toronto: University of Toronto Press, 1998.

Con, Harry. *From China to Canada: A History of the Chinese in Canada.* Toronto: McClelland and Stewart, 1982.

Djao, Angela, Lily Tingley, and Roxana Ng. *Doubly Disadvantaged: The Women Who Immigrate to Canada.* Saskatoon: Immigrant Women of Saskatchewan, 1985.

Donnelly, Murray S. *Dafoe of the Free Press.* Toronto: Macmillan, 1968.

_____. *The Government of Manitoba.* Toronto: University of Toronto Press, 1963.

Dutka, June. *St. Nicholas Ukrainian Catholic Church: Celebrating 100 Years: Together for Tomorrow.* Winnipeg: St Nicholas Ukrainian Catholic Church, 2006.

Ediger, Gerald C. *Crossing the Divide: Language Transition among Canadian Mennonite Brethren, 1940–1970.* Winnipeg: Centre for Mennonite Brethren Studies, 2001.

Edwards, Justin D., and Douglas Ivison, eds. *Downtown Canada: Writing Canadian Cities.* Toronto: University of Toronto Press, 2005.

Epp, Marlene. *Mennonite Women in Canada: A History.* Winnipeg: University of Manitoba Press, 2008.

_____. *Women Without Men: Mennonite Refugees of the Second World War.* Toronto: University of Toronto Press, 2000.

_____, Franca Iacovetta, and Frances Swyripa, eds. *Sisters or Strangers? Immigrant, Ethnic, and Radicalized Women in Canadian History.* Toronto: University of Toronto Press, 2004.

Foner, Nancy. *From Ellis Island to JFK: New York's Two Great Waves of Immigration.* New Haven: Yale University Press, 2000.

Frager, Ruth A. *Sweatshop Strife: Class, Ethnicity, and Gender in the Jewish Labour Movement of Toronto, 1900–1939.* Toronto: University of Toronto Press, 1992.

Friesen, Gerald. *The Canadian Prairies: A History.* Toronto: University of Toronto Press, 1984.

_____. *Citizens and Nation: An Essay on History, Communication, and Canada.* Toronto: University of Toronto Press, 2000.

_____, and Richard Lebrun, eds. *St. Paul's College, University of Manitoba: Memories and Histories.* Winnipeg: St Paul's College, 1999.

Gabaccia, Donna. *From the Other Side: Women, Gender and Immigrant Life in the U.S., 1820–1990*. Bloomington: Indiana University Press, 1994.

Geertz, Clifford. *The Interpretation of Cultures: Selected Essays*. New York: Basic Books, 1973.

Gerus, Oleh W., and Denis Hlynka, eds. *The Memoirs and Diary of Anthony Hlynka, MP: The Honourable Member for Vegreville*. Calgary: University of Calgary Press, 2005.

Gibbon, John Murray. *Canadian Mosaic: The Making of a Modern Nation*. 1938. Reprint, New York: Dodd, Mead, 1939.

Giles, Winona. *Portuguese Women in Toronto: Gender, Immigration and Nationalism*. Toronto: University of Toronto Press, 2002.

Gilroy, Paul. *Between Camps: Nations, Cultures, and the Allure of Race*. 2000. Reprint, London: Allen Lane Penguin Press, 2001.

Gordon, Charles W. *Postscript to Adventure: The Autobiography of Ralph Connor*. New York: Farrar and Rinehart, 1938.

Gray, James. *The Boy from Winnipeg*. Toronto: Macmillan, 1970.

_____. *The Roar of the Twenties*. Toronto: Macmillan, 1975.

_____. *The Winter Years: The Depression on the Prairies*. Toronto: Macmillan, 1966.

Grekul, Lisa. *Leaving Shadows: Literature in English by Canada's Ukrainians*. Edmonton, University of Alberta Press, 2005.

Grenke, Arthur. *The German Community in Winnipeg, 1872–1919*. New York: AMS Press, 1991.

Gumpp, Ruth. *Ethnicity and Assimilation: German Postwar Immigrants in Vancouver, 1945–1970*. Vancouver: University of British Columbia Press, 1989.

Hall, Stuart, and Paul du Gay, eds. *Questions of Cultural Identity*. London: Sage, 1996.

Harney, Robert F. *Gathering Place: Peoples and Neighbourhoods of Toronto, 1834–1945*. Toronto. Multicultural History Society of Ontario, 1985.

Harvey, David. *The Condition of Postmodernity: An Enquiry into the Origins of Cultural Change*. Oxford: Blackwell, 1989.

_____. *Spaces of Hope*. Berkeley: University of California Press, 2000.

Hébert, Raymond. *Manitoba's French-language Crisis: A Cautionary Tale*. Montreal: McGill Queen's University Press, 2004.

Helmes-Hayes, Rick, and James Curtis. *The Vertical Mosaic Revisited*. Toronto: University of Toronto Press, 1998.

Hobsbawm, Eric. *The Age of Extremes: A History of the World, 1914–1991*. New York: Pantheon, 1994.

Hoerder, Dirk. *Creating Societies: Immigrant Lives in Canada*. Montreal: McGill-Queen's University Press, 1999.

Iacovetta, Franca. *Gatekeepers: Reshaping Immigrant Lives in Cold War Canada*. Toronto: Between the Lines, 2006.

_____. *Such Hardworking People: Italian Immigrants in Postwar Toronto.* Montreal and Kingston: McGill-Queen's University Press, 1992.

Isajiw, Wsevolod W., ed. *Ukrainians in the Canadian City.* Calgary: Research Centre for Canadian Ethnic Studies, 1980.

Jacobson, Matthew Frye. *Special Sorrows: The Diasporic Imagination of Irish, Polish and Jewish Immigrants in the United States.* Berkeley: University of California Press, 2002.

_____. *Whiteness of a Different Color: European Immigrants and the Alchemy of Race.* Cambridge MA: Harvard University Press, 1998.

Jones, Esyllt W. *Influenza 1918: Disease, Death, and Struggle in Winnipeg.* Toronto: University of Toronto Press, 2007.

Kelley, Ninette, and Michael Trebilcock. *The Making of the Mosaic: A History of Canadian Immigration Policy.* Toronto: University of Toronto Press, 1998.

Kinnear, Mary. *A Female Economy: Women's Work in a Prairie Province, 1870–1970.* Montreal and Kingston: McGill-Queen's University Press, 1999.

Kirkconnell, Watson. *The European Heritage: A Synopsis of European Cultural Achievement.* London: J.M. Dent, 1930.

Klassen, Henry C. *A Business History of Alberta.* Calgary: University of Calgary Press, 1999.

Kostash, Myrna. *All of Baba's Children.* Edmonton: Hurtig, 1977.

Kymlicka, Will. *Finding Our Way: Rethinking Ethnocultural Relations in Canada.* London: Oxford University Press, 1998.

Lasch, Christopher. *Haven in a Heartless World: The Family Besieged.* New York: Basic Books, 1979.

Leeson, Lynn Hershman, ed. *Clicking In: Hot Links to a Digital Culture.* Seattle: Bay Press, 1996

Loewen, Royden. *Diaspora in the Countryside: Two Mennonite Communities and Mid-Twentieth-Century Rural Disjuncture.* Toronto: University of Toronto Press, 2006.

_____. *Family, Church and Market: A Mennonite Community in the Old and the New Worlds, 1850–1930.* Urbana: University of Illinois Press, 1993.

_____. *From the Inside Out: The Rural Worlds of Mennonite Diarists, 1863–1929.* Winnipeg: University of Manitoba Press, 1999.

_____. *Hidden Worlds: Revisiting the Mennonite Migrants of the 1870s.* Winnipeg: University of Manitoba Press, 2001.

Lower, A.R.M. *Canadians in the Making: A Social History of Canada.* Toronto: Longmans, Green, 1958.

_____. *My First Seventy-Five Years.* Toronto: Macmillan, 1967.

Lucassen, Jan, and Leo Lucassen, eds. *Migration, Migration History, History: Old Paradigms and New Perspectives.* Bern: Peter Lang, 1997.

Lucassen, Leo. *The Immigrant Threat: The Integration of Old and New Migrants in Western Europe since 1850.* Urbana: University of Illinois Press, 2005.

Makabe, Tomoko. *The Canadian Sansei.* Toronto: University of Toronto Press, 1998.

Marlyn, John. *Under the Ribs of Death.* 1957. Reprint, Toronto: McClelland and Stewart, 1971.

Martynowych, Orest T. *Ukrainians in Canada: The Formative Period, 1891–1924.* Edmonton: Canadian Institute of Ukrainians Press, 1991.

Mazower, Mark. *Dark Continent: Europe's Twentieth Century.* New York: A.A. Knopf, 1999.

McGown, Rima Berns. *Muslims in the Diaspora: The Somali Communities of London and Toronto.* Toronto: University of Toronto Press, 1999.

McKeown, Adam. *Chinese Migrant Networks and Cultural Change: Peru, Chicago and Hawaii, 1900–1936.* Chicago: University of Chicago Press, 2001.

Mills, Allen. *Fool for Christ: The Political Thought of J.S. Woodsworth.* Toronto: University of Toronto Press, 1991.

Mindel, Charles H., Robert W. Habenstein, and Roosevelt Wright Jr., eds. *Ethnic Families in America: Patterns and Variations.* New Jersey: Prentice Hall, 1998.

Morton, W.L. *Manitoba: A History.* Toronto: University of Toronto Press, 1957.

Mulder, Marlene, and Bojan Korenic. *Portraits of Immigrants and Ethnic Minorities in Canada: Regional Comparisons.* Edmonton: Prairie Centre of Excellence for Research on Immigration and Integration, 2005.

Myers, Tamara. *Caught: Montreal's Modern Girls and the Law, 1869–1945.* Toronto: University of Toronto Press, 2006.

Ng, Wing Chung. *The Chinese in Vancouver, 1945–80: The Pursuit of Identity and Power.* Vancouver: University of British Columbia Press, 1999.

Palmer, Howard. *Patterns of Prejudice: A History of Nativism in Alberta.* Toronto: McClelland and Stewart, 1982.

_____, and Tamara Palmer, eds. *Peoples of Alberta: Portraits of Cultural Diversity.* Saskatoon: Western Producer Prairie Books, 1985.

Parekh, Bhikhu. *A New Politics of Identity: Political Principles for an Interdependent World.* Basingstoke: Palgrave Macmillan, 2008.

Parr, Joy. *The Gender of Breadwinners: Women, Men and Change in Two Industrial Towns, 1880–1950.* Toronto: University of Toronto Press, 1990.

Patalas, Kazimierz. *Providence Watching: Journeys from Wartorn Poland to the Canadian Prairies.* Winnipeg: University of Manitoba Press, 2003.

Petroff, Lillian. *Sojourners and Settlers: The Macedonian Community in Toronto to 1940.* Toronto: Multicultural History Society of Ontario, 1995.

Poonwassie, Deo H., and Anne Poonwassie, eds. *Adult Education in Manitoba: Historical Aspects.* Mississauga: Canadian Educators' Press, 1997.

Porter, John. *The Vertical Mosaic: An Analysis of Social Class and Power in Canada.* Toronto: University of Toronto Press, 1965.

Ramirez, Bruno. *On the Move: French-Canadian and Italian Migrants in the North Atlantic Economy, 1860–1914.* Toronto: McClelland and Stewart, 1991.

Regehr, T.D. *Mennonites in Canada: A People Transformed.* Toronto: University of Toronto Press, 1996.

Robinson, Ira, and Mervin Butovsky, eds. *Renewing Our Days: Montreal Jews in the Twentieth Century.* Montreal: Véhicule, 1995.

Roediger, David R. *The Wages of Whiteness: Race and the Making of the American Working Class.* 1991. Revised edition, London: Verso, 1999.

_____. *Working Toward Whiteness: How America's Immigrants Became White: The Strange Journey from Ellis Island to the Suburbs.* New York: Basic Books, 2005.

Rotundo, E. Anthony. *American Manhood: Transformation in Masculinity from the Revolution to the Modern Era.* New York: Basic Books, 1993.

Roy, Gabrielle. *La Détresse et l'enchantement.* 1984. Translated by P. Claxton as *Enchantment and Sorrow: The Autobiography of Gabrielle Roy.* Toronto: Lester and Orpen Dennys, 1987.

Royal Commission on Bilingualism and Biculturalism. *Report Book IV: The Cultural Contribution of the Other Ethnic Groups.* Ottawa: The Author, 1969.

Russell, Frances. *The Canadian Crucible: Manitoba's Role in Canada's Great Divide.* Winnipeg: Heartland Books, 2004.

_____. *Mistehay Sakehegan: The Great Lake: The Beauty and Treachery of Lake Winnipeg.* Winnipeg: Heartland Publications, 2000.

Said, Edward W. *Culture and Imperialism.* 1993. Reprint, New York: Vintage Books, 1994.

_____. *Humanism and Democratic Criticism.* New York: Columbia University Press, 2004.

Salverson, Laura. *Confessions of an Immigrant's Daughter.* Toronto: University of Toronto Press, 1981.

Satterthwaite, Ann. *Going Shopping: Consumer Choices and Community Consequences.* New Haven: Yale University Press, 2001.

Shover, John L. *First Majority, Last Minority: The Transforming of Rural Life in America.* Dekalb, IL: Northern Illinois University Press, 1976.

Sisler, W.J. *Peaceful Invasion.* Winnipeg: Ketchen Printing Company, 1944.

Smith, Allan. *Canada – An American Nation?: Essays on Continentalism, Identity, and the Canadian Frame of Mind.* Montreal: McGill-Queen's University Press, 1994.

Smith, Denis. *Rogue Tory: The Life and Legend of John G. Diefenbaker.* Toronto: Macfarlane Walter and Ross, 1995.

Sturino, Franc. *Forging the Chain: A Case Study of Italian Migration to North America, 1880–1930.* Toronto: Multicultural History Society of Ontario, 1990.

Swyripa, Frances. *Wedded to the Cause: Ukrainian-Canadian Women and Ethnic Identity, 1891–1991*. Toronto: University of Toronto Press, 1993.

Sylvester, Kenneth. *The Limits of Rural Capitalism: Family, Culture, and Markets, Montcalm Manitoba, 1870–1940*. Toronto: University of Toronto Press, 2000.

Taylor, Charles. *Multiculturalism: Examining the Politics of Recognition*. Princeton: Princeton University Press, 1994.

Thompson, John Herd. *Forging the West*. Toronto: Oxford University Press, 1998.

Thor, Jonas. *Icelanders in North America: The First Settlers*. Winnipeg: University of Manitoba Press, 2002.

Troper, Harold, and Morton Weinfeld. *Old Wounds: Jews, Ukrainians and the Hunt for Nazi War Criminals in Canada*. Markham: Penguin, 1989.

Tulchinsky, Gerald. *Branching Out: The Transformation of the Canadian Jewish Community*. Toronto: Stoddart, 1998.

_____. *Taking Root: The Origins of the Canadian Jewish Community*. Toronto: Lester, 1992.

Urry, James. *Mennonites, Politics, and Peoplehood: Europe – Russia – Canada, 1525–1980*. Winnipeg: University of Manitoba Press, 2006.

Van Herk, Aritha. *Mavericks: An Incorrigible History of Alberta*. Toronto: Penguin, 2001.

Waiser, Bill. *Saskatchewan: A New History*. Saskatoon: Fifth House, 2005.

Werner, Hans Peter. *Imagined Homes: Soviet German Immigrants in Two Cities*. Winnipeg: University of Manitoba Press, 2007.

Westfall, William. *Two Worlds: The Protestant Culture of Nineteenth-Century Ontario*. Montreal and Kingston: McGill-Queen's University Press, 1989.

Wilder, Joseph E. *Read All about It: Reminiscences of an Immigrant Newsboy*, edited by F.C. Dawkins and M.C. Brodeur. Winnipeg: Peguis, 1978.

Whitaker, Reg. *Canadian Immigration Policy Since Confederation*. Ottawa: Canadian Historical Association, 1991.

Wiseman, Adele. *Memoirs of a Book Molesting Childhood and Other Essays*. Toronto: Oxford University Press, 1987.

_____. *The Sacrifice*. Toronto: Macmillan, 1956.

Wolf, Kirsten, ed. *Writings by Western Icelandic Women*. Winnipeg: University of Manitoba Press, 1997

_____, and Árný Hjaltadóttir, eds. and trans. *Western Icelandic Short Stories*. Winnipeg: University of Manitoba Press, 1992.

Wood, Patricia K. *Nationalism from the Margins: Italians in Alberta and British Columbia*. Montreal and Kingston: McGill-Queen's University Press, 2002.

Woodsworth, James S. *Strangers Within Our Gates or Coming Canadians*. Toronto: F.C. Stephenson, Missionary Society of the Methodist Church, Canada, 1909.

Yee, Paul. *Struggle and Hope: The Story of the Chinese in Canada.* Toronto:
    Umbrella, 1996.
Yuzyk, Paul. *The Ukrainians of Manitoba: A Social History.* Toronto: University of
    Toronto Press, 1953.
Zucchi, John. *Italians in Toronto: Development of a National Identity, 1875–1935.*
    Montreal and Kingston: McGill-Queen's University Press, 1988.

Articles or Book Chapters

Abella, Irving. 'Jews, Human Rights, and the Making of a New Canada.' *Journal
    of the Canadian Historical Association/Revue de la Société historique du Canada*
    (2000): 3–15.
Abu-Laban, Yasmeen, and Judith A. Garber. 'The Construction of Immigration
    as a Policy Problem.' *Urban Affairs Review* 40 (2005): 520–61.
Agozino, Biko. Introduction. In *Maintaining our Differences: Minority Families in
    Multicultural Societies,* edited by C.D.H. Harvey. Hampshire, England:
    Ashgate, 2001.
Aliaga, David. 'Italian Immigrants in Calgary: Dimensions of Cultural Identity.'
    Canadian Ethnic Studies 26 (1994): 141–8.
Artibise, Alan F.J. 'Divided City: The Immigrants in Winnipeg Society, 1874–
    1921.' In *The Canadian City: Essays in Urban History,* edited by G. Stelter and
    A. Artibise, 300–36. 1966. Reprint, Toronto: McClelland and Stewart, 1979.
Ayukawa, Midge. 'From Japs to Japanese Canadians to Canadians.' *Journal of the
    West* 38 (1999): 41–8.
Backhouse, Constance. 'White Chinese Help and Chinese-Canadian Employers:
    Race, Class, Gender and Law in the Case of Lee Clun [Regina], 1924.'
    Canadian Ethnic Studies 26 (1994): 34–52.
Bai, David H. 'Canadian Immigration Policy and the Voluntary Sector: The
    Case of the Edmonton Immigrant Services Association.' *Human Organization*
    51 (1992): 23–34.
Bailey, A.G. 'Retrospective Thoughts of an Ethnohistorian.' *Canadian Historical
    Association Historical Papers/Communications Historiques* (1977): 15–29.
Balakrishnan, T.R. 'Ethnic Residential Segregation in the Metropolitan Areas of
    Canada.' *Canadian Journal of Sociology* 4 (1995): 1–20.
Barkan, E.R. 'Race, Religion, and Nationality in American Society: A Model of
    Ethnicity – From Contact to Assimilation.' *Journal of American Ethnic History*
    14 (1995) 38–75.
Barsky, Percy. 'How "Numerus Clausus" Was Ended in the Manitoba Medical
    School.' In *Jewish Life and Times: A Collection of Essays.* Vol. 3, 123–7.
    Winnipeg: Jewish Historical Society of Western Canada, 1983.

Barth, Fredrik. 'Ethnic Groups and Boundaries.' Originally published as 'Introduction' to Fredrik Barth, ed., *Ethnic Groups and Boundaries: The Social Organization of Culture Difference*. Bergen: Universitetsforlaget; London: Allen and Unwin, 1969.

Baureiss, Gunter. 'Ethnic Resilience and Discrimination: Two Chinese Communities in Canada.' *Journal of Ethnic Studies* 10 (1982): 69–87.

———, and Leo Driedger. 'Winnipeg China Town: Demographic, Ecological and Organizational Change, 1900–1980.' *Urban History Review* 15 (1982): 3–28.

Bhabha, Homi K. 'Frontlines/Borderposts,' In *Displacements: Cultural Identities in Question*, edited by Angelika Bammer, 269–72. Bloomington: Indiana University Press, 1994.

Boyd, Monica, and Doug Norris. 'Who Are the "Canadians"?: Changing Census Responses, 1986–1996.' *Canadian Ethnic Studies* 33 (2001): 1–24.

Bramadat, Paul. 'Beyond Christian Canada: Religion and Ethnicity in a Multicultural Society.' In *Religion and Ethnicity in Canada*, edited by P. Bramadat and D. Seljack, 1–29. Toronto: Pearson Longman, 2005.

———. 'Religion, Social Capital and "The Day that Changed the World."' *Journal of International Migration and Integration* 6 (2005): 201–18.

Breton, Raymond. 'Institutional Completeness of Ethnic Communities and the Personal Relations of Immigrants.' *American Journal of Sociology* 70 (1964): 193–205.

Buchignani, Norman. 'South Asian Canadians and the Ethnic Mosaic: An Overview.' *Canadian Ethnic Studies* 11 (1979): 48–68.

———. 'South Asians in Alberta.' In *Peoples of Alberta: Portraits of Cultural Diversity*, edited by H. Palmer and T. Palmer, 413–36. Saskatoon: Western Producer Prairie Books, 1985.

Careless, J.M.S. '"Limited Identities" in Canada.' *Canadian Historical Review* 50 (1969): 1–11.

Chen, Zhonping. 'Chinese Minority and Everyday Racism in Canadian Towns and Small Cities: An Ethnic Study of the Case of Peterborough, Ontario, 1892–1951.' *Canadian Ethnic Studies* 36 (2004): 71–91.

Cinotto, Simone. 'Leonard Covello, the Covello Papers, and the History of Eating Habits Among Italian Immigrants in New York.' *Journal of American History* 91 (2004): 497–521.

Conzen, Kathleen Neils, David A. Gerber, Ewa Morawska, George E. Pozzetta, and Rudolph J. Vecoli. 'The Invention of Ethnicity: A Perspective from the U.S.A.' *Journal of American Ethnic History* (Fall 1992): 3–41.

Cook, G.R. 'Church, Schools and Politics in Manitoba, 1902–1912.' *Canadian Historical Review* 39, 1 (March 1958): 1–23.

Cumbo, Enrico Carlson. '"Your Old Men Will Dream Dreams": The Italian Pentecostal Experience in Canada, 1912–1945.' *Journal of American Ethnic History* 19 (2000): 35–81.

Darroch, Gordon. 'Urban Ethnicity in Canada: Personal Assimilation and Political Communities.' *Canadian Review of Sociology and Anthropology* 18 (1981): 93–100.

DePass, Cecille. 'Centering on Changing Communities: The Colours of the South in the Canadian Vertical Mosaic.' *Canadian Ethnic Studies* 24 (1992): 99–112.

Driedger, Leo. 'Attitudes of Winnipeg University Students towards Immigrants of European and Non-European Origin.' *Prairie Forum* 7 (1982): 213–25.

_____, and Richard A. Mezoff. 'Ethnic Prejudice and Discrimination in Winnipeg High Schools.' *Canadian Journal of Sociology* 6 (1981): 1–16.

Duara, Prasenjit. 'Transnationalism and the Predicament of Sovereignty: China 1900–1945.' *American Historical Review* 102 (1997): 1030–51.

Epp, Marlene. 'The Mennonite Girls' Homes of Winnipeg: A Home Away From Home.' *Journal of Mennonite Studies* 6 (1988), 100–14.

Esau-Klippenstein, Frieda. 'Doing What We Could: Mennonite Domestic Servants in Winnipeg, 1920s–1950s.' *Journal of Mennonite Studies* 7 (1989): 145–66.

Espirtu, Yen Le. '"We Don't Sleep Around like White Girls Do": Family, Culture and Gender in Filipina American Lives.' In *American Dreaming, Global Realities: Rethinking U.S. Immigration History*, edited by D.R. Gabaccia and V.L. Ruiz, 484–503. Urbana: University of Illinois Press, 2006.

Fairbairn, Kenneth J., and Hafzia Khatun. 'Residential Segregation and the Intra-Urban Migration of South Asians in Edmonton.' *Canadian Ethnic Studies* 21 (1981): 45–64.

Fass, Paula S. 'Children and Globalization.' *Journal of Social History* 38 (2005): 937–53.

Fletcher, Robert. 'The Language Problem in Manitoba's Schools.' *Manitoba Historical Society Transactions,* Series 3, number 6, 1949–50. <http://www.mhs.mb.ca/docs/transactions/3/languageproblem.shtml>.

Freund, Alexander. 'German Immigrants and the Nazi Past: How Memory Has Shaped Intercultural Relations.' *Inroads. A Journal of Public Opinion* 15 (2004): 106–17.

Frideres, Jim, and Sheldon Goldenberg. 'Hyphenated Canadians: Comparative Analysis of Ethnic, Regional and National Identification of Western Canadian University Students.' *Journal of Ethnic Studies* 5 (1981): 91–100.

Friesen, Gerald. 'Immigrant Adaptation and Canadian Multiculturalism: Introducing a Prairie Case Study 1900–1975.' *Zeitschrift für Kanada-Studien* Band 41 (2002): 71–85.

_____. 'Stuart Garson, Harold Innis, and Adult Education in Manitoba.' In P. James Giffen, *Rural Life: Portraits of the Prairie Town, 1946*, 201–77. Winnipeg: University of Manitoba Press, 2004.

_____, and Royden Loewen. 'Romantics, Pluralists and Post-Modernists.' In Gerald Friesen, *River Road: Essays on Manitoba and Prairie History*, 183–96. Winnipeg: University of Manitoba Press, 1996.

Gabaccia, Donna R. 'Is Everywhere Nowhere? Nomads, Nations and the Immigrant Paradigm of United States History.' *Journal of American History* 86 (1999): 1115–34.

_____, and Franca Iacovetta. 'Work, Women and Protest in the Italian Diaspora: An International Research Agenda.' *Labour/le travail* 42 (1998) 161–81.

Gordon, Milton. 'Assimilation in America: Theory and Reality.' In *The Shaping of Twentieth Century America*, edited by R. Abrams and L. Levine, 70–89. Boston: Little, Brown and Company, 1965.

Grenke, Arthur. 'The German Community of Winnipeg and the English-Canadian Responses to World War I.' *Canadian Ethnic Studies* 20 (1988): 21–37.

Habermas, Jurgen. 'Opening up Fortress Europe.' >. Accessed 16 November 2006.

Harasymiw, Bohdan. 'Political Participation of Ukrainian Canadians Since 1945.' In *A Heritage in Transition: Essays in the History of Ukrainians in Canada*, edited by M.R. Lupul, 126–42. Toronto: McClelland and Stewart, 1982.

Hareven, Tamara K. 'The History of the Family and the Complexity of Social Change.' *American Historical Review* 96 (1991): 95–124.

Harney, Robert. '"So Great a Heritage as Ours": Immigration and the Survival of the Canadian Polity.' *Daedalus* 117 (1988). Reprint, in *Constructing Modern Canada: Readings in Post-Confederation History*, edited by C. Gaffield, 529–66. Toronto: Copp Clark Longman, 1994.

Henderson, Stuart. '"While there is Still Time ...": J. Murray Gibbon and the Spectacle of Difference in Three CPR Folk Festivals, 1928-1931.' *Journal of Canadian Studies* 39, 1 (2005): 139–74.

Hiebert, Daniel. 'Class, Ethnicity and Residential Structure: The Social Geography of Winnipeg, 1901–1921.' *Journal of Historical Geography* 17 (1991): 56–86.

Hinther, Rhonda L. 'Raised in the Spirit of the Class Struggle: Children, Youth, and the Interwar Ukrainian Left in Canada.' *Labour/le travail* 60 (2007): 43–76.

Hoerder, Dirk. 'Historians and Their Data: The Complex Shift from Nation-State Approaches to the Study of People's Transcultural Lives.' *Journal of American Ethnic Studies* (Summer 2006): 85–96.

Howe, R. Brian. 'The Evolution of Human Rights Policy in Ontario.' *Canadian Journal of Political Science* 24, 4 (1991): 783–802.

Husain, Fatima, and Margaret O'Brien. 'South Asian Muslims in Britain: Faith, Family and Community.' In *Maintaining Our Differences: Minority Families in Multicultural Societies*, edited by C.D.H. Harvey, 15–28. Hampshire, England: Ashgate, 2001.

Iacovetta, Franca. 'Making New Canadians: Social Workers, Women and the Reshaping of Immigrant Families.' In *A Nation of Immigrants: Women, Workers and Communities in Canada, 1840s–1960s*, edited by F. Iacovetta, P. Draper, and R. Ventresca, 482–513. Toronto: University of Toronto Press, 2002.

Indra, Doreen. 'Khmer, Lao, Vietnamese and Vietnamese Chinese in Alberta.' In *Peoples of Alberta: Portraits of Cultural Diversity*, edited by H. Palmer and T. Palmer, 437–63. Saskatoon: Western Producer Prairie Books, 1985.

Isaacs, Harold R. 'Basic Group Identity: The Idols of the Tribe.' *Ethnicity* 1 (1974): 15–41.

Johnson, Stuart D., and Cornelia B. Johnson. 'Institutional Origins in the Chilean Refugee Community in Winnipeg.' *Prairie Forum* 7 (1982): 227–35.

Karakayali, Nedim. 'Duality and Diversity in the Lives of Immigrant Children: Rethinking the "Problem of the Second Generation" in Light of Immigrant Autobiographies.' *Canadian Review of Sociology & Anthropology* 42 (2005): 325–43.

Kazal, Russell A. 'Revisiting Assimilation: The Rise, Fall, and Reappraisal of a Concept in American Ethnic History.' *American Historical Review* 100 (1995): 437–71.

Korneski, Kurt, ed. 'Citizenship Ceremony, 10 January 1947.' *Manitoba History* 51 (2006): 34–9.

Kwong, Julia. 'Ethnic Organizations and Community Transformation: The Chinese in Winnipeg.' *Ethnic and Racial Studies* 7 (1984): 374–85.

Kymlicka, Will. 'The Canadian Model of Diversity in a Comparative Perspective.' Eighth Standard Life Visiting Lecture, 29 April 2004, Canadian Studies, Edinburgh University. <http://www.cst.ed.ac.uk/documents/ Kymlickalecture.rtf>. Accessed 20 April 2009.

Lai, Daniel Wing Leung, and J.R. McDonald. 'Life Satisfaction of Chinese Elderly Immigrants in Calgary.' *Canadian Journal of Aging* 14 (1995): 536–52.

Lai, David Chuenyan, Jordan Paper, and Li Chuang Paper. 'The Chinese in Canada: Their Unrecognized Religion.' In *Religion and Ethnicity in Canada*, edited by P. Bramadat and D. Seljak, 89–110. Toronto: Pearson, 2005.

Li, Peter. 'Prejudice Against Asians in a Canadian City.' *Canadian Ethnic Studies* 11 (1979): 70–7.

Loewen, Royden. 'The Fragmented: Trends in American Urban Immigration History: A Review Essay.' *Urban History Review* 27 (1999): 60–3.

_____. 'Poetics of Peoplehood: Mennonites and the Ethnic Question.' In *Christianity and Ethnicity in Canada,* edited by P. Bramadat and D. Seljack, 330–61. Toronto: University of Toronto Press, 2008.

_____. 'Rurality, Ethnicity, and Gender Patterns of Cultural Continuity during the "Great Disjuncture" in the R.M. of Hanover, 1945–1961.' *Journal of the Canadian Historical Association* 4 (1993): 161–82.

Lucassen, Jan, and Leo Lucassen. 'Migration, Migration History, History: Old Paradigms and New Perspectives.' In *Migration, Migration History, History,* edited by J. Lucassen and L. Lucassen. Bern: Peter Lang, 1997.

Lukawiewicz, Krystyna, 'Ethnicity, Politics and Religion: Polish Societies in Edmonton in the Inter-war Period.' *Alberta History* 50 (2001): 2–12.

Lunn, Kenneth. 'Immigration and Reaction in Britain, 1880–1950: Rethinking the "Legacy of Empire."' In *Migration, Migration History, History: Old Paradigms and New Perspectives,* edited by J. Lucassen and L. Lucassen. Bern: Peter Lang, 1997.

Martin, Paul. 'Citizenship and the People's World.' In *Belonging: The Meaning and Future of Canadian Citizenship,* edited by W. Kaplan, 64–78. Montreal: McGill-Queen's University Press, 1993.

Martynowych, Orest T., and Nadia Kazymyra. 'Political Activity in Western Canada, 1896–1923.' In *A Heritage in Transition: Essays in the History of Ukrainians in Canada,* edited by M.R. Lupul, 85–107. Toronto: McClelland and Stewart, 1982.

Matejko, Joanna. 'The Polish Experience in Alberta.' In *Peoples of Alberta: Portraits of Cultural Diversity,* edited by H. Palmer and T. Palmer, 274–96. Saskatoon: Western Producer Prairie Books, 1985.

Matthiasson, John S. 'Icelandic Canadians in Central Canada: One Experiment in Multiculturalism.' *Western Canadian Journal of Anthropology* 4, 2 (1974): 49–61.

Matwijiw, Peter. 'Ethnicity and Urban Residence in Winnipeg, 1941–1971.' *The Canadian Geographer* 23 (1979): 45–61.

Maynard, Steven. 'Rough Work and Rugged Men: The Social Construction of Masculinity in Working Class History.' *Labour/le travail* 23 (1989): 159–69

McCormack, A. Ross. 'Networks among British Immigrants and Accommodation to Canadian Society: Winnipeg, 1900–1914.' *Histoire Sociale/Social History* 17 (1984): 357–74.

McDonough, Sheila, and Homa Hoodfar. 'Muslims in Canada: From Ethnic Groups to Religious Community.' In *Religion and Ethnicity in Canada,* edited by P. Bramadat and D. Seljack, 133–53. Toronto: Pearson, 2005.

McInnis, Marvin. 'Canada's Population in the Twentieth Century.' In *A Population History of North America,* edited by M.R. Haines and R.H. Steckel, 529–99. Cambridge: Cambridge University Press, 2000.

Moodley, Kogila A. 'Multicultural Education in Canada: Historical
    Development and Current Status.' In *Handbook of Research on Multicultural
    Education,* edited by J.A. Banks, 801–19. New York: Simon & Schuster
    Macmillan, 1995.
Montgomery, R. 'The Economic Adaptation of Vietnamese Refugees in Alberta,
    1979–84.' *International Migration* 24 (1986): 749–62.
Morrish, Margot. 'The Origins of the Citizenship Council of Manitoba /
    International Centre.' In *Adult Education in Manitoba: Historical Aspects,* edited
    by D.H. Poonwassie and A. Poonwassie, 57–94. Mississauga: Canadian
    Educators' Press, 1997.
Morton, W.L. 'Manitoba Schools and Canadian Nationality 1890–1923.'
    Canadian Historical Association Annual Report. 1951. <http://www.erudit.org/
    revue/ram/1951/v30/n1/290034ar.pdf>.
Nunoda, Peter. 'Harold Hirose on Integration and Citizenship for Japanese
    Manitobans, 1942–52.' *Prairie Forum* 27, 2 (2002): 209–20.
Orsi, Robert. 'The Center Out There, In Here, And Everywhere Else: The
    Nature of Pilgrimage to the Shrine of Saint Jude, 1929–1965.' *Journal of
    Social History* 25 (1991): 213–32.
Palmer, Howard. 'Patterns of Immigration and Ethnic Settlements in Alberta.'
    In *Peoples of Alberta: Portraits of Cultural Diversity,* edited by H. Palmer and T.
    Palmer, 28–49. Saskatoon: Western Producer Prairie Books, 1985.
_____, and Tamara Palmer. 'Estonians in Alberta.' In *Peoples of Alberta: Portraits
    of Cultural Diversity,* edited by H. Palmer and T. Palmer, 193–213. Saskatoon:
    Western Producer Prairie Books, 1985.
_____, and Tamara Palmer. 'The Icelandic Experience in Alberta.' In *Peoples of
    Alberta: Portraits of Cultural Diversity,* edited by H. Palmer and T. Palmer,
    174–94. Saskatoon: Western Producer Prairie Books, 1985.
_____, and Tamara Palmer. 'The Religious Ethic and Spirit of Immigration: The
    Dutch in Alberta.' In *Peoples of Alberta: Portraits of Cultural Diversity,* edited by
    H. Palmer and T. Palmer, 143–73. Saskatoon: Western Producer Prairie
    Books, 1985.
_____, and Tamara Palmer. 'The Romanian Community in Alberta.' In *Peoples of
    Alberta: Portraits of Cultural Diversity,* edited by H. Palmer and T. Palmer,
    243–73. Saskatoon: Western Producer Prairie Books, 1985.
Palmer, Tamara. 'Ethnic Responses to the Canadian Prairies, 1900–1950: A
    Literary Perspective of the Physical and Social Environment.' *Prairie Forum* 12
    (1987): 49–74.
Pankiw, Bohdanna, and Rita M. Bienvenue. 'Parental Responses to Ethnic
    Name-Calling: A Sociological Inquiry.' *Canadian Ethnic Studies* 22 (1990):
    78–98.

Parr, Joy. 'Gender History and Historical Practice.' *Canadian Historical Review* 76
   (1995): 354–76.
Patrias, Carmela. 'Socialists, Jews, and the 1947 Saskatchewan Bill of Rights.'
   Canadian Historical Review 87, 2 (June 2006): 265–92.
Patrias, Carmela, and Ruth A. Frager. '"This Is Our Country, These Are Our
   Rights": Minorities and the Origins of Ontario's Human Rights Campaigns.'
   Canadian Historical Review 82 (2001): 1–35.
Pitsula, James M. 'The Mixed Economy of Unemployment Relief in Regina
   during the 1930s.' *Journal of the Canadian Historical Association* 15 (2004):
   97–122.
Pohorecky, Zenon S., and Alexander Royick. 'Anglicization of Ukrainian in
   Canada between 1895 and 1970: A Case Study of Linguistic Crystallization.'
   Canadian Ethnic Studies 1 (1969): 141–94.
Quarterman, John S. 'Telecomputing in the New Global Networks.' In
   Communication in History: Technology, Culture, Society, edited by D. Crowley and
   P. Heyer, 341–8. White Plains, NY: Longman, 1995.
Ralston, Helen. 'Organizational Empowerment among South Asian Immigrant
   Women in Canada.' *International Journal of Canadian Studies* 11 (1995): 121–46.
Ramraj, Victor J. 'West Indian Canadian Writing in English.' *International
   Journal of Canadian Studies* 13 (1996): 163–68.
Rasporich, Anthony. 'Utopian Ideals and Community Settlements in Western
   Canada, 1880–1914.' In *The Canadian West: Social Change and Economic
   Development*, edited by H. Klassen, 37–62. Calgary: Comprint, 1977.
Reitz, Jeffrey, and Margaret Ashton. 'Ukrainian Language and Identity
   Retention in Urban Canada.' *Canadian Ethnic Studies* 12 (1980): 33–54.
Roediger, David. *The Wages of Whiteness: Race and the Making of the American
   Working Class*. London and New York: Verso, 1999.
Romsa, Gerald. 'Jewish-Mennonite-Ukrainian Intergroup Perspectives.' In *A
   Sharing of Diversities: Proceedings of the Jewish Mennonite Ukrainian Conference,
   Building Bridges*, edited by F. Stambrook and B. Friesen, 123–34. Regina:
   Canadian Plains Research Center, 1999.
Rubin, Max. 'Alberta's Jews: The Long Journey.' In *Peoples of Alberta: Portraits of
   Cultural Diversity*, edited by H. Palmer and T. Palmer, 328–47. Saskatoon:
   Western Producer Prairie Books, 1985.
Sager, Eric W., and Christopher Morier. 'Immigrants, Ethnicity, and Earnings in
   1901: Revisiting Canada's Vertical Mosaic.' *Canadian Historical Review* 83
   (2002): 196–229.
Sanders, Harry M. 'The Jews of Alberta.' *Alberta History* 47 (1999): 20–6.
Sandwell, R.W. 'The Limits of Liberalism: The Liberal Renaissance and the
   History of the Family in Canada.' *Canadian Historical Review* 84 (2003): 423–50.

Sangster, Joan. 'Creating Social and Moral Citizens: Defining and Treating Delinquent Boys and Girls in English Canada, 1920–65.' In *Contesting Canadian Citizenship: Historical Readings*, edited by R. Adamoski, D.E. Chun, and R. Menzies, 337–58. Peterborough: Broadview, 2002.

Satzewich, Vic. 'Whiteness Limited: Racialization and the Social Construction of "Peripheral Europeans."' *Histoire Sociale/Social History* 33 (2006): 271–89.

Sauer, Angelika. 'Being German in Western Canada: The German-Speaking Population of the Prairie Provinces, 1880s to 1980s.' *Journal of the West* 38 (1999): 49–55.

Schiller, Nina Glick, and Linda Bash. 'From Immigrant to Transmigrant: Theorizing Transnational Migration.' *Anthropological Quarterly* 68 (1995): 48–63.

Shack, Sybil. 'The Education of Immigrant Children During the First Two Decades of This Century.' *Historical and Scientific Society of Manitoba Transactions*. Series III. 30 (1973–4). <http://www.mhs.mb.ca/docs/transactions/3/immigranteducation.shtml>.

Siddique, Chaudry M. 'Structural Separation and Family Change: An Exploratory Study of the Immigrant Indian and Pakistani Community of Saskatoon, Canada.' *International Review of Modern Sociology* 7 (1977): 13–34.

Siddique, Muhammad. 'Changing Family Patterns: A Comparative Analysis of Immigrant Indian and Pakistani Families of Saskatoon, Canada.' *Journal of Comparative Family Studies* 8 (1977): 179–200.

Silverman, Eliane Leslau. 'Lena Hanen and the Conflicts of Leadership in the Twentieth Century.' In *Unsettled Pasts: Reconceiving the West through Women's History*, edited by S. Carter, L. Erickson, P. Roome, and C. Smith, 363–70. Calgary: University of Calgary Press, 2005.

Sissons, C.B. 'Illiteracy in the West.' *University Magazine* 12 (1913): 440–51.

Smith, Donald B. 'A History of French-Speaking Alberta.' In *Peoples of Alberta: Portraits of Cultural Diversity,* edited by H. Palmer and T. Palmer, 84–109. Saskatoon: Western Producer Prairie Books, 1985.

Smith, J.E. 'Our Own Kind: Family and Community Networks in Providence.' *Radical History Review* 17 (1978): 99–108.

Smith, Timothy L. 'Religion and Ethnicity in America.' *American Historical Review* 83 (1978): 1155–85.

Sololyck, K.W. 'The Role of Ukrainian Sports Teams, Clubs and Leagues, 1924–1952.' *Journal of Ukrainian Studies* 16 (1991): 131–46.

Switzer, Jack. 'Whoa Emma!! An Anarchist Visits Calgary, 1907.' *Alberta History* 55 (2007): 6–12.

Szach, Jerry. 'Playing in the Shadow of the Ukrainian Labour Temple,' edited by N. Reilly. *Manitoba History* 60 (Spring 2009): 28–46.

Tatsoglou, E., and G. Stubos. 'The Greek Immigrant Family in the United States and Canada: The Transition from an "Institutional" to a "Relational" Form, 1945–1970.' *International Migration* 30 (1992): 155–74.

Taves, Krista M. 'Dividing the Righteous: Soviet Mennonites as Cultural Icons in the Canadian Russian Mennonite Narrative, 1923–1938.' *Journal of Mennonite Studies* 16 (1998): 101–27.

Taylor, K.W., and Nelson Wiseman. 'Class and Ethnic Voting in Winnipeg: The Case of 1941.' *Canadian Review of Sociology and Anthropology* 14 (1977): 174–87.

Thompson, John Herd, and Ian MacPherson. 'The Business of Agriculture: Prairie Farmers and the Adoption of Business Methods, 1880–1950.' *Canadian Papers in Business History* 1 (1989): 245–69.

Tilly, Charles. 'Contentious Repertoires in Great Britain, 1758–1834.' *Social Science History* 17 (1993): 253–80.

Tötösy de Zepetnek, Steve. 'A History of the Hungarian Cultural Society of Edmonton, 1946–1986.' *Canadian Ethnic Studies* 25 (1993): 100–17.

Varzally, Allison. 'Romantic Crossings, Making Love, Family and Non-Whiteness in California, 1925–1950.' *Journal of American Ethnic History* 23 (2003): 3–54.

Wei, Li. 'Building Ethnoburbia: The Emergence and Manifestation of the Chinese Ethnoburbia in Los Angeles's San Gabriel Valley.' *Journal of Asian American Studies* 2 (1999): 1–28.

Wiens, Jason. 'The Prairies as Cosmopolitan Space: Recent "Prairie" Poetry.' In *Toward Defining the Prairies: Region, Culture and History*, edited by R. Wardhaugh, 151–64. Winnipeg: University of Manitoba Press, 2001.

Wilkinson, Lori. 'Visualizing Canada, Identity and Belonging among Second Generation Youth in Winnipeg.' *Canadian Diversity/Diversité Canadienne* 6, 2 (Spring 2008): 84–6.

Wiseman, Adele. 'Old Markets, New World.' In *Memoirs of a Book Molesting Childhood and Other Essays*. Toronto: Oxford University Press, 1987.

Wiseman, Nelson, and K.W. Taylor. 'Class and Ethnic Voting in Winnipeg During the Cold War.' *Canadian Review of Sociology and Anthropology* 16 (1979): 60–76.

_____. 'Ethnic vs Class Voting: The Case of Winnipeg, 1945.' *Canadian Journal of Political Science* 7 (1974): 314–28.

_____. 'Voting in Winnipeg During the Depression.' *Canadian Review of Sociology and Anthropology* 19 (1982): 215–36.

Woodsworth, J.S. 'The Strangers Within Our Gates.' *Methodist Magazine* (July 1905).

Xiao, Hong. 'Chinese Language Maintenance in Winnipeg.' *Canadian Ethnic Studies* 30 (1998): 86–96.

Young, Jon, and Robert J. Graham. 'School and Curriculum Reform: Manitoba Frameworks & Multicultural Teacher Education.' *Canadian Ethnic Studies* 32 (2000): 142–55.

Yu, Henry. 'Refracting Pacific Canada: Seeing Our Uncommon Past.' *BC Studies* 156–7 (2007–08): 5–10.

Zolf, Larry. 'Larry Zolf,' interviewed by Danny Finkleman. In *Speaking of Winnipeg*, edited and introduced by J. Parr, 135–49. Winnipeg: Queenston House, 1974.

Web Sites

<http://ethio-calgary.ab.ca/cecahistory.html>, accessed 24 December 2006.

<http://moia.gov.in>, accessed 24 December 2006.

<http://www.edkor.org>, accessed 24 December 2006.

<http://www.manilawinnipeg.com>, accessed 24 December 2006.

<http://www.reginahungarianclub.com/Main.html>, accessed 24 December 2006.

<http://www.sfn.saskatoon.sk.ca/arts/chinese>, accessed 24 December 2006.

<http://www.lycos.com/info/emma-goldman–women.html>, accessed 30 January 2009.

<http://www.mhs.mb.ca/docs/transactions/3/immigranteducation.shtml>.

<http://www.mhs.mb.ca/docs/transactions/3/languageproblem.shtml>.

<www.usda.gov/agency/nass/pubs/trends/farmpop/-labor.csv,>, accessed 17 April 2005.

<http://www40.statcan.ca/l01/cst01/demo34c.htm>, accessed 22 January 2008.

<http://www.calgarymandir.com/History.htm>; <islamiccenter.sk.ca/community_1.htm>, accessed 24 January 2008.

<www.policyalternatives.ca>, accessed 20 January 2009.

<www.signandsight.com/features/1048.html>, accessed 16 November 2006.

<http://www.cst.ed.ac.uk/documents/Kymlickalecture.rtf, accessed 20 April 2009.

<http://www.erudit.org/revue/ram/1951/v30/n1/290034ar.pdf>.

Index

Rome Mutual Benefit Society, 30
Ross, Brian, 18, 30, 161, 188n4,
189n23, 191n72, 218n14
Rousseau, Jean-Jacques, 146, 215n17
Roy, Gabrielle, 38–40, 42, 193n8
Royal Commission on Bilingualism
and Biculturalism, 7, 117
Royick, Alexander, 65, 197n27,
197n30
Rubin, Max, 62, 166, 195n1, 196n17,
197n21, 219n32
Russia (and Soviet Union), immigrants from, 6, 24, 28–9, 31, 32,
38, 51, 71, 78, 160–1, 200n10,
220n42
Russian Germans (Volksdeutsche), 6,
29, 32, 71, 79, 168

Said, Edward, 4, 176, 183, 186n5,
221n1, 221n10
St Jean Baptiste Society, 30
Salverson, Laura Goodman, 16,
188n9, 188n12, 190n32, 190n38
Sandwell, R. W., 122, 207n9
Sangster, Joan, 130, 209n42
Saskatoon, 6, 15–20, 26, 57–75,
101–2, 121, 128–38, 160, 162,
172, 189n13, 195n1, 196, n14,
196n18, 197n29, 197n31, 198n32,
207n16, 209n40, 210n53,
211n67–8
Saskatoon Branch, Chinese Cultural
Association of Saskatchewan, 172
Scandinavia, immigrants from, 6–7,
38, 49, 75, 107
schools: 17, 19, 30, 42–50, 54, 69,
79–80, 82, 84–5, 90, 93, 95, 106,
108, 111, 114, 116, 127, 131, 136,
140–2, 145–6, 150–1, 155, 162,
167–8, 178–80; languages of

instruction, 45–9, 180, 194n24,
194n28; Manitoba schools
question, 45–9. See also integration
secularism, 30–2
Selvon, Sam, 119
Semchyshyn, Cecil, 147, 215n20
sexuality, 122, 131, 133. See also
health
Shack, Sybil, 44, 193n14, 193n17,
193n21
Siddique, Muhammad, 130, 209n40
Sisler, W. J., 44–8, 193n18, 193n20
Smith, Donald, 165, 219n31
Snider, Howard, 67, 198n38
social safety net, 58, 90, 93, 101,
104–5, 109, 113, 115–16, 126, 128,
130,134, 179, 182. See also health
South America, immigrants from, 8,
103, 105, 128, 179, 205n64,
207n10, 209n39, 210n46
Southeast Asia, immigrants from,
103, 105, 110, 111, 179, 203n17,
203n24
southern hemisphere (Global South),
8, 101–20, 150, 179, 181, 202
sports, 13, 19, 32, 42, 45, 79, 102,
112, 119, 135, 172
Sri Lanka, immigrants from, 111
Sweden, immigrants from, 17, 110
Swyripa, Frances, 19, 64, 161,
189n27, 190n50, 197n28, 218n18,
218n21
Sylvester, Kenneth, 5, 199n1

Taras Shevchenko Educational
Society, 30
Taylor, Charles, 146, 153, 154–5,
187n21, 215n17, 217n29
Taylor, Wayne, 52–3, 195n36–7,
195n39